HOW TO BECOME HUMAN CALCULATOR?

with the magic of Vedic Maths

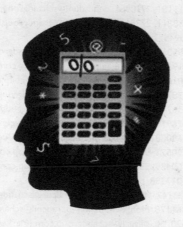

Aditi Singhal

Guinness World Record Holder
3 Records in the Limca Book
(For Memory & Calculation)

Eurasia Publishing House

EURASIA PUBLISHING HOUSE
(An imprint of S. Chand Publishing)
A Division of S. Chand & Co. Pvt. Ltd.
7361, Ram Nagar, Qutab Road, New Delhi-110055
Phone: 23672080-81-82, 9899107446, 9911310888
Fax: 91-11-23677446
www.schandpublishing.com; e-mail : helpdesk@schandpublishing.com

Branches :

Ahmedabad	:	Ph: 27541965, 27542369, ahmedabad@schandgroup.com
Bengaluru	:	Ph: 22268048, 22354008, bangalore@schandgroup.com
Bhopal	:	Ph: 4274723, 4209587, bhopal@schandgroup.com
Chandigarh	:	Ph: 2725443, 2725446, chandigarh@schandgroup.com
Chennai	:	Ph. 28410027, 28410058, chennai@schandgroup.com
Coimbatore	:	Ph: 2323620, 4217136, coimbatore@schandgroup.com (Marketing Office)
Cuttack	:	Ph: 2332580; 2332581, cuttack@schandgroup.com
Dehradun	:	Ph: 2711101, 2710861, dehradun@schandgroup.com
Guwahati	:	Ph: 2738811, 2735640, guwahati@schandgroup.com
Haldwani	:	Mob. 09452294584 (Marketing Office)
Hyderabad	:	Ph: 27550194, 27550195, hyderabad@schandgroup.com
Jaipur	:	Ph: 2219175, 2219176, jaipur@schandgroup.com
Jalandhar	:	Ph: 2401630, 5000630, jalandhar@schandgroup.com
Kochi	:	Ph: 2378740, 2378207-08, cochin@schandgroup.com
Kolkata	:	Ph: 22367459, 22373914, kolkata@schandgroup.com
Lucknow	:	Ph: 4076971, 4026791, 4065646, 4027188, lucknow@schandgroup.com
Mumbai	:	Ph: 22690881, 22610885, mumbai@schandgroup.com
Nagpur		Ph: 2720523, 2777666, nagpur@schandgroup.com
Patna	:	Ph: 2300489, 2302100, patna@schandgroup.com
Pune	:	Ph: 64017298, pune@schandgroup.com
Raipur	:	Ph: 2443142, Mb. : 09981200834, raipur@schandgroup.com (Marketing Office)
Ranchi		Ph: 2361178, Mob. 09430246440, ranchi@schandgroup.com
Siliguri	:	Ph. 2520750, siliguri@schandgroup.com (Marketing Office)
Visakhapatnam	:	Ph. 2782609 (M) 09440100555, visakhapatnam@schandgroup.com
		(Marketing Office)

First Edition 2012 Reprint with corrections 2014
Second Revised Edition 2015

ISBN : 978-81-219-3921-8   **Code : 1014B 642**

PRINTED IN INDIA
By Vikas Publishing House Pvt. Ltd., Plot 20/4, Site-IV, Industrial Area Sahibabad, Ghaziabad-201010 and Published by EURASIA PUBLISHING HOUSE., 7361, Ram Nagar, New Delhi -110 055.

Dedicated with reverence to
Almighty GOD,
The Supreme father of
All Souls and the Source of
True Knowledge.

FOREWORD

The history of Vedic Mathematics dates back to the golden aged India, where calculations were done mentally. There was perfect coordination of both parts of the brain. Faculty of mind was used by each individual upto 100%. In due course of time, mind power and mental calculation reduced. The sages and saints knew the secrets of numbers and they devised a unique system of fast calculations during the Vedic age. Since this system was devised in Vedic age, we call it 'Vedic Mathematics'.

This book provides very interesting techniques to calculate fast. I found this book unique in the following respects:

1. This book comprehensively and systematically presents the steps of calculation in a layman language. It can be easily understood by students, housewives or anyone.

2. The book also clearly highlights the techniques of calculations for ease of students, especially those aspiring for competitive examinations. Students can take maximum benefits of these techniques as enumerated in this book.

Aditi Singhal is known to me personally for the last three years. She is a simple woman of high thinking. She has various experiences of applying the Vedic Mathematics techniques which she fondly calls Math-E-Magic. She also provides tips to students to overcome their exam fear and better their performances by improving memory and mind power. Aditi is also the visiting faculty to the "Invisible Doctors Solutions Pvt Ltd", Faridabad.

She has put sincere efforts to present the knowledge of Vedic Mathematics in a simple book form worth emulating for the benefits of the student community. Her efforts are an eye-opener for all of us. I hope this book will prove beneficial for the students to harness their talents and release their true potential. I wish her Good Luck in this endeavour and many successes in her life.

BK Chandra Shekhar
(Director SIGFA Solutions, Rajyogi, Author and Spiritual Healer)

Can I Become a Human Calculator?

Students find maths cumbersome and difficult at school level.

Is it because they are afraid of Mathematics?

Your answer may be Yes or you might find mathematics as the most interesting subject. No matter what the answer is, the reason is the same, i.e. 'the universal nature of Mathematics'. The solution of any maths problem is very unique and to the point. If I ask you *what is 4+5?*, your immediate answer will be *9*. If I ask a Japanese the same question, he will also answer the same. Infact anybody from any part of the world if asked the same question, will answer 9; nobody will answer it as 8.5 or 9.1 or anything else. It is this universality of answer that makes Maths so interesting or at the same time can develop a phobia in some, because even a single small mistake at any calculation stage can result in a wrong answer.

That is why, students, and adults too, find a rescue in the use of a calculator. But I can assure you that after reading this book and with little practice, you can calculate on your own – infact much faster than a calculator!

You might wonder if anyone can really calculate like a calculator. But the truth is, *'we all can'*. **Our brain has the potential to work even faster than the world's fastest computer.** We all have heard this, but can you think of even one incident where you find an evidence of this.

Let's analyze the following situation:

When we cross the road, we estimate the ever changing speed of different vehicles on road, keep in mind the fixed distance of the road and adjust our own speed with the changing distance of other vehicles. While calculating all this in mind at one time, don't we cross the road successfully each time? Imagine how difficult it would be if all these calculations have to be done on a computer! A slight mistake in these calculations may not have let us even read this book today!

This proves that our brain definitely has the potential to work much better than any other computer. Research shows that a person uses only 1% - 3% of his brain, while intelligent people, like Einstein, also used only upto 10% of his brain. Can you imagine what magic could be created if we are able to unleash even 50% of our brain's potential.

But the million dollar question is *how to use this potential? How to really become as fast as a computer?*

Definitely hard work alone cannot help. Otherwise also, nobody has more than 24 hours to perform work. So, obviously **some smart work is required** to calculate fast. And that's where the Vedic Maths techniques help us. Learning these techniques is extremely simple and interesting. And anybody, **even a person from non-maths background can learn these.** Someone who knows basic mathematical operations of addition, subtraction, multiplication and division, can calculate many times faster by learning these simple techniques.

And I can say this confidently because *I too studied formal maths till high school only.* Having graduated as a B.Sc. (Home Science) Hons. and after 10 years of married life, it was almost 16 years since I left Maths, when one day, I was drawn into reading about Vedic Mathematics. What started as a pass time, could not be resisted. Soon I was practicing the techniques in my day-to-day life. Gradually, the whole system of Vedic Mathematics generated a new passion in me to know more and more about it and discover its magic.

Vedic Maths techniques were so absorbing that I could not get over the temptation of sharing them with my friends and relatives. I practiced teaching the techniques to children of my relatives staying nearby. Observing their enthusiasm and the positive change in their interest for Maths, I extended these techniques to secondary and higher secondary students & teachers in my workshops at various schools. Even the Principals were surprised how these simple Vedic Maths techniques kept their highly qualified maths teachers awestruck!

With time, the workshops were attended by people from all walks of life – students, doctors, housewives, MBAs, CAs, teachers and many others. After numerous workshops, a need was felt to present these techniques in simpler language, especially for school students and those appearing for different competitive exams, or aspiring for an MBA, Banks, etc. Their tremendous response and thirst for a guide-cum-reference book inspired me to write this book.

A conscious effort has been made to explain the techniques of Vedic Maths in simple language with enough step-by-step solved examples at each point and with sufficient practice exercises given after each technique. Different colours have been used to highlight the key points and steps for a gist of the techniques at a glimpse.

It is important to emphasize that you must be thorough with a chapter before moving on to the next chapter. Many chapters are interlinked, like multiplication should be understood first before division and square roots cannot be understood before understanding division. The sequence of the chapters are designed in such a way so that easier and basic techniques are taught earlier and some higher level chapters are dealt later.

On the request of the readers, we have added chapters on algebra using vedic mathematics, in this second edition. So for your convenience, the book is divided in two parts – *Arithmetic and Algebra*. A reader needs ample revision work in the basics as an ongoing practice and this has been taken into account in the framing of exercises.

Finally, consolidated test papers are given at the end of the book, comprising problems from all chapters for thorough revision. Maths is more of a practical subject than theoretical. So, a workbook with exhaustive exercises on each topic is also available to facilitate more practice. Any suggestions that may help to improvise the book are heartily welcomed.

Let me assure you that it was only by the use of these easy and wonderful techniques, that I now hold a National Record for the fastest calculation and even got my name registered in the '*Limca*

Book of Records' and the *'India Book of Records'*. Using these techniques along with the memory techniques, we have developed a methodology to workout tables till 99 mentally. Infact, me and my husband, Mr. Sudhir Singhal have made a **Guinness World Record** in teaching the *"Largest Maths Class"* involving 2,312 students, where we taught them to memorize tables till 99. We have also written a very illustrative book on the same "Mastering tables from 2 to 99", a ready handbook for all who want to master tables.

What I want to emphasize is that **if I can do it; I am confident, anybody can do it.**

You should just believe that you can do it
and have the will to do it! The rest is easy.

All the best for your adventurous, magical and entertaining journey of Vedic Mathematics!

-Aditi Singhal
(email: mvedica@gmail.com)

ACKNOWLEDGEMENT

I thank the Almighty God who empowered me with the intellect and the belief to write this book.

A heartfelt thanks to my parents for the ever encouraging role they have always been playing in my life and standing like a pillar besides me, always.

With two little kids to look after, it really was a herculean task to even think of writing the book. But my mother-in-law's support was a big help in not only encouraging the writing but also in working on seminars. Her care and timely adjustments throughout my journey of this book are something that cannot be described in words.

A very special thanks to Mr. B.K. Chandra Shekhar Tiwari for motivating me to take the first step towards writing this book and for believing in my potential much before I started believing in myself.

A very special thanks to Mr. Biswaroop Roy Chowdhury, for being an ideal to me and for always boosting my confidence with his valuable inputs and support.

I express my thanks to Mr. Antriksh Johri, for always believing in me and inspiring me to think high while maintaining a balance between the professional and family life.

This book couldn't have been made more interesting without the valuable suggestions of Mr. Ravi Gupta. I thank him for his constant support and guidance throughout the making of this book.

Apart from being a qualified Trainer, I could also play the role of a successful housewife; thanks to my husband, Sudhir Singhal's limited expectations and unlimited encouragement.

The book could not have been written in the simplest manners had I not learnt from the experiences of teaching my students. Their persistent questions and ever surprising looks helped me to develop better and simpler ways of explanation. I thank the students and their parents for believing in me.

Finally I also thank those whose names have not been mentioned, but have lent their support in any way.

Author

We have witnessed phenomenal technological changes in the recent years leading better and faster applications in life. Approach to Mathematics, a subject that brings focus and precession in our life also needs a fresh look. "How to become a Human Calculator" is a book which teaches us the means for such learning and application. It is felt that the book should be a must for all students in schools and colleges.

– Retd. Air Marshal Mr. P.S. Bhangu

I know the author of this book, Aditi Singhal, personally. I have attended some of her lectures and she is extremely good. She is an asset, a great trainer. Vedic Mathematics is a very useful tool not only for school students, but also for students aspiring for different competitive exams. I am sure whoever read this book will get extremely benefited. I wish her all the best.

– Prof. Dr. S. Viswanathan
(Secretary, International Medical Sciences Academy (IMSA)
Director, Center for Yoga Studies, Annamalai University)

The techniques mentioned in this book create a paradigm shift from hard work to smart work. This book is written in a very simple way to understand the ancient system of calculations. The whole emphasis is laid on the fact that mathematics is a process to be enjoyed and cherished.

– Sushil Chandra
(Scientist 'E' & Head Department of Biomedical Engineering
Institute of Nuclear Medicine & Allied Sciences, DRDO)

This book is a compilation of series of easy methods to do fast calculations. I am hopeful that this book will help children to fight Maths phobia effectively. My sincere appreciation for Ms. Aditi Singhal for her commendable work in helping out the students with the skill sets needed for effective studies .

– Rupam Sah
(Principal, Bosco Public School)

The techniques mentioned in this book should be a part of every school and college curriculum.

– Arvind Gupta
(Chairman, Dolphin College, Dehradun)

Vedic Mathematics is the reorganized and revealed presentation of ancient mathematics techniques. I appreciate Mrs Aditi Singhal's sleepless and consistent efforts towards bringing back the past events towards present time with lucid and accessible method in this book "HOW TO BECOME A HUMAN CALCULATOR?" which will be helpful not only for the students but for everyone in some or many ways.

– Dr. Santanu Kumar Sahu, Orissa

I attended few lectures of Aditi Singhal and I appreciate that her thoughts and expressions, both are very clear and this beauty of clarity is expressed in the lucid presentation of this book also. A perfect blend of a good writer as well as a good speaker, I appreciate her effort for bringing these techniques in such a simple language for the benefit of all. These techniques help bring out a child in me and reminded me of my own student's life. I recommend this book for people of all age groups.

– Dr. V.P. Bhutani
(Prof. of College of Pharmacy)

WHY SHOULD I CALCULATE MENTALLY WHEN I HAVE A CALCULATOR?

Just like our body needs exercise to stay fit, our brain is also like a muscle which needs exercise and doing mental calculations is the best exercise for the brain.

We know that people go to the gym for exercising, to tone their muscle and to remain healthy and active. In the same way, it has been researched that if exercised and used very often, our brain weight may increase upto 5%. Our brain behaves like plastic. As plastic once expanded does not return to its original size, in the same way, brain weight once increased cannot be reduced.

Just as a machine works smoothly only when used regularly with proper oiling, in the same way, we can ensure the smooth functioning of our brain when proper oiling in the form of mental work in the right direction, is provided to it.

Exercising brain not only helps to calculate fast, but also in our daily activities. The efficiency of the whole process of thinking and taking action is accelerated substantially in our day-to-day decisions.

A research has shown that people who perform mental calculations are able to think fast and arrive at right decisions after analyzing different situations much quicker than those who are dependent on computers and calculators for their mental work.

While doing calculations with a calculator, our involvement in the process of calculation is nil. This is highly dangerous in the long run, as we lose our ability to calculate in day-to-day life and our thinking ability is also affected. Mental maths, on the contrary, helps to sharpen our calculating ability.

So, to have a smart and fast brain, we must exercise it as often as possible and performing mental calculations serves as a mental gym for our brain, keeping it fit and active.

According to anatomists, our brain has 2 halves: the left and the right. The left half of our brain is used to collect information, analyze it and arrive at logical conclusions. Only the left part of the brain is activated and developed by the present Maths education being taught in schools and colleges. We use the right half of the brain for creative works, pattern recognition and sensing intuition, but unfortunately this intuitive faculty remains undeveloped in most of the students.

The techniques taught in this book, based on Vedic Mathematics, help to develop both parts of the brain. The very first step in this system is to recognize the pattern of the problem and pick up the most efficient Vedic method from the multiple choices available at each stage of working.

Secondly, because of the simplicity and the availability of more than one method, it provides varied opportunities for the development of innovation in young students. At the same time, the job of calculating becomes easy and interesting.

Not only do the calculations become easier, they can be done with less mental energy and in a short time. At the same time, unlike calculators, there is full involvement, which is very important. This approach provides a corrective methodology to the problem of mental slavery to the calculators.

CONTENTS

Preface – Can I Be a Human Calculator?   vi

Why should I calculate mentally when I have a calculator?   xii

What is Vedic Mathematics?   xv

Chapters	Pages

PART I – ARITHMETIC

0.	Vedic Math-E-Magic	3 – 8
1.	Two basic concepts of Vedic Mathematics	9 – 12
2.	Multiplications with 99999…. in less than 5 seconds	13 – 18
3.	Magic with 11	19 – 24
4.	Multiplying by 12 (without using 12)	25 – 31
5.	Subtraction at one look	32 – 39
6.	Checking your answers (*removing silly mistakes*)	40 – 47
7.	Multiplication of numbers near the bases	48 – 68
8.	Multiplication by 5, 25, 50, 250, 500….	69 – 70
9.	Vertical & Crosswise Multiplication	71 – 80
10.	Interesting squares	81 – 88
11.	Finding squares in one line	89 – 96
12.	Fractions	97 – 106
13.	Division	107 – 124
14.	Long division in one line (the crowning glory)	125 – 143
15.	Square roots in one line	144 – 154
16.	Cube roots at a Glance	155 – 158
17.	Cubes	159 – 169
18.	Magic Division	170 – 186
19.	Checking Divisibility by prime number	187 – 198
20.	500 years Calendar	199 – 206

PART II – ALGEBRA

21.	Algebraic Multiplication	209 – 214
22.	Factorizing Quadratic Expressions	215 – 223
23.	Linear Equations In One Variable	224 – 228
24.	Linear Equations (Special Types)	229 – 238
25.	Simultaneous Linear Equations	239 – 249
26.	Application of Vedic Maths in Competition Exams	250 – 254
	Speed Enhancement Test papers	255 – 257
	Vedic Maths Sutras and Sub-Sutras	258 – 260
	Vedic Mathematics Sutras (with their applications)	261 – 262
	Answers	263 – 274
	Testimonials	275 – 276
	Author's profile	277 – 278

WHAT IS VEDIC MATHEMATICS?

Vedic Mathematics is a super fast way of making all Mathematical Calculations easy and fast.

About 5000 years. back, an era which was also known as the Golden Age Period, people used to calculate mentally and very accurately, without even using pen and paper, in no time. At that time, education was imparted in verbal form only. As time passed by, a need was felt to document the knowledge of that time for future generations and different Vedas were being written. With time that knowledge also got scattered.

We all know that there are four main Vedas – *Rigveda, Samveda, Yajurveda and Atharvaveda*. Each of these deals with a specific set of subject. Out of these, *Atharvaveda* contains all kinds of knowledge related to all kinds of sciences, be it architectural science, astronomical science or engineering science or science of mathematics. At the beginning of the 20th century, great interest was shown in the ancient Sanskrit texts, especially in Europe. However, certain texts called '*Ganit Sutras*' in *Atharvaveda*, which contained Mathematical deductions, were ignored, because no one could find any Mathematics in them.

Vedic Maths is the result of intuitive work of **Late Swami Shri Bharti Krishna Tirthaji** *(1884 – 1960),* the Shankaracharya of Puri, who himself was a great scholar of Sanskrit, English, Mathematics, History and Philosophy. He studied these texts called '*Ganit Sutras*' in deep silence in the forests of Shingeri for a period of 8 long years. There in deep meditation and through intuitive revelation from scattered references, he was able to reconstruct 16 main Sutras or Formulae and 13 Sub-Sutras, which cover a wide range of mathematical operations from arithmetic to analytical cones. Through these formulae, he presented a glimpse of the high tech methods used in earlier times in the form of a system, now popularly known as "Vedic Mathematics".

Bharti Krishna ji wrote 16 volumes, one on each of these 16 formulae, but these were unaccountably lost and when the loss was confirmed in his final years, he wrote a single volume, "Vedic Mathematics", which was published 5 years after his death.

These formulae are short, easy to remember and very easy to apply.

These shortcut formulae save a lot of time. They make it possible for students to multiply a 20-digit number by a 19-digit number, without using pen and paper. The process boosts confidence in one's ability to tackle mathematical problems, which is necessary for a sustained interest in Mathematics. The speed, distinctness and directness with which one arrives at the answer make Vedic Mathematics a class by itself.

One wonders at the supreme simplicity and ease of the Vedic Method, which is lacking in most of our usual methods.

While performing arithmetical calculations, we deal with only ten numbers, i.e. 0 to 9. We can also call them the alphabets of mathematics by which the whole infinite number system is created. Each one of these has got peculiar properties and patterns of behavior. If we understand these patterns and make these numbers our friends, then the whole mathematics is just like playing with numbers. These properties can be used to develop newer and newer methods of calculation because Vedic Maths looks at numbers from different angles. When 39 is seen as 39, it has some properties. But as soon as we look at it as 40-1(=39), we have an altogether new world opened up for calculations.

Therefore, Vedic Mathematics is the gift of the Veda to solve the problem of "Maths anxiety" faced in Maths education all over the world.

In a nutshell, we can say that owing to its very special and universal features, Vedic Maths system converts the dry and tedious Maths into a playful and joyful subject, which children enjoy to learn with a smile.

PART I :

ARITHMETIC

Vedic Math-E-Magic

An interest in a subject is important to understand it. But what if the subject itself is like a MAGIC? Magic – a term that has always fascinated us as kids and even as grown-ups, for some!

Our journey of Vedic Math-E-Magic begins with chapter zero as it is the first digit of maths language. During our journey, you'll not only improve your maths skills, you'll increase your love of numbers. So, before actually beginning it, let's set the stage for the magic tricks by trying out how much time you take to carry out the following multiplication by using the old conventional method:

Example 1:

47328 × 99999

This calculation by the usual long multiplication method, which is the only method taught in schools, will take about 4–5 minutes. So try it out and check yourself:

$$
\begin{array}{r}
4\,7\,3\,2\,8 \\
\times\,9\,9\,9\,9\,9 \\
\hline
4\,2\,5\,9\,5\,2 \\
4\,2\,5\,9\,5\,2\,\times \\
4\,2\,5\,9\,5\,2\,\times\,\times \\
4\,2\,5\,9\,5\,2\,\times\,\times\,\times \\
4\,2\,5\,9\,5\,2\,\times\,\times\,\times\,\times \\
\hline
4\,7\,3\,2\,7\,5\,2\,6\,7\,2 \\
\end{array}
$$

You must have taken 4–5 minutes or even more to solve this sum.

Now, get ready for the magic !

What if the answer to this calculation can be found in one step and in one line only?

Take 2 minutes to read and understand the following method and then see, it is a matter of few seconds only.

47328 × 99999

We shall find the answer in 2 parts: LHS (Left Hand Side) and RHS (Right Hand Side).

For **LHS** answer, subtract 1 from the original number, i.e.

47328 − 1 = **47327**

For **RHS** answer, subtract all the digits of the LHS answer from 9, i.e.

$$\begin{array}{r} 99999 \\ -47327 \\ \hline 52672 \end{array}$$

Combine both LHS and RHS parts of the answer, to get the final answer as:

47328 × 99999 = **4732752672**

Now, you might wonder "if this is mathematics or magic" ?

And the answer is: It is both.

> "It is magic until you understand it;
> And it is mathematics thereafter".
> That is why I call it "**Math-E-Magic**".

Example 2:

32497 × 99999

LHS = 32497 − 1 = 32496

RHS = 99999 − 32496 = 67503

So, the final answer is **3249667503**.

Now, you can also try one example using this technique and again check how long you take this time:

Example 3:

2375 × 9999

The answer can be directly written as:

2375 × 9999 = **23747625**

Isn't it amazing to find answers of such long multiplications through small subtractions in few seconds only!

Let's try some other examples:

Example 4:

Find the square of 35

Conventional method:

$$35^2 = \begin{array}{r} 35 \\ \times\ 35 \\ \hline 175 \\ 105\times \\ \hline 1225 \end{array}$$

Vedic Method:

35^2

Answer comes in 2 parts: LHS and RHS

LHS = first number × next consecutive number, i.e. $3 \times 4 = 12$

RHS = $5^2 = 25$

So, $35^2 = 3\times4\ /\ 5^2 = 1225$

Example 5:

Find the square of 75

The answer can be directly written as:

$75^2 = 7\times8\ /\ 5^2 = 5625$

       LHS RHS

So you see, instead of carrying out long cumbersome steps of working, answer to difficult sums can also be given in a single and simple step of work by the Vedic Method. It's like you merely have to go on tossing off the digits one after the other by mere mental arithmetic without needing pen, pencil or paper.

There are some more illustrations given to compare the two methods – the Vedic one line method and the Conventional method, involving long and tedious computational steps. *However, a detailed methodology and practice of each technique is explained in their corresponding chapters.*

Some more magical illustrations of Vedic Maths:

Example 6:   **Find the square of 9989**

Vedic Method	*Conventional Method*
$9989^2 = 99780121$	9989
	× 9989
	89901
	79912×
	89901××
	89901×××
	99780121

Example 7:   **Find the cube of 996**

Vedic Method	*Conventional Method*
$996^3 = 988 / 048 / \overline{064}$	996
$= 988047936$	× 996
	5976
	8964×
	8964××
	992016
	992016
	× 996
	5952096
	8928144×
	8928144××
	988047936

Example 8:   **Find 24372 × 53014**

Vedic Method	*Conventional Method*
24372	24372
× 53014	×53014
1292057208	97488
	24372×
	00000××
	73116×××
	121860××××
	1292057208

Example 9:

Find the full recurring decimal for $\dfrac{3}{19}$

Vedic Method   *Conventional Method*

$\dfrac{3}{19} = 0.\dot{1}5789473684210526\dot{3}$ $19\overline{)30}(0.\dot{1}5789473684210526\dot{3}$

$$
\begin{array}{r}
\underline{19} \\
110 \\
\underline{95} \\
150 \\
\underline{133} \\
170 \\
\underline{152} \\
180 \\
\underline{171} \\
90 \\
\underline{76} \\
140 \\
\underline{133} \\
70 \\
\underline{57} \\
130 \\
\underline{114} \\
160 \\
\underline{152} \\
80 \\
\underline{76} \\
40 \\
\underline{38} \\
20 \\
\underline{19} \\
100 \\
\underline{95} \\
50 \\
\underline{38} \\
120 \\
\underline{114} \\
60 \\
\underline{57} \\
30
\end{array}
$$

Example 10:

Divide 6732045 by 738942 upto 4 decimal places

Vedic Method	*Conventional Method*

Vedic Method

738942 | 67 3 2 0 4 5
  4 9 10 8 10

9.1103

Conventional Method

738942)6732045(9.1103

6650478

815670
738942

767280
738942

2833800
2216826

616974

Example 11:

Find the square root of 24.365 upto 3 decimal places

Vedic Method

8 | 24. 3 6 5 0
  8 11 11 13

4. 936

Conventional Method

4.936

24.365

16

89 | 836
801

986 | 3550
2949

60100
59196

904

So now that you have already taken the test drive of Vedic Maths,

Are you ready to go for the magical and adventurous roller coaster ride!

Two Basic Concepts of Vedic Mathematics

Let's start the amazing and wonderful journey of Vedic Mathematics with the two basic concepts — Base and Complements.

BASE

The whole number system is made up of only 10 numbers (0 to 9). All these numbers repeat themselves in a specific order after numbers like 10, 100, 1000, and so on, which are called Bases.

> Bases are the numbers starting with 1 and followed by any number of 0's e.g. 10, 100, 1000, 10000 and so on.

Base numbers are the first number for 'those many digits' like 10 is the first number for 2-digit numbers, 100 is the first number for 3-digit numbers and so on.

A base number should not have any other digit at the starting except 1 and it should be followed only by 0's. So, numbers such as 200, 1001, 1200 are not bases.

EXERCISE 1.1

Say whether the following numbers are bases or not:

1.	1001	**2.**	1100	**3.**	201	**4.**	10
5.	1000	**6.**	4000	**7.**	1000100	**8.**	1500
9.	10000	**10.**	2900				

COMPLEMENTS

The concept of complement is important to understand because these complements are very useful in making many kinds of calculations easy and interesting which includes subtraction, multiplication, division, finding squares, cubes and many more.

So, first we understand what complements are and in the following chapters, we shall see their use in different types of calculations.

> Those two numbers which when added with each other results in the next nearest base, are called Complements of each other. e.g. 48 + 52 = 100, 23 + 77 = 100.
>
> So, 48 is the complement of 52 and 52 is the complement of 48.

In other words, a complement of a number can be calculated by subtracting it out from its nearest base, like:

complement of 76 = 100 – 76 = 24

complement of 358 = 1000 – 358 = 642

But, finding complements of bigger numbers means subtraction from bigger bases, like finding the complement of 24368 means 100000 – 24368 which requires the borrowing process at each column.

In Vedic Maths, to simplify this, we use the formula "*All from 9 and last from 10*". This means that:

> To find the complement of any number, subtract all the digits from 9 and the last digit from 10 (where the last digit means the unit's place digit.)

Example 1: **Find the complement of 4356.**

Complement of 4356 can be found by subtracting each of 4, 3 and 5 from 9 and the last digit 6 from 10, i.e.

$$\begin{array}{r} 9\ \ 9\ \ 9\ \ 10 \\ -\ \ 4\ \ 3\ \ 5\ \ \ 6 \\ \hline 5\ \ 6\ \ 4\ \ \ 4 \end{array}$$

So complement of 4356 is **5644**.

Example 2: **Find the complement of 8375.**

Complement of **8375 = 1 6 2 5**

(9–8) (9–3) (9–7) (10–5)

Similarly, complement of **4397 = 5603**

and complement of **9158 = 0842**

When a 0 comes in between the number

When a 0 comes in between the number, treat this 0 as any other digit, i.e. subtract it from 9 like other digits.

Example 3: **Find the complement of 3059.**

Complement of 3059 can simply be found as:

$$
\begin{array}{r}
9\ 9\ 9\ 10 \\
-\ 3\ 0\ 5\ \ 9 \\
\hline
6\ 9\ 4\ \ 1
\end{array}
$$

So, the complement of 3059 = **6941**

When a 0 comes at the end of the number

When a 0 comes at the end of the number, write that 0 as it is in the complement and treat the last non-zero digit as the last digit, i.e. subtract the last non-zero digit from 10 and rest of the numbers from 9.

Example 4: **Find the complement of 3420.**

It can be found by subtracting digits 3 and 4 from 9 and considering 2 as the last digit, subtract it from 10 and write the 0 as it is, as shown below:

$$
\begin{array}{r}
9\ \ 9\ \ 10 \\
-\ 3\ \ 4\ \ \ 2\ \ 0 \\
\hline
6\ \ 5\ \ \ 8\ \ 0
\end{array}
$$

So, the complement of **3420** = **6580**.

Similarly, complement of **25390** is **74610**.

And complement of **7400** is **2600**.

EXERCISE 1.2

Find the complements of the following numbers:

1.	243	**2.**	731	**3.**	1298	**4.**	4763
5.	84056	**6.**	7060	**7.**	700	**8.**	80900
9.	9100	**10.**	80050				

When a decimal comes in between the number

Numbers with decimals are treated like any other numbers, but the decimal point must come at its place in the complement.

Example 5: **Find the complement of 437.26**

$$
\begin{array}{r}
9\ 9\ 9\ \ \ 9\ 10 \\
-\ 4\ 3\ 7.\ 2\ \ \ 6 \\
\hline
5\ 6\ 2.\ 7\ \ \ 4 \\
\hline
\end{array}
$$

So, complement of the **437.26 = 562.74**

Similarly, complement of **830.25 = 169.75**

complement of **523.043 = 476.957**

EXERCISE 1.3

Find the complements of the following numbers:

1.	638.26	**2.**	724.850	**3.**	9306.002	**4.**	29346.83
5.	58600	**6.**	28309	**7.**	81819	**8.**	1201.050
9.	82650	**10.**	6409.20				

Multiplication with 99999...
in Less than 5 Seconds

In the whole number series, 9 is the most interesting number, and so multiplication by 9 is also very interesting in itself.

If a number is to be multiplied by another number consisting of only 9's or a series of 9, the answer can be arrived in a very easy and amazing way.

The formulae used for these calculations are:

    1. *By one less than the one before*

    2. *All from nine and last from ten*

*When two numbers are multiplied, any one of them is the **multiplicand** and the other is the **multiplier**. e.g. 23 × 99, here, we consider 23 as multiplicand and the other number, i.e. 99 as multiplier.*

In this chapter, whenever we are talking about the number having 9's, we will consider that number as a multiplier.

We have categorized the multiplication by 9's in 3 types according to the number of 9's present in the multiplier.

TYPE I: Multiplicand digits = Multiplier digits

When the number of digits in the multiplicand (number to be multiplied), are equal to the number of 9's in the multiplier.

The answer comes in two parts; LHS & RHS.

For **LHS**, we apply the formula: *by one less than the one before*, i.e. subtract one from the multiplicand.

For **RHS**, we write the complement of the multiplicand, by using the formula: *"all from nine and last from ten"*.

Example 1:   **46 × 99**

46 is a 2 digit number and 99 also has two 9's in it.

For **LHS**, subtract 1 from 46, *i.e.* 46 – 1 = **45**

For **RHS**, write the complement of 46, *i.e.* **54**

So, the answer is **4554.**

Example 2: **389 × 999**

The answer can be directly written in two parts as:

$$388 / 611$$

by subtracting 1   complement of
from 389   389

So, 389 × 999 = **388611**

Isn't it amazing to find the answer of such a big calculation through a simple subtraction.

The same formula can be applied to any number of digits provided that the number of digits in the multiplicand and the multiplier (number of 9's) are the same.

Example 3: **942678 × 999999**

LHS = 942678 – 1 = **942677**

RHS = complement of 942678 = **057322**

So, the answer is 942678 × 999999 = **942677057322.**

EXERCISE 2.1

Multiply the following:

1. 24 × 99   2. 732 × 999   3. 401 × 999

4. 67 × 99   5. 832 × 999   6. 1765 × 9999

7. 9988 × 9999   8. 85671 × 99999   9. 3924 × 9999

10. 789526 × 999999

TYPE II: Multiplicand digits < Multiplier digits

When the number of digits in the multiplicand, is less than the number of 9's in the multiplier.

The same formula as in Type 1 will be applied in this type also, but with a little modification.

Make the number of digits in the multiplicand equal to the number of 9's by adding required 0's, before the multiplicand.

For **LHS**, subtract 1 from the multiplicand;

For **RHS**, write the complement of the multiplicand (obtained by adding required 0's).

Example 4: **67 × 999**

Since, the multiplier here has three 9's, so convert the multiplicand 67 also into a 3 digit number, by adding a 0 in front of it. So it becomes:

067 × 999

The answer can be directly written in two parts as:

066 / 933

by subtracting 1   complement of
from 067   067

So, the answer is 67 × 999 = **66933**.

The process can be simplified even more in the following 3 steps:

1. Reduce 1 from the multiplicand,
2. Write the extra 9('s), (number of 9's in the multiplier more than the number of digits in the multiplicand);
3. Write the complement of multiplicand.

The above will become clearer by the following example:

Example 5: **243 × 9999**

Here the multiplicand 243 has 3 digits and multiplier 9999 has 4 digits, so in this case, there is one 9 extra in the multiplier.

The answer can be arrived directly as

$$242 / 9 / 757 = \mathbf{2429757}$$

One extra 9 of the multiplier

***Example 6*:** $\mathbf{58 \times 9999}$

$$= 57 / 99 / 42$$
$$= \mathbf{579942.}$$

***Example 7*:** $\mathbf{645 \times 9999999}$

$$= 644 / 9999 / 355$$
$$= \mathbf{6449999355.}$$

EXERCISE 2.2

Multiply the following:

1. 42×999 2. 37×999 3. 901×9999

4. 76×9999 5. 813×9999 6. 179×9999

7. 982×9999 8. 567×99999 9. 64×9999

10. 38001×999999

TYPE III: Multiplicand digits > Multiplier digits

When the number of digits in the multiplicand are more than the number of 9's in the multiplier.

***Example 8*:** $\mathbf{378 \times 99}$

We do this multiplication in 3 steps:

Step 1: Divide the multiplicand into 2 parts, such that the number of digits on RHS of multiplicand is equal to the number of 9's in the multiplicand.

i.e. $\mathbf{3} / \mathbf{78} \times 99$

Step 2: Add 1 to the **LHS** of multiplicand and subtract the number obtained from whole of the multiplicand to get the LHS of answer.

i.e. $3 + 1 = 4$; subtract 4 from 378 to get **374**

Step 3: For **RHS** part answer, write the complement of RHS of the multiplicand.

i.e. complement of 78 = **22**

So, the answer is 378 ×99 = 374 / 22 = **37422**

Example 9:   **4276 × 999**

Step 1: Divide multiplicand 4276 in 2 parts, as shown:

4 / 276 × 999

3 digits   three 9's

Step 2: For **LHS** answer, add 1 to LHS of the multiplicand

4 + 1 = 5

Subtract this 5 from whole of the multiplicand
i.e. 4276 − 5 = **4271**

Step 3: For **RHS** answer, write the complement of 276, i.e. **724**

So, the answer is 4276 × 999 = **4271724**

Example 10:   **3274 × 99**

Step 1: Divide multiplicand 3274 in 2 parts, as shown: **32 / 74 × 99**

Step 2: For **LHS**: 32 + 1 = 33

3274 − 33 = 3241   3241 /

Step 3: For **RHS**: complement of 74 = 26   3241 / **26**

So, the answer is 3274 × 94 = **324126.**

Example 11:	***Example 12:***
425 × 99	**7428 × 99**
4 / 25	74 / 28
− 5	− 75
4 2 0 / 75	73 5 3 / 72
So, the answer is **42075.**	So, the answer is **735372.**

EXERCISE 2.3

Multiply the following:

1. 946 × 99   2. 73 × 9   3. 192 × 99   4. 1639 × 99

5. 427 × 99   6. 8437 × 999   7. 526 × 99   8. 5568 × 999

9. 3927 × 99   10. 90145 × 999

GENERAL GUIDELINES

1. When the number of multiplicand digits = number of 9's, subtract 1 from the multiplicand for LHS answer and write the complement of the multiplicand for RHS answer.

2. When the number of multiplicand digits are less than the number of 9's, the procedure is the same explained above, except that we place extra 9's in between LHS and RHS. (extra 9's means number of 9's in the multiplier more than the number of digits in the multiplicand).

3. When the number of multiplicand digits are more than the number of 9's, divide the multiplicand into 2 parts, so that the number of digits on the RHS of multiplicand is equal to the number of 9's in the multiplier. Add 1 to the LHS of the multiplicand and subtract that number from the multiplicand to get LHS of the answer.

4. Write the complement of the digits on the right of the multiplicand to get the RHS of the answer.

Magic with 11

By now, just as the multiplication by 9 seems a simple calculation to you, multiplication by number 11 is also very interesting and fast in itself.

In many cases, the answers can be given by just a look only.

Example 1: **25 × 11**

The answer can be given at a glance, i.e. 275.

Here's how:

Write 2 & 5 of 25 as it is and the sum of 2 & 5 (i.e. 7) in between.

$$25 \times 11$$
$$2\ 7\ 5$$
add

So, 25 × 11 = **275**

Similarly, **71 × 11 = 781** (sum of 7 & 1, i.e. 8 in between)

Example 2: **42631 × 11**

In longer calculations like this, we first write the border numbers, i.e. 4 & 1 as it is and then write the sum of next successive pairs in between as shown below:

i.e.   4 2 6 3 1 × 11
        4 6 8 9 4 1

4 & 1 as it is, as two border numbers. Then, starting from the left side, we keep writing the sum of the two digits:

4 + 2 = 6, 2 + 6 = 8, 6 + 3 = 9, 3 + 1 = 4

So, the answer is **468941**.

This system of 'calculation at a glance' is more comfortable when the addition of numbers do not require carry over. When it needs carry over, we make use of the formula known as *"only the last two"*.

In such a case, we simplify the calculation by making it as a **Dot Sandwich**, i.e. one Dot on both the sides of the number.

The application of this can be better understood in the following example:

Example 3:   354 × 11

Make a **Dot Sandwich** of the number by putting a dot on both sides of the number, like this:

· **354** · (where the value of dot is 0).

Step 1: Starting from the RHS dot, keep on adding two digits at a time, until we reach the LHS dot.

$$· 354 · × 11 \qquad 4 + 0 = \mathbf{4} \rightarrow \text{unit's digit}$$
$$\mathbf{4}$$

Step 2: $\qquad · 354 · × 11 \qquad 5 + 4 = \mathbf{9} \rightarrow \text{ten's digit}$
$$\mathbf{9}4$$

Step 3: $\qquad · 354 · × 11 \qquad 3 + 5 = \mathbf{8} \rightarrow \text{hundred's digit}$
$$\mathbf{8}\,9\,4$$

Step 4: $\qquad · 354 · × 11 \qquad 0 + 3 = \mathbf{3} \rightarrow \text{thousand's digit}$
$$\mathbf{3}\,8\,9\,4$$

So, the answer is 354 × 11 = **3894**.

Example 4: 4573 × 11

First we convert it into a dot sandwich like: ·**4573**· and then just keep adding the last 2 digits, starting from the right dot as shown below:

Step 1: $\qquad ·4573 · \qquad 3 + 0 = \mathbf{3}$
$$\mathbf{3}$$

Step 2: $\qquad ·4573· \qquad 7 + 3 = {}_1\mathbf{0} \text{ (1 is carried to the next step)}$
$${}_1 03$$

Step 3: $\qquad ·4573· \qquad 5 + 7 = 12$
$${}_1 303 \qquad 12 + 1(\text{carry}) = {}_1\mathbf{3} \text{ (1 is carried to the next step)}$$

Step 4: $\cdot 4\underset{\smile}{57}3\cdot$ $4 + 5 = 9$

        $_10303$ $9 + 1 \text{(carry)} = {}_1\mathbf{0}$ (1 is carried to the next step)

Step 5: $\cdot 4\underset{\smile}{57}3\cdot$ $0 + 4 = 4$

        50303 $4 + 1 \text{(carry)} = \mathbf{5}$

So, the answer is $4573 \times 11 = \mathbf{50303}$.

Note: *If at any step, we get a two digit number, we write down the unit's digit and carry over the ten's digit to be added in the next step.*

Example 5:   **28346 × 11**

        $\cdot 28346\cdot = 3\underset{1}{}1\underset{1}{}18\underset{1}{}06 = \mathbf{311806}$

Example 6:   **32419 × 11**

        $\cdot 32419\cdot = 3566\underset{1}{}09 = \mathbf{356609}$

Once the technique for multiplication by 11 is mastered, multiplication of a number by 22, 33, 44, etc. (multiples of 11), can be carried out quickly by splitting the multiplicand as 11 × 2, 11 × 3 or 11 × 4.

First the number is multiplied by 2, 3 or as the case may be and then, that obtained number multiplied by 11.

Example 7:   **4362 × 33**

It can be written as: $4362 \times 3 \times 11$

First multiply 4362 by 3 to get the result as 13086 and then in the second step, multiply this 13086 by 11, through the dot sandwich method:

$$\cdot 13086\cdot \times 11 = 143946$$

So, the answer is $4362 \times 33 = \mathbf{143946}.$

EXERCISE 3.1

Multiply the following:

1. 32 × 11   **2.** 451 × 11   **3.** 489 × 11   **4.** 4721 × 11

5. 1496 × 11   **6.** 283 × 44   **7.** 736 × 66   **8.** 8046 × 11

9. 6781 × 11   **10.** 342 × 77

This formula can also be modified further to carry out calculations with 111, 1111, etc.

<u>*Example 8*</u>:   **3582 × 111**

In this case we will make the dot sandwich with **two dots on each side** of the number and take the **sum of 3 digits** at a time, starting from the right dot, as shown below:

Step 1: $\cdot\cdot$ 3 5 8 2 $\cdot\cdot$ $2 + 0 + 0 = 2$
                    $\underset{2}{\smile}$

Step 2: $\cdot\cdot$ 3 5 8 2 $\cdot\cdot$ $8 + 2 + 0 = {}_1 0$
                    $\underset{{}_1 02}{\smile}$

Step 3: $\cdot\cdot$ 3 5 8 2 $\cdot\cdot$ $5 + 8 + 2 = 15$
                    $\underset{{}_1 602}{\smile}$ $15 + 1 \text{ (carry)} = {}_1 6$

Step 4: $\cdot\cdot$ 3 5 8 2 $\cdot\cdot$ $3 + 5 + 8 = 16$
                    $\underset{{}_1 7602}{\smile}$ $16 + 1 \text{ (carry)} = {}_1 7$

Step 5: $\cdot\cdot$ 3 5 8 2 $\cdot\cdot$ $0 + 3 + 5 = 8$
                    $\underset{9 7602}{\smile}$ $8 + 1 \text{ (carry)} = 9$

Step 6: $\cdot\cdot$ 3 5 8 2 $\cdot\cdot$ $0 + 0 + 3 = 3$
                    $\underset{397602}{\smile}$

So, the answer is $3582 \times 111 = \textbf{397602.}$

<u>*Example 9*</u>:   **8732 × 111** $= \cdot\cdot 8732 \cdot\cdot = 9\ \underset{1}{6}\ \underset{1}{9}\ \underset{1}{2} 52 = \textbf{969252}$

<u>*Example 10*</u>:   **5924 × 111** $= \cdot\cdot 5924 \cdot\cdot = 6\ \underset{1}{5}\ \underset{1}{7}\ \underset{1}{5} 64 = \textbf{657564}$

Let's take one example of multiplication by 1111 also:

<u>*Example 11*</u>:   **2473 × 1111**

We make dot sandwich with **3 dots on each side** of the number and take **the sum of 4 digits** at a time, starting from the right dot.

Note: *The number of digits in a group taken for addition is always equal to the number of digits in the multiplier (11, 111, 1111, etc.)*

Step 1: $\cdots 2\ 4\ 7\ 3 \cdots$ $3 + 0 + 0 + 0 = 3$

                        $\underbrace{\quad}$

                           3

Step 2: $\cdots 2\ 4\ 7\ 3 \cdots$ $7 + 3 + 0 + 0 = {}_1 0$

                        $\underbrace{\quad}$

                          $_1 03$

Step 3: $\cdots 2\ 4\ 7\ 3 \cdots$ $4 + 7 + 3 + 0 = 14$

                        $\underbrace{\quad}$ $14 + 1$ (carry) $= {}_1 5$

                         $_1 503$

Step 4: $\cdots 2\ 4\ 7\ 3 \cdots$ $2 + 4 + 7 + 3 = 16$

                        $\underbrace{\quad}$ $16 + 1$ (carry) $= {}_1 7$

                        $_1 7503$

Step 5: $\cdots 2\ 4\ 7\ 3 \cdots$ $0 + 2 + 4 + 7 = 13$

                        $\underbrace{\quad}$ $13 + 1$ (carry) $= {}_1 4$

                       $_1 47503$

Step 6: $\cdots 2\ 4\ 7\ 3 \cdots$ $0 + 0 + 2 + 4 = 6$

                        $\underbrace{\quad}$ $6 + 1$ (carry) $= 7$

                       747503

Step 7: $\cdots 2\ 4\ 7\ 3 \cdots$ $0 + 0 + 0 + 2 = 2$

                        $\underbrace{\quad}$

                      $2\ 747503$

So, the answer is $2473 \times 1111 = $ **2747503.**

EXERCISE 3.2

Multiply the following:

1. 389×111 2. 43×111 3. 546×111 4. 3224×111

5. 213×1111 6. 702×1111 7. 8152×111 8. 2091×1111

9. 493×1111 10. 1739×111

GENERAL GUIDELINES

1. Make a dot sandwich of the given number by putting a dot on either side of the number, where the value of the dot is 0.

2. When multiplying with 11, starting from the right dot, keep on adding 2 digits at a time, until we reach the LHS dot.

3. When multiplying with 111, two dots on each side of the number are placed and starting from RHS dot, keep on adding 3 digits at a time, until we reach the LHS dot.

4. In any step, if addition gives a 2 digit number, write down the unit's digit only and carry over the other digit to the next step.

5. As the number of 1's in the multiplication increases, the dots on each side of the number increase accordingly. Also the number of digits in a group taken for addition is always equal to the number of 1's in the multiplier.

MULTIPLYING BY 12
(Without Using 12)

Students generally find it difficult to memorise the tables from 12 to 19 and even after mugging up these tables, they often get confused. But now using the following method, there is no need to memorize them at all.

You can mentally multiply any number by 12 if you know the table of 2 or multiply any number by 17, if you know the table of 7. That means by using tables from 2 – 9, you can actually multiply by tables of 12 – 19 in an easy way by using the following formula: *"twice the penultimate and the ultimate"*, where ultimate stands for the last digit and penultimate for the second last digit.

Let's understand this better, through the following example:

▌ MULTIPLICATION BY 12

Example 1:   **43 × 12**

Step 1:	· **4 3** ·	We first make the **dot sandwich** of 43 by putting a dot on both the sides of 43.
Step 2:	· 4 3 · ‿ **6**	Staring from RHS dot, **taking 2 digits at a time**, we see dot is the last digit and 3 is the second last digit. **Keep on adding, twice the second last digit and the last digit,** i.e. $(2 \times 3) + 0 = \mathbf{6}$.
Step 3:	· 4 3 · ‿ 16 $_1$	Considering the next pair, i.e. 43 (4 is the second last digit and 3 is the last digit), we get: $(2 \times 4) + 3 = 8 + 3 = {}_1 1$
Step 4:	· 4 3 · ‿ **5** 16	Considering the next pair, *i.e.* ·4 (dot is the second last and 4 is the last digit), we get:

$$(2 \times 0) + 4 = 4$$
$$4 + 1(\text{carry}) = \mathbf{5}$$

So, the answer is $43 \times 12 = \mathbf{516}$

Example 2: 3785×12

$\cdot 3\,7\,8\,5 \cdot$
$\underbrace{}$
$4\,5\,4\,2\,0$
$_1\;_2\;_2\;_1$

Step 1: $(2 \times 5) + 0 = {}_1\mathbf{0}$

Step 2: $(2 \times 8) + 5 = 21$
$21 + 1(\text{carry}) = {}_2\mathbf{2}$

Step 3: $(2 \times 7) + 8 = 22$
$22 + 2(\text{carry}) = {}_2\mathbf{4}$

Step 4: $(2 \times 3) + 7 = 13$
$13 + 2(\text{carry}) = {}_1\mathbf{5}$

Step 5: $(2 \times 0) + 3 = 3$
$3 + 1(\text{carry}) = \mathbf{4}$

So, the answer is $3785 \times 12 = \mathbf{45420}$.

Example 3:

$$5732 \times 12 = \cdot 5732 \cdot = 6_18_1784 = \mathbf{68784}$$

Example 4:

$$93264 \times 12 = \cdot 93264 \cdot = 11_219_11_168 = \mathbf{1119168}$$

GENERAL GUIDELINES

1. We make a dot sandwich by putting a dot on each side of the number.

2. Starting from the RHS dot and taking two digits at a time, keep on adding the twice of the second last digit and the last digit.

3. Continue it till we reach the LHS dot.

EXERCISE 4.1

Multiply the following:

1. 24×12 2. 72×12 3. 453×12 4. 216×12

5. 342×12 6. 8912×12 7. 4764×12 8. 21432×12

9. 5734×12 10. 30958×12

MULTIPLICATION BY 112

This method can further be extended to multiply any number by 112, 1112, etc. For 112, we will make **2 dots on both the sides** of the number to be multiplied and a **group of 3 digits** is taken at a time, starting from RHS dot.

Twice of third last digit is added to the sum of last & second last digit.

Example 5: **432 × 112**

Convert it first into dot sandwich as below:

$$\cdot\cdot 4\ 3\ 2\ \cdot\cdot$$

Step 1:	$\cdot\cdot 4\ 3\ 2\ \cdot\cdot$ $\underset{4}{\smile}$	considering the group 2 $\cdot\cdot$ $(2 \times 2) + (0 + 0) = \mathbf{4}$
Step 2:	$\cdot\cdot 4\ 3\ 2\ \cdot\cdot$ $\underset{8\ 4}{\smile}$	next group is 32$\cdot$ $(2 \times 3) + (2 + 0) = \mathbf{8}$
Step 3:	$\cdot\cdot 4\ 3\ 2\ \cdot\cdot$ $\underset{{}_1 3\ 8\ 4}{\smile}$	next group is 432 $(2 \times 4) + (3 + 2) = {}_1 3$
Step 4:	$\cdot\cdot 4\ 3\ 2\ \cdot\cdot$ $\underset{8{}_1 3\ 8\ 4}{\smile}$	next group is $\cdot$43 $(2 \times 0) + (4 + 3) = 7$ $7 + 1$ (carry) $= \mathbf{8}$
Step 5:	$\cdot\cdot 4\ 3\ 2\ \cdot\cdot$ $\underset{4\ 8{}_1 3\ 8\ 4}{\smile}$	next group is $\cdot\cdot$4 $(2 \times 0) + (0 + 4) = \mathbf{4}$

So, the answer is 432 × 112 = **48384**.

MULTIPLICATION BY 1112

The steps for multiplication with 1112 can be summarized as:

1. Put three dots on either side.
2. Take a group of 4 digits at a time.
3. Twice of 4th last digit, plus the earlier 3 digits (starting from the right side dot).

Example 6:   **5321 × 1112**

Step 1: $\cdots 5\,3\,2\,\underset{\smile}{1}\cdots$ $(2 \times 1) + (0 + 0 + 0) = \mathbf{2}$
                        2

Step 2: $\cdots 5\,3\,\underset{\smile}{2\,1}\cdots$ $(2 \times 2) + (1 + 0 + 0) = \mathbf{5}$
                        $5\,2$

Step 3: $\cdots 5\,\underset{\smile}{3\,2}\,1\cdots$ $(2 \times 3) + (2 + 1 + 0) = \mathbf{9}$
                        $9\,5\,2$

Step 4: $\cdots \underset{\smile}{5\,3}\,2\,1\cdots$ $(2 \times 5) + (3 + 2 + 1) = {}_1\mathbf{6}$
                        ${}_1 6\,9\,5\,2$

Step 5: $\cdots \underset{\smile}{5}\,3\,2\,1\cdots$ $(2 \times 0) + (5 + 3 + 2) = {}_1 0$
                                                    $10 + 1 \text{ (carry)} = {}_1\mathbf{1}$
                        ${}_1 6\,9\,5\,2$

Step 6: $\cdots \underset{\smile}{}\,5\,3\,2\,1\cdots$ $(2 \times 0) + (0 + 5 + 3) = 8$
                                                    $8 + 1 \text{ (carry)} = \mathbf{9}$
                        $9\,1\,6\,9\,5\,2$

Step 7: $\cdots \underset{\smile}{}\,5\,3\,2\,1\cdots$ $(2 \times 0) + (0 + 0 + 5) = \mathbf{5}$
                        $5\,9\,1\,6\,9\,5\,2$

So, the answer is 5321 × 1112 = **5916952**

Similarly, **842 × 1112** = $\cdots 842 \cdots$ = $9\,{}_1 3\,{}_1 6\,{}_2 3\,{}_1 04$ = **936304**.

So, you can see just how by a simple multiplication and adding few digits to it, we can make such big calculations in one line.

EXERCISE 4.2

Multiply the following:

1. 71 × 112   **2.** 84 × 112   **3.** 534 × 112   **4.** 1692 × 112

5. 426 × 1112   **6.** 916 × 1112   **7.** 834 × 1112 **8.** 2732 × 1112

9. 709 × 1112   **10.** 5861 × 1112

▌MULTIPLICATION BY TABLES OF 13 TO 19

The same formula, as for 12, can be applied when multiplying any number by 13 to 19, with a little modification.

When a number is multiplied by 13, 14, 15, 16, 17, 18 or 19, then instead of doubling the second last digit, as in the case of 12, we multiply it with 3, 4, 5, 6, 7, 8 and 9 respectively.

Let's understand it better with the following example:

Example 7:   24 × 13

Step 1: We make a dot sandwich as ·24·

Since, it is to be multiplied by 13, so we multiply the second last digit by 3.

Starting from the right, we multiply the second last digit, *i.e.* 4 by 3:

$$·2\underset{\smile}{4}· \qquad (3 \times 4) + 0 = {}_1 2$$
$$_1 2$$

Step 2: $·\underset{\smile}{2}4· \qquad (3 \times 2) + 4 = 10$

$\quad _1 12 \qquad\qquad\qquad 10 + 1(\text{carry}) = {}_1 1$

Step 3: $·2\,4· \qquad (3 \times 0) + 2 = 2$

$\quad \underset{\smile}{}$

$\mathbf{3}12 \qquad\qquad\qquad 2 + 1(\text{carry}) = \mathbf{3}$

So, the answer is 24 × 13 = **312**.

Example 8:   735 × 14

In this case, we will multiply the second last digit by 4.

Step 1: $·7\,3\underset{\smile}{5}· \qquad (4 \times 5) + 0 = {}_2 0$

$\qquad\quad _2 0$

Step 2: $·7\underset{\smile}{3}5· \qquad (4 \times 3) + 5 = 17$

$\qquad\quad _1 9\,0 \qquad\qquad 17 + 2\,(\text{carry}) = {}_1 9$

Step 3: $·\underset{\smile}{7}3\,5· \qquad (4 \times 7) + 3 = 31$

$\qquad\quad _3 2\,90 \qquad\qquad 31 + 1(\text{carry}) = {}_3 2$

Step 4: $\cdot 7\,3\,5 \cdot$ $(4 \times 0) + 7 = 7$

                   $1029\ 0$ $7 + 3(\text{carry}) = \mathbf{10}$

So, the answer is $735 \times 14 = \mathbf{10290}$.

EXERCISE 4.3

Multiply the following:

1. 438×16 2. 502×13 3. 8315×17 4. 10016×18

5. 372×14 6. 312×15 7. 9012×9 8. 543×13

9. 2961×12 10. 36041×16

Similarly, calculations by 113, 114, 1116, 1119, etc. can be made easy and the answer can be obtained in one line.

Example 9: 473×119

In this case, we will take the group of 3 digits at a time.

Multiply the third last digit of group by 9 and add the second last and the last digit to it.

Step 1: $\cdot\cdot 4\,7\,3\cdot\cdot$ $(9 \times 3) + 0 + 0 = {}_2 7$

                   ${}_2 7$

Step 2: $\cdot\cdot 4\,7\,3\cdot\cdot$ $(9 \times 7) + 3 + 0 = 66$

                   ${}_6 87$ $66 + 2(\text{carry}) = {}_6 8$

Step 3: $\cdot\cdot 4\,7\,3\cdot\cdot$ $(9 \times 4) + 7 + 3 = 46$

                   ${}_5 287$ $46 + 6(\text{carry}) = {}_5 2$

Step 4: $\cdot\cdot 4\,7\,3\cdot\cdot$ $(9 \times 0) + 4 + 7 = 11$

                   ${}_1 6287$ $11 + 5(\text{carry}) = {}_1 6$

Step 5: $\cdot\cdot 4\,7\,3\cdot\cdot$ $(9 \times 0) + 0 + 4 = 4$

                   56287 $4 + 1(\text{carry}) = 5$

So, the answer is $473 \times 119 = \mathbf{56287}$.

Multiplying By 12 (Without Using 12)   **31**

Some more solved examples:

Example 10: **932 × 16** = ·932· = $14_59_21_12$ = **14912**

Example 11: **481 × 117** = ··481·· = $5_16_42_577$ = **56277**

Example 12: **596 × 18** = ·596· = $10_57_82_48$ = **10728**

Example 13: **239 × 1115** = ···239··· = $26_16_24_28_45$ = **266485**

EXERCISE 4.4

Multiply the following:

1. 43 × 13   2. 87 × 16   3. 247 × 17   4. 845 × 19

5. 621 × 114   6. 372 × 115   7. 123 × 118   8. 7234 × 1113

9. 932 × 117   10. 216 × 113

Subtraction at One Look

Subtraction of a number can be categorized as follows:

1. Subtraction of any number from bases (10, 100 , 1000...)
2. General Subtraction

Subtraction of a number from its Base

The formula for finding complements *"All from 9 and last from 10"* can be made use of in subtracting any number from any base or from multiples of bases.

Example 1:

If a sum is like **10000 – 3246**, it is similar to finding complement of 3246. So applying the formulae "all from nine and the last from ten", we get

Complement of 3246 as 6754

So, 10000 – 3246 = **6754**

Note: The number of digits in the number to be subtracted should be equal to the number of 0's in the base.

This method of subtraction **removes the mental strain of borrowing** at each column which exists in the method taught in schools.

Similarly, **100 – 23** = complement of 23 = **77**

Also, **1000 – 426** = complement of 426 = **574**

EXERCISE 5.1

Subtract the following sums using complements:

1. 100 – 46	**2.** 100 – 94	**3.** 100 – 59	**4.** 100 – 28
5. 1000 – 246	**6.** 10000 – 4285	**7.** 1000 – 142	**8.** 1000 – 396
9. 10000 – 4908	**10.** 100 – 37		

Subtraction of a number from a bigger base

If the subtraction of the number is from a bigger base, then make the number of digits in the number to be subtracted equal to the number of 0's in the base, by adding the required 0's at the beginning of the number.

Example 2: **10000 – 23**

Here base 10000 has four 0's and 23 is a 2-digit number, so put two 0's in front of 23 to write it as 0023 and find its complement to get the answer.

i.e. 10000 – 23 = 10000 – 0023
$$= \text{complement of } 0023$$
$$= \mathbf{9977}$$

Addition of 0's can be done mentally also.

Similarly, **1000 – 46** can be written as 1000 – 046 = **954**

If the sum has decimals involved, then also the same formula is applied.

It should be checked that the number of digits before the decimal should be equal to the number of 0's in the base.

Example 3: **100 – 36.398 = 63.602**

Similarly, **1000 – 24.35** = 1000 – 024.35 = **975.65**

EXERCISE 5.2

Subtract the following sums:

1. 1000 – 77   **2.** 10000 – 65   **3.** 100000 – 637 **4.** 10000 – 3

5. 1000 – 8.05 **6.** 1 – 0.238   **7.** 10000 – 874.9 **8.** 10 – 2.9964

9. 100 – 72.42 **10.** 100000 – 172.246

Subtraction of a number from multiple of bases (200, 3000, etc.)

Split the multiple of base to the nearest base as shown in the following example:

Example 4:   **400 – 63**

Here 400 can be split as   300 + 100

So, the sum can be written as: 300 + 100 – 63

$$= 300 + (100 – 63)$$
$$= 300 + 37 \text{ (i.e. complement of 63)}$$
$$= 337$$

You need not do all the steps. These steps are just to make you understand the concept.

> Simply, reduce 1 from the multiple of base and write the complement of the number to be subtracted.
>
> *Note: Make sure that number of digits in the number to be subtracted should be equal to the number of 0's in the base.*

Example 5:   **5000 – 248**

Reduce 1 from 5 to get **4** at the thousand's place.

Write the complement of 248 as **752**

So, 5000 – 248 = **4752**

Example 6:   **8000 – 43**

It can be written as 8000 – 043 = **7 957**

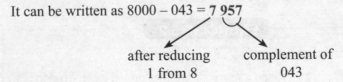

after reducing   complement of
1 from 8   043

When both the numbers have same number of digits

> When the number of digits in the number, to be subtracted, is equal to the number of digits in the multiple of base;
>
> Subtract the digits on the left most side of both the numbers. Further reduce it by 1 and take the complement of other digits of the number to be subtracted.

Example 7: 9000 – 5246

Considering the thousand's place, 9 will be reduced by 5 (9 – 5) = 4 and now reduce 1 more from 4. Then find the complement of 246.

So, 9000 – 5246 = **3 754**

[(9–5) – 1] complement of 246

EXERCISE 5.3

Subtract the following sums:

1. 600 – 88	**2.** 50000 – 2331	**3.** 8000 – 38	**4.** 300 – 132
5. 2000 – 979	**6.** 4000 – 285.36	**7.** 700 – 32.043	**8.** 9000 – 2435
9. 7000 – 23.6	**10.** 6000 – 1238		

General Subtraction without Borrowing

Formulae used are:

1. *All from nine and last from ten*

2. *By one more than the one before (Ekadhika Purvena)*

You are already familiar with the above first formulae. Let's see what the second formula means.

It is one of the first few amongst the 16 main formulae.

We get our whole number system using this formula. The first number of the number system is 0 and by using this formula or by *ekadhika*, one more than 0 is 1.

1 more than 1 is 2,

1 more than 2 is 3,

1 more than 3 is 4, and so on.

So, *ekadhika* of any number is the number one more than that.

i.e. *ekadhika* of 7 is 8,

ekadhika of 43 is 44

ekadhika of 247 is 248 and so on.

In the last chapter, we saw how easy it is to subtract any number from any base or its multiple without the process of borrowing. But other than bases, if we have to subtract any number from any other number, then also it is very easy to subtract without using the conventional borrowing method.

Let's see how:

Example 8:

Suppose the sum is:

4156 – 2679

> **Conventional Method**
>
> $4\,{}^1 1\,{}^1 5\,{}^1 6$
> $-2\ \ 6\ \ 7\ \ 9$
> $\overline{\ \ 1\ \ 4\ \ 7\ \ 7\ }$

Vedic Method:

Step 1: Starting from the right side, consider the one's digits. We can see that 6 on top is smaller digit and 9 below is a larger digit. So, 9 cannot be subtracted from 6.

So, instead of subtracting, we take the complement of 9, i.e. 1 and add it to 6 to get 7 as the answer at one's place digit. Also make *ekadhika* of the number before 9 by putting a dot on it (as a symbol of *ekadhika*), i.e. $\dot{7}$, now its value is equal to 8. It can be considered as carryover of conventional method.

$$4\ 1\ 5\ 6$$
$$-2\ 6\ \dot{7}\ 9 \qquad \text{complement of } 9 = 1$$
$$\phantom{-2\ 6\ \dot{7}\ }7 \qquad 1 + 6 = 7 \text{ at one's place}$$

Step 2: In ten's place again, upper digit 5 is smaller and lower digit 8 (i.e. $\dot{7}$ = 8) is larger. So add the complement of 8 i.e. 2 to 5 to get 7 as ten's digit of the answer.

$$4\ 1\ 5\ 6$$
$$-2\ \dot{6}\ \dot{7}\ 9 \qquad \text{complement of } \dot{7}, \text{ i.e. } 8 = 2$$
$$\phantom{-2\ \dot{6}\ }7\ 7 \qquad 2 + 5 = 7 \text{ at ten's place}$$

Make the *ekadhika* of the number before 7, i.e. 6 as $\dot{6}$

Step 3: In hundred's place again, upper digit 1 is smaller than lower digit $\dot{6}$ =7. So, add the complement of 7 (i.e. 3), to 1 to get 4 as the hundred's digit of the answer.

$$4\ 1\ 5\ 6$$
$$-\dot{2}\ \dot{6}\ \dot{7}\ 9 \qquad \text{complement of } \dot{6}, \text{ i.e. } 7 = 3$$
$$\phantom{-\dot{2}\ }4\ 7\ 7 \qquad 3 + 1 = 4 \text{ at hundred's place}$$

Make the *ekadhika* of the number before 6, i.e. 2 as $\overset{\bullet}{2}$

Step 4: In thousand's place, here 4 is bigger than 2 (i.e. 3), so it can be subtracted normally as:

$$
\begin{array}{r}
4\ 1\ 5\ 6 \\
\overset{\bullet}{-2}\ \overset{\bullet}{6}\ \overset{\bullet}{7}\ 9 \\
\hline
1\ 4\ 7\ 7
\end{array}
\qquad
\begin{array}{l}
4 - \overset{\bullet}{2},\ \text{i.e. } 4 - 3 = \mathbf{1} \\
\text{at thousand's place.}
\end{array}
$$

So, $4156 - 2679 = \mathbf{1477}$.

Example 9:   3895 – 1926

Step 1: In one's place, upper digit 5 < lower digit 6, so add the complement of 6, (i.e. 4) to the upper digit 5, to give 9 as one's place answer.

Now, make the *ekadhika* of the number before 6, i.e. 2 as $\overset{\bullet}{2}$, as shown below:

$$
\begin{array}{r}
3\ 8\ 9\ 5 \\
-1\ 9\ \overset{\bullet}{2}\ 6 \\
\hline
9
\end{array}
\qquad
\begin{array}{l}
\text{complement of } 6 = 4 \\
4 + 5 = \mathbf{9} \text{ at one's place}
\end{array}
$$

Step 2: In ten's place, lower digit $\overset{\bullet}{2} = 3$ and upper digit 9 > 3. So it can be subtracted normally and there is no need of making *ekadhika* of 9 at hundred's place.

$$
\begin{array}{r}
3\ 8\ 9\ 5 \\
-1\ 9\ \overset{\bullet}{2}\ 6 \\
\hline
\mathbf{6}\ 9
\end{array}
\qquad
9 - \overset{\bullet}{2} = 9 - 3 = \mathbf{6} \text{ at ten's place}
$$

Step 3: In hundred's place, again upper digit 8 < lower digit 9, so add the complement of 9 (i.e. 1) to 8, to give 9 as hundred's place answer. And make *ekadhika* of 1 as $\overset{\bullet}{1}$ (*at thousand's place*):

$$
\begin{array}{r}
3\ 8\ 9\ 5 \\
-\overset{\bullet}{1}\ 9\ \overset{\bullet}{2}\ 6 \\
\hline
\mathbf{9}\ 6\ 9
\end{array}
\qquad
\begin{array}{l}
\text{complement of } 9 = 1 \\
1 + 8 = \mathbf{9} \text{ at hundred's place}
\end{array}
$$

***Step 4*:** In thousand's place, here $3 > \overset{\bullet}{1}$, so we do normal subtraction.

$$\begin{array}{r} 3\ 8\ 9\ 5 \\ -\ \overset{\bullet}{1}\ 9\ \overset{\bullet}{2}\ 6 \\ \hline 1\ 9\ 6\ 9 \end{array}$$ $3 - 1 = 3 - \overset{\bullet}{2} = \mathbf{1}$ at thousand's place

So, $3895 - 1926 = \mathbf{1969}$

***Example 10*:**   **96247 – 28519**

***Step 1*:** $\begin{array}{r} 9\ 6\ 2\ 4\ 7 \\ -\ 2\ 8\ 5\ \overset{\bullet}{1}\ 9 \\ \hline 8 \end{array}$ complement of 9 = 1

                                                 1 + 7 = **8** at one's place,

                                                 ekadhika of $1 = \overset{\bullet}{1}$

***Step 2*:** $\begin{array}{r} 9\ 6\ 2\ 4\ 7 \\ -\ 2\ 8\ 5\ \overset{\bullet}{1}\ 9 \\ \hline 2\ 8 \end{array}$ $4 - \overset{\bullet}{1} = 4 - 2 = \mathbf{2}$ at ten's place
(As we have done normal subtraction here, so we would not take *ekadhika* of next digit, i.e. 5)

***Step 3*:** $\begin{array}{r} 9\ 6\ 2\ 4\ 7 \\ -\ 2\ \overset{\bullet}{8}\ 5\ 1\ 9 \\ \hline 7\ 2\ 8 \end{array}$ complement of 5 = 5
$5 + 2 = \mathbf{7}$ at hundred's place and *ekadhika* of $8 = \overset{\bullet}{8}$

***Step 4*:** $\begin{array}{r} 9\ 6\ 2\ 4\ 7 \\ -\ \overset{\bullet}{2}\ \overset{\bullet}{8}\ 5\ \overset{\bullet}{1}\ 9 \\ \hline 7\ 7\ 2\ 8 \end{array}$ complement of 8 (i.e. 9) = 1
$1 + 6 = \mathbf{7}$ at thousand's place and *ekadhika* of $2 = \overset{\bullet}{2}$

***Step 5*:** $\begin{array}{r} 9\ 6\ 2\ 4\ 7 \\ -\ \overset{\bullet}{2}\ \overset{\bullet}{8}\ 5\ \overset{\bullet}{1}\ 9 \\ \hline 6\ 7\ 7\ 2\ 8 \end{array}$ $9 - \overset{\bullet}{2}$, i.e. $9 - 3 = \mathbf{6}$ at ten thousand's place.

So, $96247 - 28519 = \mathbf{67728}$

This method is extremely useful in eliminating the phobia amongst students for subtraction through the usual process.

Vedic method gives a totally different perspective to the sum. Now the problem does not look like a subtraction sum; rather it seems to be an addition sum.

EXERCISE 5.4

Subtract the following sums:

1. 4256
    – 2837

2. 2374
    – 768

3. 8425
    – 1785

4. 9123
    – 4587

5. 3742
    – 2759

6. 7326
    – 5289

7. 58347
    – 29416

8. 8591
    – 6085

9. 57324
    – 19062

10. 903654
    – 587146

CHAPTER

6

Checking Your Answers
(Removing Silly Mistakes)

After performing any calculation, we re-check it through the same procedure of calculation all over again. It is human tendency that many-a-times, if we have made a mistake, we tend to repeat it during re-checking as well.

For example, in an addition sum, if by mistake we have calculated 2 + 3 = 6, then we sometimes tend to make that mistake again while re-checking the answer.

Vedic mathematics techniques not only help us to give answers in straight steps which are very fast and accurate but also help us to check the answers effectively without repeating the actual calculation by the use of **Digit Sum**.

> Digit Sum of a number is obtained by adding all the digits in a number, until we get a single digit.
>
> Digit Sum of a number is always from 1 to 9 and never a 0. It is denoted by D.S.

Example 1:

Digit Sum of **5021** = 5 + 0 + 2 + 1 = **8**

Example 2:

Digit Sum of **7324** = 7 + 3 + 2 + 4 = 16

Since, 16 is a two digit number, add its digits again to get the final D.S., i.e. 1 + 6 = **7**.

Since, value of Digit Sum of a number can only be from 1 to 9, that means after every 9 numbers, D.S. repeats itself. That further means adding or subtracting 9 to any number should not affect its D.S., i.e. 5, 59, 95, 959, 9959 all have the Digit Sum as 5.

All 9's or groups of digits in a number that add up to 9 can be cancelled out or casted out from the number and the remaining digits can be added to get the Digit Sum of that number.

Example 3:   **643891**

We can cancel out: 9, (8,1), (6, 3), i.e. $\cancel{6}\,4\,\cancel{3}\,\cancel{8}\,\cancel{9}\,\cancel{1}$

Since, we are left with 4

So, the D.S. of 643891 = **4**

Example 4:   **2576415**

We can cancel out: (2,7), (5, 4), i.e. $\cancel{2}\,\cancel{5}\,\cancel{7}\,6\,\cancel{4}\,1\,5$

Since, we are left with 6, 1 and 5

So, the D.S. of 2576415 = 6 + 1 + 5 = 12 $\rightarrow$ 1 + 2 = **3**.

In case, all the digits in the number are cancelled out and we don't have any other digit left, the Digit Sum of that number will not be 0. Since, adding 9 to a number does not affect its Digit Sum, so, in that case we add 9 to 0 and the Digit Sum will be 9.

Example 5:   **9345672**

We can cancel out: 9, (3, 6), (4, 5), (7, 2)

Since, D.S. can not be 0, adding 9 to it gives the final D.S. as 9.

So, D.S. of 9345672 = **9**.

EXERCISE 6.1

Find the Digit Sum of the following numbers:

1. 24962   **2.** 38145   **3.** 863145   **4.** 12736

5. 93852   **6.** 78781   **7.** 638922   **8.** 290851

9. 42756318   **10.** 53429801

Checking the answers by the use of Digit Sum

Digit Sum can be used to check answers, involving mathematical operations like addition, subtraction, multiplication, division, squaring, square roots, cube roots, etc. To verify our answers, we perform the same mathematical operation on the Digit Sums of the numbers as done in the problem, and the answer obtained should be equal to the Digit Sum of the answer of the sum.

If both do not match, then the answer is incorrect.

Let's see how Digit Sums help us in verifying the answers with different mathematical operations:

■ ADDITION

If the sum of the Digit Sums of the numbers to be added is equal to the D.S. of the answer, then the answer is correct.

Example 6:

$$4\,2\,8 \quad \text{D.S.} \quad 4{+}2{+}8 = 14 = \;5$$
$$\underline{+\;7\,3\,6} \quad \underline{\text{D.S.}} \quad 7{+}3{+}6 = 16 = \underline{+7}$$
$$\underline{11\,6\,4} \qquad\qquad\qquad\quad 12 \longrightarrow 3$$

D.S. of answer $1164 = 1 + 1 + 6 + 4 = 12 \longrightarrow 3$

Since, this is an addition sum, so we add the D.S. of the numbers, to get 3 as final D.S. (i.e. $5 + 7 = 12 \longrightarrow 3$)

Since both D.S. are same, so the answer is correct.

Example 7:

$$\qquad\qquad\qquad\qquad\qquad \text{D.S.}$$
$$7\,2\,8\,3\,2\,9 \quad\longrightarrow\quad 4$$
$$\underline{+\;3\,6\,9\,4\,7\,6} \quad\longrightarrow\quad \underline{+8}$$
$$\underline{1\,0\,8\,7\,7\,9\,5} \qquad\quad 12 \qquad 3$$

D.S. of the answer $1087795 = \mathbf{1} \longleftarrow$

not same

So, the answer is incorrect.

Note: *Sometimes there might be such conditions where D.S. are the same, still the answer is not right.*

Example 8:

$$
\begin{array}{rcl}
& & \text{D.S.} \\
2\,9\,7 & \longrightarrow & 9 \\
+\,3\,8\,4 & \longrightarrow & +6 \\
\hline
5\,9\,1 & & 15 \longrightarrow 6 \\
\end{array}
$$

D.S. of the answer 591 = 6

same

The D.S. are matching, which suggests that the answer is correct, but actually the answer is incorrect. The correct answer is 297 + 384 = 681.

Therefore, if the D.S. are matching, it doesn't give a 100% assurance that the answer is correct (the chances of which are very low), but if the D.S. are not matching that assures that definitely the answer is incorrect.

SUBTRACTION

If the difference of the Digit Sums of the numbers is equal to the Digit Sum of the answer, then the answer is correct.

Example 9:

$$
\begin{array}{rcl}
& & \text{D.S.} \\
4\,2\,8 & \longrightarrow & 5 \\
-\,3\,4\,6 & \longrightarrow & -4 \\
\hline
8\,2 & & 1 \\
\end{array}
$$

(since, this is subtraction sum, so we subtract the D.S. of the numbers)

D.S. of the answer 82 = 1

same

So, the answer is correct.

In some cases, we may get the difference of the Digit Sums in negative also, then we will add 9 to it to make it positive (since adding 9 to any number doesn't affect its D.S.).

Example 10:

$$
\begin{array}{rcl}
& & \text{D.S.} \\
3\,4\,8\,5 & \longrightarrow & 2 \\
-\,2\,8\,1\,6 & \longrightarrow & -8 \\
\hline
6\,6\,9 & & -6 \\
\end{array}
$$

Add 9 to (–6) to get **3** (i.e. 9+ (–6)) as final D.S.

D.S. of the answer 669 = **3**

Since, the D.S. of the answer matches the difference of the D.S. so, the answer is correct.

MULTIPLICATION

If the product of the Digit Sums of the numbers is equal to the Digit Sum of the answer, then the answer is correct.

Example 11:

$$D.S.$$

$$3\ 1\ 2 \longrightarrow 6 \quad \text{(since, it is a multiplication sum, so we}$$

$$\underline{\times\quad 2\ 4} \longrightarrow \underline{\times\ 6} \quad \text{multiply the D.S. of the numbers)}$$

$$7\ 4\ 8\ 8 \qquad 36 \longrightarrow 3+6 = 9$$

D.S. of the answer 7488 = **9**

So, the answer is correct.

DIVISION

If the product of the D.S. of the quotient and the divisor plus the D.S. of the remainder is equal to the D.S. of the dividend, then the answer is correct.

Example 12:

73421 ÷ 3

On division, we get:

  Quotient = 24473

  Remainder = 2

D.S. of the Quotient (24473) = 2

D.S. of the Divisor (3)   = 3

D.S. of Remainder (2)   = 2

Multiplying the D.S. of the Quotient with D.S. of the Divisor and adding the D.S. of remainder, we get: $(2 \times 3) + 2 = \mathbf{8}$

D.S. of dividend 73421 = **8**

So, the answer is correct.

We have just verified the answers of same involving addition, subtraction, multiplication and division. In the same way, we can check the answers obtained by other mathematical operations too, like squaring, square roots, cubing, etc.

Below is the summarized table of the mathematical operations involved and the method for checking the answer by Digit Sums.

Mathematical Operation	Method for checking the answer
Addition $a + b = c$	D.S. (a) + D.S. (b) = D.S. (c)
Subtraction $a - b = c$	D.S. (a) − D.S. (b) = D.S. (c)
Multiplication $a \times b = ab$	D.S. (a) × D.S. (b) = D.S. (ab)
Division a (dividend) ÷ b (divisor) = c (quotient) & d (remainder)	D.S. (quotient c) × D.S. (divisor b) + D.S. (remainder d) = D.S. (dividend a)
Squaring $a^2 = b$ e.g. $41^2 = 1681$	D.S. [D.S. (a)]^2 = D.S. (b) e.g. D.S. (41) = 5 and D.S. (5^2 i.e.25) = 7; D.S. of 1681 = 7 D.S. of square of D.S. of 41 is same as D.S. of 1681
Cubing $a^3 = b$ e.g. $12^3 = 1728$	D.S. [D.S.(a)]^3 = D.S. (b) e.g. D.S. (12) = 3 and D.S. (3^3 i.e.27) = 9, D.S. of 1728 = 9 D.S. of cube of D.S.12 is same as D.S. of 1728

EXERCISE 6.2

Verify whether the following answers are correct or not using Digit Sums:

1. $2372 + 5384 = 7756$ **2.** $45382 - 29635 = 15247$

3. $3892 \times 1629 = 6341068$ **4.** $56381 - 48962 = 7419$

5. $37625 + 24839 + 65431 = 127895$ **6.** $78^2 = 6084$

7. $53^2 = 2806$ **8.** $2.386 \times 0.342 = 0.816012$

9. $81623 \div 7352 = Q : 11, R : 751$ **10.** $243658 \div 294 = Q:838, R: 226$

▌ CHECKING DIVISIBILITY BY 3 AND 9

Digit Sums are also useful in checking the divisibility of any number by 9 and 3.

Checking divisibility by	Conventional Method	Vedic Method
9	If sum of all the digits in the number is divisible by 9, then the number is divisible by 9.	If the Digit Sum of the number is 9, then the number is divisible by 9.
3	If sum of all the digits in the number is divisible by 3, then the number is divisible by 3.	If the Digit Sum of the number is 3, 6, or 9, then the number is divisible by 3.

Example 13:

Verify whether 4736982 is divisible by 9 and 3.

Instead of adding all the digits, find Digit Sum of the number, casting out 9's gives:

$4\cancel{7}\cancel{3}\cancel{6}\cancel{9}8\cancel{2} = 3$ as D.S.

So, 4736982 is not divisible by 9, but divisible by 3.

The D.S. of the number is also the remainder which we get when that number is divided by 9, i.e. in the above example, we get 3 as the remainder when 4736982 is divided by 9.

Example 14:

What number should be added or subtracted from 537629, so that the number is divisible by 9?

Solution:

   Remainder of 537629 ÷ 9 = D.S. of 537629

   i.e. Remainder = 5

So, either 5 should be subtracted or 4 should be added to 537629, so that it is divisible by 9.

EXERCISE 6.3

Verify using Digit Sums, the divisibility of the following numbers by 3 and 9.

1. 42183   2. 2715   3. 3916   4. 80133

5. 943056

Multiplication of Numbers Near the Bases

So far we have seen special multiplication formulae to multiply by the series of 9's, 11, 12 and other teens. Now we shall learn another special multiplication which involves multiplying numbers near their bases.

If you are asked to do calculations like: 997 × 996, you would at once baffle at seeing the question. But using Vedic Maths method, this can be calculated quickly, using the formula: *"All from nine and the last from ten"*.

When talking about numbers near the base, 3 types of cases may appear:

1. Numbers below the base (e.g. 95, 997)
2. Numbers above the base (e.g. 104, 112)
3. Mixed; one above and one below the base (e.g. 98, 103)

CASE I: Multiplying numbers below the base

Let's first take the examples, where the numbers are near base 100:

Example 1: **98 × 97**

Step 1:

In Vedic Method, we write the two numbers one below the other and write their differences from the base or their complements, opposite them with a negative (-) sign as:

98 – 2 (difference of 98 from its base is 2)

97 – 3 (difference of 97 from its base is 3)

Conventional Method

```
    98
  × 97
   686
   882×
  9506
```

Step 2:

The answer will come in 2 parts – RHS & LHS.

For **LHS** answer, subtract the complement of the first number from the second number or vice-versa, i.e. either 98–3 or 97–2, both ways the answer is **95** as shown below:

98 – 2 cross
97 – 3 subtract
95

Step 3:

For **RHS** answer, multiply the differences from the base or complements (–2 × –3) to get **06** as RHS answer, i.e.

98 – 2 ⎤ multiply
97 – 3 ⎦
95 / **06**

Remember that digits on RHS of answer should be equal to the number of 0's in the base. Since, in this case the base is 100, so we put a 0 to the left of 6 to make 2 digits on the right side. That's why, it is 06 and not 6.

So, the final answer is 98 × 97 = **9506**

<u>*Example 2*</u>: **91 × 96**

91 – 9   **LHS** = 91 – 4 or 96 – 9 = **87**
96 – 4   **RHS** = 9 × 4 = **36**
87 / 36   Answer = **8736**

<u>*Example 3*</u>: **89 × 88**

89 – 11   **LHS** = 89 – 12 or 88 – 11 = **77**
88 – 12   **RHS** = 11 × 12 = **132**
77 / 32₁

Since on RHS, there can be only 2 digits (as base 100 has 2 zeros), so 1 at hundred's place on RHS is carried over towards LHS and added to 77 to get 78 as the final LHS answer.

So, the final answer is 89 × 88 = 77 / 32₁ = **7832**

Important points to remember :

1. Always identify the base first and see that number of digits on RHS should always be equal to the number of 0's in the base.

2. Suppose the base is 100, if after multiplication of complements, we get a single digit, then we add 0 to its left to make 2 digits on RHS which is equal to the number of 0's in the base.

3. If number of digits is more, say 3 on RHS, then the 3rd most digit on left is shifted to the LHS part of answer and added to it. *(see example 3 above).*

Consider some more examples with larger bases:

Example 4:   **994 × 992**

$$
\begin{array}{ll}
994 & -6 \\
992 & -8 \\
\hline
986 & /\,048
\end{array}
$$

Base is 1000
LHS = 994 – 8 or 992 – 6 = **986**
RHS = 6 × 8 = **048**
(3 digits on RHS as three 0's in base)

So, 994 × 992 = **986048**

Example 5: **9989 × 9888**

$$
\begin{array}{ll}
9989 & -\ \ 11 \\
9888 & -112 \\
\hline
9877 & /\,1232
\end{array}
$$

Since base is 10000, so there should be 4 digits on RHS.
So, 9989 × 9888 = **98771232**

EXERCISE 7.1

Multiply the following:

1. 98 × 91   2. 89 × 92   3. 998 × 989   4. 999 × 901

5. 9898 × 9997

CASE II: Multiplying numbers above the base

Example 6: **104 × 106**

Step 1: We write one number below the other and write their surpluses from the base with a positive (+) sign:

$$104 \quad +4$$
$$106 \quad +6$$

Step 2: For the **LHS** answer, cross add either of the two, i.e. either 104 + 6 or 106 + 4. Both ways it is **110**.

Step 3: For **RHS** answer, multiply the surpluses from the base, i.e. 4 × 6 to get **24**.

$$104 \quad + \quad 4$$
$$106 \quad + \quad 6$$
$$110 \ / \ 24$$

So, the answer is 104 × 106 = **11024**.

In this case also, we have to ensure that the number of digits on RHS should be equal to the number of 0's in the base.

To understand it, see the example given below:

Example 7: **1002 × 1007**

1002 + 2	Base is 1000
1007 + 7	LHS = 1002 + 7 or 1007 + 2 = **1009**
1009 / 014	RHS = 2 × 7 = **014**

So, the answer is 1002 × 1007 = **1009014**

Note: _We add an extra 0 on RHS to make it 3 digits, as here base (1000) has three 0's._

Example 8: **112 × 109**

112 + 12	Base is 1000
109 + 9	LHS = 112 + 9 or 109 + 12 = **121**
121 / 08	RHS = 12 × 9 = **108**

This 1 is carried to the LHS to get 122 as final LHS answer. So the final answer is 112 × 109 = 121 / 08 = **12208**.

EXERCISE 7.2

Multiply the following:
1. 106×109 2. 101×108 3. 1011×1012
4. 10008×10012 5. 117×106

CASE III: Mixed Base Multiplication

It involves the multiplication amongst numbers, where one number is below the base and the other is above the base.

Example 9: **96 × 107**

Both the numbers are near the base 100. So, 96 is below 100 and 107 is above 100.

Step 1:

Since 96 is 4 less than 100, we write –4 opposite to 96 and as 107 is 7 more than 100, so we write +7 opposite 107, as shown below:

    96 –4
    107 +7

Step 2:

For LHS answer, we either cross add (96 + 7) or cross-subtract (107 – 4). Both ways it will be 103.

For RHS answer, multiply –4 and 7 to get –28, which can be written as $\overline{28}$.

    96 – 4   LHS = (96 + 7) or (107 – 4) = **103**
    107 + 7   RHS = –4 × 7 = **$\overline{28}$**
    103 / $\overline{28}$

Step 3:

Since RHS answer cannot be negative, so to make this side positive we take 1 from LHS (i.e. equivalent to 100 in this case, as the base is 100) and carry it to RHS to get:

    96 – 4   LHS = 103 – 1 = **102**
    107 + 7   RHS = 100 – 28 = **72**
    102 / 72   *(All from nine and last from ten)*

So, the final answer is $96 \times 107 = $ **10272**.

Note that whenever we get a negative in an answer, then to make it positive:

• Reduce 1 from the digit left to it.

• Write the complement of the negative number.

For example, if the number is $56\overline{32}$, to make $\overline{32}$ positive, reduce 1 from 6

(i.e. $6 - 1 = 5$) and write the complement of 32, i.e. 68.

So, $56 / \overline{32} = 55 / 68 = 5568$.

It is like carrying 100 from LHS to the RHS, to find the complement of 32.

Once again, care should be taken that number of digits on RHS is equal to the number of 0's in the base. *If any adjustment of adding 0's or carrying over to the left is required, then that should be done before taking out the complement.*

This would be clearer by the following example:

Example 10: **111 × 88**

Step 1:

Write the difference or surplus of the given number from the base 100 with their respective signs as shown below:

$$111 \quad + \quad 11 \qquad\qquad \textbf{LHS} = (111 - 12) \text{ or } (88 + 11) = \textbf{99}$$
$$\underline{88 \quad - \quad 12} \qquad\qquad \textbf{RHS} = 11 \times -12 = \overline{\textbf{132}}$$
$$99 \quad / \underset{1}{\overline{32}}$$

Step 2:

Since base is 100 and only 2 digits are allowed on RHS, so before taking out complement to make RHS positive, move $^{-}$ of $\overline{132}$ to the left so that it becomes 98 (i.e. $99 + \overline{1}$) on LHS and $\overline{32}$ on RHS

$$111 \quad + \quad 11$$
$$\underline{88 \quad - \quad 12}$$
$$99 \quad / \underset{1}{\overline{32}} \quad = \quad \textbf{98 / } \overline{\textbf{32}}$$

Step 3:

To make RHS positive, less 1 from 98 to get 97 on LHS and write the complement of 32, i.e. 68 on RHS.

i.e. $98 / \overline{32} = 97 / 68$

So, the final answer is $111 \times 88 = \mathbf{9768}.$

Example 11: **92 × 104**

  Base = 100

  $\begin{array}{r} 92 \quad - \ 8 \\ 104 \quad + 4 \\ \hline 96 \ / \ \overline{32} \end{array}$

  = 95 / 68

  Answer is **9568**

Example 12: **989 × 1011**

  Base = 1000

  $\begin{array}{r} 989 \quad - \ 11 \\ 1011 \quad + \ 11 \\ \hline 1000 \quad / \ \overline{121} \end{array}$

  = 999 / 879

  Answer is **999879**

Example 13: **117 × 94**

  Base = 100

  $\begin{array}{r} 117 \quad + \ 17 \\ 94 \quad - \ 6 \\ \hline 111 \ / \ \overline{102} \end{array}$

  = 110 / $\overline{02}$

  = 109 / 98

  Answer is **10998**

Example 14: **9997 × 10008**

  Base = 10000

  $\begin{array}{r} 9997 \quad - \ 3 \\ 10008 \quad + \ 8 \\ \hline 10005 / 0024 \end{array}$

  4 digits on RHS
  as base is 10,000

  = 10004 / 9976

  Answer is **100049976**

EXERCISE 7.3

Multiply the following:

1. 98 × 103   **2.** 987 × 1017   **3.** 89 × 111

4. 1012 × 996   **5.** 10102 × 9997

DECIMAL MULTIPLICATION

If the multiplication involves decimals, multiply the numbers as usual and after arriving at the answer, simply place the decimal point at the right place.

Example 15: **998 × 99.2**

First we consider the sum as 998 × 992 and solve it as usual:

$$998 \quad - 2$$
$$\underline{992 \quad - 8}$$
$$990 \ / \ 016$$

cross subtract   multiply
(998 – 8) or   vertically (–2 × –8)
(992 – 2)

Since the original numbers have one digit in the decimal place, we place the decimal point one digit from the right and get the final answer as **99001.6**

EXERCISE 7.4

Multiply the following:
1. 93 × 8.9   **2.** 997 × 0.993   **3.** 97.9 × 1005
4. 87 × 1.02   **5.** 9.989 × 10013

WORKING BASE MULTIPLICATION

We discussed multiplication of numbers close to any base, but what if both the numbers are not close to a convenient power of 10 but are close to a multiple of the base? For such cases, we make use of the formula: "*proportionately*".

We take the convenient multiple or sub-multiple of a suitable base as our "working base", perform the necessary operation and then multiply or divide the result proportionately, i.e. in the same proportion, as used to get the working base from the actual base.

This will be clearer from the following example:

50 as working base

Example 16: **48 × 42**

Since, both these numbers are not near any particular base, but are near 50, so we assume 50 as working base and we may take either 10 or 100 as the actual base.

CASE I: Let's take 10 as actual base and 50 (10 × 5) as working base.

Step 1: Since 50 is working base, write the difference of 48 and 42 from 50 next to them, as shown below:

$$48 - 2$$
$$\underline{42 - 8}$$
$$40 \;/\; 16$$

LHS = (48 – 8) or (42 – 2) = **40**
RHS = 2 × 8 = **16**

Step 2: As we have multiplied actual base 10 by 5 to get working base 50, so we multiply the LHS answer proportionately by 5, i.e.

$$48 - 2$$
$$\underline{42 - 8}$$
$$40 \;/\; 16$$
$$\underline{\times 5 \quad}$$
$$200 \;/\; 16$$

LHS = 40 × 5 = **200**

Step 3: Since, actual base is 10, only one digit is allowed on RHS. So, 1 of 16 will be carried over to the LHS and added to 200 to make it 201.

So, the answer is 48 × 42 = 200 / 16 = 201 / 6 = **2016**.

CASE II: Let's take 100 as the actual base

Actual base = 100

Working base = $100 \times \dfrac{1}{2} = 50$

Step 1: Initially the sum is done as shown below:

$$48 - 2$$
$$\underline{42 - 8}$$
$$40 \;/\; 16$$

Step 2: Since, working base is half the actual base 100, we therefore divide LHS, i.e. 40 by 2 to get the 20 as LHS answer.

The RHS answer remains unaffected (as the base 100 has two 0's):

$$48 - 2$$
$$\underline{42 - 8}$$
$$2\overline{)40}/16$$
$$20 / 16$$

Answer is $48 \times 42 = \mathbf{2016}$

CASE III: We can also take 10 and 40 as the actual and working base respectively.

Actual base = 10

Working base = $10 \times 4 = 40$

Step 1: Write the surplus of 48 and 42 from working base 40, next to them.

$$48 + 8 \qquad\qquad LHS = (48 + 2) \text{ or } (42 + 8) = 50$$
$$\underline{\times 42 + 2} \qquad\qquad RHS = 8 \times 2 = 16$$
$$50 / 16$$

Step 2: Since, working base 40 is 4 times the actual base, so we multiply LHS with 4 to give 200 / 16.

$$48 + 8$$
$$\underline{\times 42 + 2}$$
$$50 / 16$$
$$\underline{\times \ \ 4}$$
$$200 / 16$$

Since, actual base is 10, only one digit is allowed on RHS, so 1 of 16 will carried over to LHS and added to 200 to make it 201.

Answer is $48 \times 42 = \mathbf{2016}$.

So, we see, the answer is same by taking any of the three combinations of bases.

Example 17: **58 × 63**

Actual base = 10

Working base = 10 × 6 = 60

$$\begin{array}{ll} 58 \ - \ 2 \\ \underline{63 \ + \ 3} \\ 61 \ / \ \overline{6} \\ \underline{\times \ 6} \\ 366 \ / \overline{6} \end{array}$$

LHS = (58 + 3) or (63 − 2) = **61**

RHS = −2 × 3 = $\overline{6}$

Since working base 60 is 6 times actual base 10, so we multiply LHS with 6.

To convert $\overline{6}$ into positive, reduce 1 from 366 to get 365 on LHS and write the complement of $\overline{6}$, i.e. 4, on RHS

So, the answer is 58 × 63 = 365 / 4 = **3654**.

Important points to remember:

1. We carry out the normal base method multiplication taking the convenient working base.

2. Multiply or divide LHS of the answer proportionately, i.e. in the same proportion, as used to get the working base from the actual base.

3. If there is a figure to carry from RHS to LHS or vice-versa, we first multiply or divide proportionately and then carry it over.

---

500 as working base

Example 18: **497 × 493**

When actual base is 100

Working base = 100 × 5 = 500

$$\begin{array}{ll} 497 \ - \ 3 \\ \underline{493 \ - \ 7} \\ 490 \ / \ 21 \\ \underline{\times \ 5} \\ 2450 \ / \ 21 \end{array}$$

LHS = (497−7) or (493 − 3) = **490**

RHS = (−3 × −7) = **21**

Since working base 500 is 5 times actual base 100, so we multiply the LHS proportionately by 5

So, the answer is **245021**.

When actual base is 1000

Working base = $1000 \times \dfrac{1}{2} = 500$

$$\begin{array}{r} 497 \quad -3 \\ \underline{493 \quad -7} \end{array}$$

2) $\overline{490}$ / 021 (3 digits on RHS since actual base is 1000)

245 / 021

Since working base 500 is half of actual base 1000, so we divide the LHS by 2.

So, the answer is **245021**.

---

250 as Working base

Let's take another example where numbers are near 250:

Example 19: **253 × 246**

Let's take actual base as 1000

Working base = $1000 \times \dfrac{1}{4} = 250$

$$\begin{array}{r} 253 \quad +3 \\ \underline{246 \quad -4} \end{array}$$

4) $\overline{249}$ / $\overline{012}$

62 ¼ / $\overline{012}$

Since actual base is 1000 and 62 ¼ is at thousand's place, so when we will carry ¼ from LHS to RHS. This is equal to a carryover of 250 (¼ of 1000 is 250). So we will subtract 12 from 250 to give 238 on RHS.

$$62\ ¼\ /\ \overline{012} = 62\ /\ (250 - 12) = 62\ /\ 238$$

So, the answer is 253 × 246 = **62238**.

Some more solved examples:

Example 20: **192 × 198**

Actual Base = 100
Working Base = 100 × 2 = 200

$$
\begin{array}{r}
192 \quad -8 \\
198 \quad -2 \\
\hline
190 \,/\, 16 \\
\times 2 \\
\hline
380 \,/\, 16
\end{array}
$$

Answer is 192 × 198 = **38016**

Example 21: **78 × 87**

Actual Base = 10
Working Base = 10 × 8 = 80

$$
\begin{array}{r}
78 \quad -2 \\
87 \quad +7 \\
\hline
85 \,/\, 14 \\
\times 8 \\
\hline
680 \,/\, \overline{14}
\end{array}
$$

$679 / \overline{4} = 678 / 6 = 6786$
Answer is 78 × 87 = **6786**.

Example 22: **3992 × 4011**

Actual Base = 1000
Working Base = 1000 × 4 = 4000

$$
\begin{array}{r}
3992 \quad - 8 \\
4011 \quad + 11 \\
\hline
4003 \,/\, \overline{088} \\
\times 4 \\
\hline
16012 \,/\, \overline{088} \\
16011 \,/\, 912
\end{array}
$$

Answer is 3992 × 4011
= **16011912**

Example 23: **521 × 488**

Actual Base = 100
Working Base = 100 × 5 = 500

$$
\begin{array}{r}
521 \quad + 21 \\
488 \quad - 12 \\
\hline
509 \,/\, \overline{252} \\
\times 5 \\
\hline
2545 \,/\, \underset{2}{\_}52
\end{array}
$$

$2543 / \overline{52} = 2542 / 48$
Answer is 521 × 488
= **254248**

EXERCISE 7.5

Multiply the following numbers:

1. 68 × 67   **2.** 59 × 61   **3.** 809 × 803   **4.** 312 × 293

5. 6102 × 6003   **6.** 296 × 304   **7.** 788 × 811   **8.** 398 × 396

9. 7015 × 7005   **10.** 402 × 396

MULTIPLICATION OF NUMBERS HAVING DIFFERENT BASES

When we need to multiply numbers which are near different bases, the method is almost same with a little modification.

CASE I: Both the numbers are below their respective bases

Example 24: **996 × 93**

Now, here 996 is near the base 1000 and 93 is near the base 100.

Step 1:   996 – 4   Write the differences of the numbers
                  93 – 7   from their respective bases.

Step 2:

First find the ratio of bigger base to smaller base.

$$\text{Ratio} = \frac{1000}{100} = 10$$

We can't subtract the complements right away from the given numbers, as bases are different.

So, **LHS** can be obtained in 2 ways:

(a) To subtract the complement of 93, i.e. 7 whose base is 100, from 996, whose base is 1000, first we have to multiply 7 by the ratio of bigger base to smaller base, i.e. 10, so 7 × 10 = 70 and then 996 – 70 = **926** = LHS answer

(b) or to subtract complement 4 (which is according to base 1000) from 93 (according to base 100), first we have to multiply 93 by the ratio of the two bases, i.e. 93 × 10 = 930 and then 930 – 4 = **926** = LHS answer.

Step 3:

RHS answer can be obtained by multiplying the two complements 4 and 7 to get **28**.

So, the answer is 996 × 93 = 926 28 = **92628**.

Remember that numbers of digits on RHS should always be equal to the number of 0's in the smaller base.

Since, in the above case, smaller base is 100, so two digits on RHS are fine.

Alternatively, we can also multiply the smaller number by the ratio of two bases, i.e. 10, so as to make the bases of both the numbers same.

i.e. $996 \times (93 \times 10) = 996 \times 930$

Now, following the usual base multiplication method, we get:

$$
\begin{array}{r}
996 \ - \ 4 \\
930 \ -70 \\
\hline
926 \ / \ 280
\end{array}
$$

Since, initially we multiplied the number by 10, so to get the final answer, we divide the obtained answer by 10.

i.e. $926280 \div 10 = 92628$.

So, the final answer is $996 \times 93 = \textbf{92628}$

Example 25: **9994 × 98**

Here, bases are 10000 and 100.

Ratio of two bases is $\dfrac{10000}{100} = 100$

So, $\begin{array}{r} 9994 \ -6 \\ 98 \ -2 \\ \hline 9794 \ / \ 12 \end{array}$ **LHS** = either $9994 - (2 \times 100) = 9794$
       or $(98 \times 100) - 6 = \underline{9794}$

       RHS = $6 \times 2 = 12$

       (2 digits on RHS as two 0's in smaller base).

So, the answer is $9994 \times 98 = \textbf{979412}$.

CASE II: Both the numbers are above their respective bases

Example 26: **1002 × 104**

Bases are 1000 and 100 and the ratio of bases is 10.

$\begin{array}{r} 1002 \ +2 \\ 104 \ +4 \\ \hline 1042 \ / \ 08 \end{array}$ **LHS** = either $1002 + (4 \times 10) = 1042$
       or $(104 \times 10) + 2 = \textbf{1042}$

       RHS = $4 \times 2 = 08$

       (2 digits on RHS as 2 0's in the smaller base).

So, the answer is $1002 \times 104 = \textbf{104208}$.

CASE III: One number below the base and one number above the different base

Example 27: **95 × 10014**

Bases are 100 and 10000 respectively and the ratio is 100

    95 – 5   **LHS** = either $(95 \times 100) + 14 = 9514$

<u>10014 + 14</u>   or $10014 - (5 \times 100) = \mathbf{9514}$

 9514 / $\overline{70}$ **RHS** = $-5 \times 14 = \overline{70}$

 9513 / 30

 = **951330.**

Some more solved examples:

Example 28: **9989 × 1005**

 Bases = (10000)   (1000)

 Ratio = 10

 9989 – 11   **LHS** = $9989 + (5 \times 10) = 10039$

<u>1005 +   5</u>   or $(1005 \times 10) - 11 = \mathbf{10039}$

10039 / $\overline{055}$ **RHS** = $-11 \times 5 = \overline{055}$

10038 / 945   (3 digits on RHS as smaller base

                        1000 has three 0's)

 = **10038945**

Example 29: **112 × 9988**

  Bases = (100)   (10000)

  Ratio = 100

  112 + 12   **LHS** = $(112 \times 100) - 12 = 11188$

<u>9988 – 12</u>   or $9988 + (12 \times 100) = \mathbf{11188}$

11188 / $\overline{144}$ **RHS** = $-12 \times 12 = \overline{144}$

11187 / $\overline{44}$ (only 2 digits are allowed on RHS as

                       smaller base is 100, so $\overline{1}$ will be

                       carried to the LHS)

 = **1118656**

Example 30: **109 × 1112**

Bases = (100)   (1000)

Ratio = 10

  109 +   9

<u>1112 + 112</u>

1202 / 1008

LHS = (109 × 10) + 112 = 1202

  or 1112 + (9 × 10) = **1202**

RHS = 9 × 112 = **1008**

(where, the first two digits will be carried to LHS, since only 2 digits are allowed in RHS as smaller base is 100)

= 1212 / 08

= **121208**

EXERCISE 7.6

Multiply the following:

1. 992 × 89
2. 1008 × 92
3. 9989 × 992
4. 11001 × 109
5. 9888 × 102
6. 10103 × 103
7. 99996 × 92
8. 10021 × 997
9. 10099 × 1001
10. 10032 × 96

MULTIPLICATION OF 3 NUMBERS NEAR THE BASE

Now, we will multiply 3 numbers near a base, altogether in a single line.

CASE I: When the 3 numbers are above a certain base

Example 31: **102 × 103 × 105**

Step1:   Base is 100

Write the surplus of the numbers next to them as shown:

102   + 2

103   + 3

105   + 5

Step 2: We get the answer in 3 parts – left, middle and right side.

For the **LHS** answer, add any one number to the surpluses of other two numbers, i.e.

either 102 + (3+5)

or   103 + (2+5)

or   105 + (2+3)

either way, it is **110**

Step 3: For the **middle part** answer, multiply the surpluses in pairs and add, i.e.

$$(2 \times 3) + (3 \times 5) + (2 \times 5) = 6 + 15 + 10 = 31$$

Step 4: For **RHS** answer, multiply the surpluses:

i.e. $2 \times 3 \times 5 = 30$

So, it can be written as:

102 + 2

103 + 3

105 + 5

110 / 31 / 30

So, the answer is $102 \times 103 \times 105 = $ **1103130**

Note: Since base is 100, there should be two digits in the middle part and the right part of the answer, as the digits in both the parts are always equal to the number of 0's in the base.

CASE II: When the 3 numbers are below a certain base

Example 32: **97 × 98 × 99**

It can be written as:

97 – 3   ***Step 1:*** Write their deficiencies from base next to them

98 – 2   ***Step 2:*** For **LHS** answer, either 97–2–1

99 – 1   or 98–3–1,

94 / 11 / $\overline{06}$ or 99–3–2

so, LHS = **94**

Step 3: For **middle part**, multiply the deficiencies in pairs and add:

$$(-3 \times -2) + (-2 \times -1) + (-3 \times -1) = 6 + 2 + 3 = 11$$

Step 4: For **RHS** answer, multiply the three deficiencies but as they are three, their product is negative $(-3 \times -2 \times -1) = -6$

But, since base is 100, so 2 digits are on RHS,

so, it is $\overline{06}$.

Answer is: $97 \times 98 \times 99 = 94 / 11 / \overline{06}$

$$= 94 / 10 / (100-06) = \mathbf{941094}$$

CASE III: When the 2 numbers are below and one number is above a certain base

Example 33: **997 × 1006 × 998**

It can be written as:

$$
\begin{array}{l}
997 \quad -3 \\
1006 \quad +6 \\
\underline{998 \quad -2} \\
1001 \;/\; \overline{024} \;/\; 036 \\
1000 \;/\; (1000-024) \;/\; 036 \\
1000 \;/\; 976 \;/\; 036
\end{array}
$$

LHS = (997 + 6 − 2)

or (1006 − 3 − 2)

or (998 − 3 + 6)

= **1001**

Middle Part

= (−3 × 6) + (6 × −2) + (−3 × −2)

= − 18 − 12 + 6 = − 24

= $\overline{024}$ (since base is 1000)

RHS = −3 × 6 × −2 = 36 = **036**

Since 1000 is base of the given 3 numbers, so, three digits in middle and right part answer.

The answer is 997 × 1006 × 998 = **1000976036**

CASE IV: When the 3 numbers are near different bases

Example 34: **105 × 107 × 14**

It can be written as:

$$
\begin{array}{ll}
105 \quad +5 & \text{Base is 100} \\
107 \quad +7 & \text{Base is 100} \\
14 \quad +4 & \text{Base is 10}
\end{array}
$$

Step 1:

For **LHS**; since 14 is near the base 10, so either 14 has to be multiplied by 10 (ratio of bigger base to smaller base, i.e. $\frac{100}{10}$) to add the surpluses of the two numbers to it, or the surplus of 14 (i.e. 4), has to be multiplied by 10 and to be added with other surplus:

i.e.   either $105 + 7 + (4 \times 10)$

    or $107 + 5 + (4 \times 10)$

    or $(14 \times 10) + 5 + 7$

    $= 152.$

Step 2:

For **middle part**; multiply the 3 pairs of surpluses and add them:

$(5 \times 7) + (5 \times 40) + (7 \times 40)$

$= 35 + 200 + 280$

$= 515$

Step 3:

For **RHS** answer; multiply the 3 surpluses:

$5 \times 7 \times 4 = 140$

Since, smaller base 10 has one 0, so RHS has 1 digit and the next bigger base is 100, so the middle part has 2 digits.

So, answer is: $105 \times 107 \times 14 = 152 / \underset{5}{15} / \underset{14}{0}$

$$= 157290$$

Some more solved examples:

<u>*Example 35*</u>: **93 × 96 × 88**

93 – 7	**LHS** $= 93 - 4 - 12 = 77$
96 – 4	**Middle Part**
88 – 12	$= (-7 \times -4) + (-4 \times -12) + (-7 \times -12)$
$77 / \underset{1}{60} / \underset{3}{\overline{36}}$	$= 28 + 48 + 84 = 160$
$= 78 / 57 / \overline{36}$	**RHS** $= -7 \times -4 \times -12 = \overline{336}$
$= 785664$	

Example 36: 1004 × 1008 × 1111

1004 + 4   **LHS** = 1004 + 8 + 111 = **1123**
1008 + 8   **Middle Part**
<u>1111 + 111</u>   = (4 × 8) + (8 × 111) + (4 × 111)
1123 / $_1$364 / $_3$552   = 32 + 888 + 444 = **1364**
= **1124367552**   **RHS** = 4 × 8 × 111 = **3552**

Example 37: 106 × 109 × 96

106   + 6   **LHS** = 106 +9 –4 = **111**
109   + 9   **Middle Part**
<u>96 – 4</u>   = (6 × 9) + (9 × –4) + (6 × –4)
111 / $\overline{06}$ / $_2\overline{16}$ = 54 –36 –24
= 111 / $\overline{08}$ / $\overline{16}$ = $\overline{–06}$ or $\overline{06}$
= 110 / 92 / $\overline{16}$ **RHS** = 6 × 9 × – 4
= **1109184**   = **–216 or $\overline{216}$**

EXERCISE 8.7

Multiply the following:

1. 91 × 92 × 93   2. 989 × 996 × 1011

3. 1001 × 1012 × 1005   4. 106 × 96 × 102

5. 112 × 101 × 103

Multiplication By 5, 25, 50, 250, 500...
(By Mere Observation)

A unique advantage of Vedic Maths is that many calculations can be done by mere observation only.

Multiplying any number by 10, 100, 1000 ....., etc.

Add that many 0s to the right of the number as there are in 10, 100, etc.

e.g. $43 \times 10 = 430$

also, $394 \times 100 = 39400$, and so on.

Multiplying any number by 5

Since, $5 = \dfrac{10}{2}$, so it means, first multiply the number by 10 and then half it.

Example 1: 24 × 5

Just put one 0 at the right of 24 and half the number obtained, i.e.

$$24 \times 5 = \frac{240}{2} = 120$$

Multiplying any number by 50

Since, $50 = \dfrac{100}{2}$, so when multiplying the number by 50, add two 0's to its right and half it:

Example 2: 47 × 50

$$47 \times 50 = \frac{4700}{2} = 2350$$

Multiplying any number by 25

Since, $25 = \dfrac{100}{4}$, so when multiplying the number by 25, add two 0's to its right and half it twice:

Example 3: **64 × 25**

$$64 \times 25 = \frac{6400}{2 \times 2} = \mathbf{1600}$$

SUMMARY			
Multiplication by	Step I	Step II	Example
a) $5 = \dfrac{10}{2}$	Add one 0 to right	Half the result once	$62 \times 5 = \dfrac{620}{2} = 310$
b) $50 = \dfrac{100}{2}$	Add two 0's to right	Half the result once	$62 \times 50 = \dfrac{6200}{2}$ $= 3100$
c) $500 = \dfrac{1000}{2}$	Add three 0's to right	Half the result once	$62 \times 500 = \dfrac{62000}{}$ $= 31000$
d) $25 = \dfrac{100}{4}$	Add two 0's to right	Half the result twice	$62 \times 25 = \dfrac{6200}{4}$ $= 1550$
e) $250 = \dfrac{1000}{4}$	Add three 0's to right	Half the result twice	$62 \times 250 = \dfrac{62000}{4}$ $= 15500$

EXERCISE 8.1

Multiply the following numbers:

1. 42×5 2. 36×5 3. 73×50 4. 84×50

5. 56×500 6. 91×500 7. 28×250 8. 132×250

9. 67×5 10. 49×50

Vertical and Crosswise Multiplication

This is the general method for multiplying any two given numbers. The formula used is *"Vertically and crosswise"*

As the name suggests, the method consists of steps including vertical multiplication and crosswise multiplication giving the answer in one straight line.

<table>
<tr><td align="center">*Conventional Method*</td><td align="center">*Vedic one-line Method*</td></tr>
<tr><td align="center">32142</td><td align="center">32142</td></tr>
<tr><td align="center">×12374</td><td align="center">×12374</td></tr>
<tr><td align="center">128568</td><td align="center">397725108</td></tr>
<tr><td align="center">2249940</td><td></td></tr>
<tr><td align="center">9642600</td><td></td></tr>
<tr><td align="center">64284000</td><td></td></tr>
<tr><td align="center">321420000</td><td></td></tr>
<tr><td align="center">397725108</td><td></td></tr>
</table>

We will consider the following patterns in this chapter and once the pattern is understood, this method can be extended to any number of digits:

1. 2×2 digit multiplication
2. 3×3 digit multiplication
3. 3×2 digit multiplication
4. 4×4 digit multiplication
5. 4×3 digit multiplication
6. 5×5 digit multiplication

Pattern I: 2 × 2 digit multiplication

We start with the multiplication of a 2 digit number by another 2 digit number. The steps involved can be explained with the help of dot diagram as shown below. Each dot represents a digit in the number and the line joining represents the digits to be multiplied.

Step 1: :| *Step 2:* ✕   *Step 3:* |:

> *Step 1:* We vertically multiply the 2 digits in the right hand column
>
> *Step 2:* We cross multiply the digits in both the columns and add the products.
>
> *Step 3:* Then we vertically multiply the digits in the left hand column.
>
> In each step we write down only one digit and carry over the other digits, if any, to the next step.

Example 1:   21 × 34

Step 1:

$$\begin{array}{r} 2\ 1 \\ \times\ 3\ 4 \\ \hline 4 \end{array}$$

Multiply vertically in the right hand column $1 \times 4 = 4$ at unit's place.

Step 2:

$$\begin{array}{r} 2\ 1 \\ 3\ 4 \\ \hline {}_1 14 \end{array}$$

Multiply crosswise and add the results for the ten's place.

$(2\times4) + (1\times3) = 8 + 3 = {}_1 1$ *(1 is carried over)*

Step 3:

$$\begin{array}{r} 2\ 1 \\ 3\ 4 \\ \hline 7\ {}_1 14 \end{array}$$

Multiply vertically in the left hand column and add 1 as carry over

$(2\times3) = 6$

$6 + 1(\text{carry}) = 7$

So, the answer is 21 × 34 = **714**

Example 2:   47 × 28

$$\begin{array}{r} 4\ 7 \\ \times\ 2\ 8 \\ \hline 13\ {}_5 1\ {}_5 6 \end{array}$$

Step 1: $7\times8 = {}_5 6$ *(5 is carried over)*

Step 2: $(4\times8)+(7\times2) = 46$

$46 + 5(\text{carry}) = {}_5 1$ *(5 is carried over)*

Step 3: $4\times2 = 8$

$8+5 \ (\text{carry}) = 13$

So, the answer is 47 × 28 = **1316**

Example 3:   **82 × 74**

8 2	*Step 1:* $2 \times 4 = 8$
× 7 4	*Step 2:* $(8 \times 4) + (2 \times 7) = {}_4 6$
60 68	*Step 3:* $8 \times 7 = 56$
4	$56 + 4 \text{ (carry)} = 60$

So, the answer is $82 \times 74 =$ **6068**

Pattern II: 3×3 digit multiplication

Example 4:   **413 × 321**

The steps can be explained with the help of the following dot diagram:

Step 1:   413
             × 321
             —————
                 3

Multiply vertically in right column

$3 \times 1 = 3$

Step 2:   413
             × 321
             —————
                73

Multiply crosswise the digits in the middle and right hand column and add the results

$(1 \times 1) + (3 \times 2) = 7$

Step 3:   413
             × 321
             —————
             ₁573

Multiply crosswise the digits in the right and left hand columns and vertically the middle digits. Then add all the three:

$(3 \times 3) + (4 \times 1) + (1 \times 2) = {}_1 5$

Step 4:   413
             × 321
             —————
             ₁2₁573

Multiply crosswise the digits in the middle and left column and add the results

$(4 \times 2) + (3 \times 1)$

$11 + 1 \text{(carry)} = {}_1 2$

Step 5:   413
             × 321
             —————
             13₁2₁573

Multiply vertically the left column digits

$4 \times 3 = 12 + 1 \text{(carry)} = 13$

So, the answer is $413 \times 321 =$ **132573**

Example 5:   **734 × 256**

```
      734
  ×   256
  18 7 9 0 4
    4 6 4 2
```

Step 1:   7 3 4
                   |
             2 5 6

$4 \times 6 = {}_2 4$

Step 2:   7 3 4
              $\times$
             2 5 6

$(3 \times 6) + (5 \times 4) = 38$
$38 + 2 \text{ (carry)} = {}_4 0$

Step 3:   7 3 4
              $\times$
             2 5 6

$(4 \times 2) + (7 \times 6) + (3 \times 5)$
$8 + 42 + 15 = 65$
$65 + 4 \text{ (carry)} = {}_6 9$

Step 4:   7 3 4
              $\times$
             2 5 6

$(7 \times 5) + (3 \times 2)$
$35 + 6 = 41$
$41 + 6 \text{ (carry)} = {}_4 7$

Step 5:   7 3 4
                   |
             2 5 6

$7 \times 2 = 14$
$14 + 4 \text{ (carry)} = \mathbf{18}$

So, the answer is 734 × 256 = **187904**

EXERCISE 9.1

Multiply the following numbers:

1. 23 × 31   2. 42 × 53   3. 71 × 86   4. 32 × 47
5. 81 × 15   6. 93 × 43   7. 216 × 374   8. 405 × 231
9. 351 × 726   10. 572 × 503

Pattern III: 3×2 digit multiplication

Example 6:   **352 × 41**

We can consider it as a 3×3 digit multiplication by adding 0 at the beginning of 41 as 041. So the sum becomes 352 × 041

```
      352
  ×   041
  1 4 4 32
   1 2 1
```

Step 1:   3 5 2
                   |
             0 4 1

$2 \times 1 = \mathbf{2}$

Step 2:   3 5 2
              0 4 1 $(5×1) + (2×4) = {}_13$

Step 3:   3 5 2 $(3×1) + (2×0) + (5×4)$
              0 4 1 $3 + 0 + 20 = 23$
                         $23 + 1(carry) = {}_24$

Step 4:   3 5 2 $(3×4) + (5×0)$
              0 4 1 $12 + 0 = 12$
                         $12 + 2(carry) = {}_14$

Step 5:   3 5 2 $3 × 0 = 0$
              0 4 1 $0 + 1(carry) = 1$

So, the answer is $352 × 41 = \mathbf{14432}$

Example 7:   **574 × 28**

Consider the sum as 3×3 multiplication by adding a 0 in front of 28.
So, the sum becomes: $574 × 028$

          574   **Step 1:**   5 7 4
      ×   028   0 2 8 $4×8 = {}_32$
      1 6 0 7 2
      1 6 6 3   **Step 2:**   5 7 4 $(7×8) + (4×2) = 64$
                                 0 2 8 $64 + 3(carry) = {}_67$

                  Step 3:   5 7 4 $(5×8) + (4×0) + (7×2)$
                                0 2 8 $40 + 0 + 14 = 54$
                                           $54 + 6(carry) = {}_60$

                  Step 4:   5 7 4 $(5×2) + (7×0)$
                                0 2 8 $10 + 0 = 10$
                                           $10 + 6(carry) = {}_16$

                  Step 5:   5 7 4 $5 × 0 = 0$
                                0 2 8 $0 + 1(carry) = 1$

So, the answer is $574 × 28 = \mathbf{16072}$

Pattern IV: 4×4 digit multiplication

The method of multiplication of two 4 digits number remains the same as for two 3 digit number except that the pattern is extended.

> *Step 1:* We always start multiplying digits in the right most column and keep adding one column in each next step, until all the columns get involved in the multiplication.
>
> *Step 2:* Then we start leaving column again from the right one at a time till we reach the single leftmost column.
>
> *Step 3:* And in each step, either we do a vertical or crosswise multiplication or both depending on the number of columns we have in that step.

Example 8:   2134 × 3261

Step 1:   2134
             × 3261
             ————
                4

$1×1$ vertical multiplication
$4 × 1 = 4$

Step 2:   2134
             × 3261
             ————
             $_2$74

$2 × 2$ cross multiplication
$(4 × 6) + (3 × 1) = {_2}7$

Step 3:   2134
             × 3261
             ————
             $_2$974

$3×3$ vertical and cross multiplication
$(4×2) + (1×1) + (3×6) = 27$
$27 + 2(carry) = {_2}9$

Step 4:   2134
             × 3261
             ————
             $_2$8974

$4×4$ vertical and cross multiplication
$(2×1)+(4×3)+(1×6)+(3×2)=26$
$26+2(carry)={_2}8$

Step 5:   2134
             × 3261
             ————
             $_2$58974

$3×3$ vertical and cross multiplication
$(2×6)+(3×3)+(1×2)=23$
$23+2(carry)={_2}5$

Step 6:   2134
             × 3261
          ──────────
             958974

2×2 cross multiplication
(2×2)+(3×1)=7
7+2(carry)=**9**

Step 7:   2134
             × 3261
          ──────────
             6958974

1×1 vertical multiplication
2×3=**6**

So, the answer is 2134 × 3261 = **6958974**

Pattern V: 4×3 digit multiplication

This multiplication can also be carried out by the same method, i.e. by converting 3 digit number as 4 digit number, by adding a 0 in front of it. Then continue like a 4×4 digit multiplication.

Example 9: 4382 × 526

It can be written as 4382 × 0526

         4382
       × 0526
    ─────────────
    2 3 0 4 9 3 2
     2 3 7 4 5 1

Step 1: $2×6 = {}_1 2$

Step 2: $(8×6) + (2×2) = 52$
$52 + 1(carry) = {}_5 3$

Step 3: $(3×6) + (5×2) + (8×2) = 44$
$44 + 5(carry) = {}_4 9$

Step 4: $(4×6) + (2×0) + (3×2) + (8×5) = 70$
$70 + 4(carry) = {}_7 4$

Step 5: $(4×2) + (8×0) + (3×5) = 23$
$23 + 7(carry) = {}_3 0$

Step 6: $(4×5) + (3×0) = 20$
$20 + 3(carry) = {}_2 3$

Step 7: $4×0 = 0$
$0 + 2(carry) = 2$

So, the answer is 4382 × 526 = **2304932**.

Pattern VI: 5 × 5 digit multiplication

The vertical and crosswise method can be extended to 5×5 digits also.

**Example 10**: **25342 × 73614**

$$25342$$
$$\times \quad 73614$$

18 6 5 5 2 5 9 88
 4 5 7 6 5 2 1

Step 1:   2 5 3 4 2 $2 \times 4 = \mathbf{8}$
              |
              7 3 6 1 4

Step 2:   2 5 3 4 2 $(4 \times 4) + (2 \times 1) = {}_1\mathbf{8}$
              7 3 6 1 4

Step 3:   2 5 3 4 2 $(3 \times 4) + (6 \times 2) + (4 \times 1) = 28$
              7 3 6 1 4 $28 + 1(\text{carry}) = {}_2\mathbf{9}$

Step 4:   2 5 3 4 2 $(5 \times 4) + (2 \times 3) + (3 \times 1) + (4 \times 6) = 53$
              7 3 6 1 4 $53 + 2(\text{carry}) = {}_5\mathbf{5}$

Step 5:   2 5 3 4 2 $(2 \times 4) + (7 \times 2) + (5 \times 1) + (4 \times 3) +$
              7 3 6 1 4 $(3 \times 6) = 57$
                                 $57 + 5(\text{carry}) = {}_6\mathbf{2}$

Step 6:   2 5 3 4 2 $(2 \times 1) + (4 \times 7) + (5 \times 6) + (3 \times 3) = 69$
              7 3 6 1 4 $69 + 6(\text{carry}) = {}_7\mathbf{5}$

Step 7:   2 5 3 4 2 $(2 \times 6) + (3 \times 7) + (5 \times 3) = 48$
              7 3 6 1 4 $48 + 7(\text{carry}) = {}_5\mathbf{5}$

Step 8:   2 5 3 4 2 $(2×3) + (5×7) = 41$
              7 3 6 1 4 $41 + 5(\text{carry}) = 6_4$

Step 9:   2 5 3 4 2 $2×7 = 14$
              7 3 6 1 4 $14 + 4(\text{carry}) = \mathbf{18}$

So, the answer is $25342 × 73614 = \mathbf{1865525988}$

EXERCISE 9.2

Multiply the following numbers:

1. $371 × 28$	**2.** $426 × 31$	**3.** $635 × 45$
4. $284 × 51$	**5.** $2413 × 1672$	**6.** $9350 × 2453$
7. $1278 × 5806$	**8.** $1234 × 431$	**9.** $8015 × 638$
10. $36124 × 20618$		

SUMMARY OF STEPS INVOLVED IN VERTICAL AND CROSSWISE MULTIPLICATION

Important points to remember:

1. The number of steps required is always 1 less than the total number of digits of the multiplier and multiplicand, e.g. 23 × 84 has 2+2, i.e. 4 digits so 3 steps are required for the answer.

2. Start from the right and keep on adding 1 digit to the left until all the digits in the multiplicand are taken care of; after that, discard the digits on the right 1 at a time.

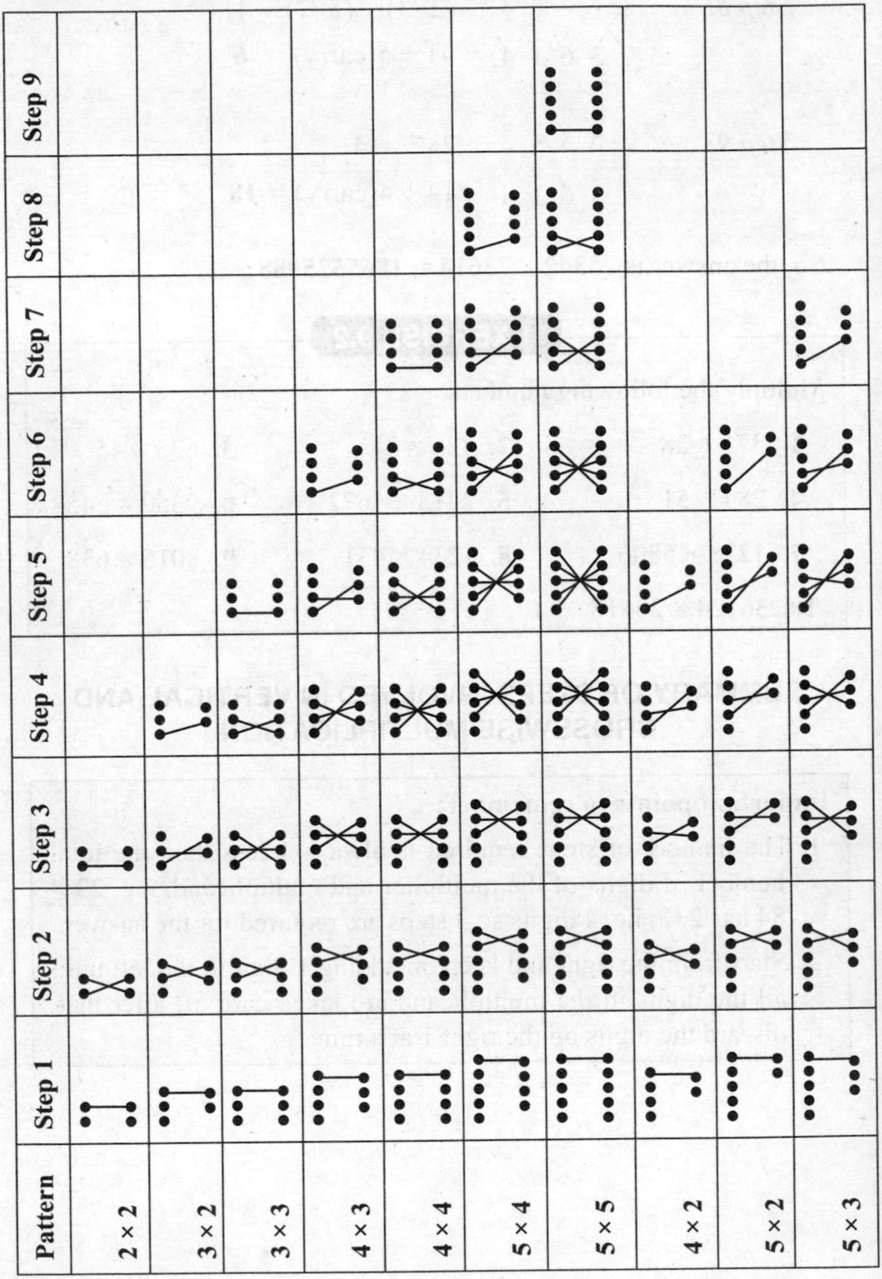
Pattern
Step 1
Step 2
Step 3
Step 4
Step 5
Step 6
Step 7
Step 8
Step 9
2 × 2
3 × 2
3 × 3
4 × 3
4 × 4
5 × 4
5 × 5
4 × 2
5 × 2
5 × 3

Interesting Squares

Squaring a number means multiplying that number by itself, i.e. 3 when multiplied by 3 gives 9 ($3 \times 3 = 9$). So, 9 is the square of 3.

In conventional maths, there is only one method available for finding squares, i.e. multiplying the number by itself through the same long multiplication process. But in Vedic Maths, there are smarter ways available to find the squares of specific numbers, like the ones ending in 5 or the ones close to bases. If a given number falls in any of the following categories, then working out the square of that number becomes very easy.

TYPE I: Squares of numbers ending in 5

The formula used for finding squares ending in 5 is *"by one more than the one before"*.

The answer comes in two parts — LHS and RHS.

LHS is computed by multiplying the digit before 5 by the digit one more than that, i.e. by its next consecutive digit.

RHS is always 5^2 as the number ends in 5, and we know that $5^2 = 25$.

Let's understand it better with the following example:

Example 1:

Find the **square of 35**

$$35^2$$
$$3 \times 4 \ / \ 5^2$$

LHS = The digit before 5 (i.e. 3) is multiplied by its next consecutive digit 4, i.e. $3 \times 4 = \mathbf{12}$

$$35^2$$
$$12 \ / \ 25$$

RHS = as the number ends in 5, so $5^2 = \mathbf{25}$

So, the final answer is $35^2 = \mathbf{1225}$

Example 2:   Find **75²**

LHS = 7 × 8 = **56**

RHS = 5² = **25**

So, 75² = **5625**.

Example 3:   Find **115²**

LHS = 11 × 12 = **132**

RHS = 5² = **25**

So, 115² = **13225**.

Some more solved examples in one line:

85² = (8 × 9) / 25 = 7225

25² = (2 × 3) / 25 = 625

15² = (1 × 2) / 25 = 225

125² = (12 × 13) / 25 = 15625

405² = (40 × 41) / 25 = 164025

EXERCISE 10.1

Find the square of the following:

1. 45²   **2.** 55²   **3.** 65²   **4.** 95²

5. 135²

Another interesting multiplication

Using the above formula along with another formula – *"last totaling to ten"*, we can also multiply two numbers, where:

1. The digits in the unit's place add upto 10

2. The digits in the ten's place are the same

In the case of multiplication of 2 numbers, where unit's digit add upto 10 and ten's digit are same, the answer come in two parts – LHS and RHS.

For LHS answer, multiply the ten's digit by the digit one more than that, i.e. by its next consecutive number.

For RHS answer, multiply together the digits in the unit's place.

Let's take an example:

Example 4:   **12 × 18**

Here, adding unit's digits, we get $2 + 8 = 10$

And ten's digit is 1 in both the numbers.

1 2	**LHS** = Multiply the ten's digit 1 by one more than that
1 8	
2 /16	i.e. $1 × (1 + 1) = 1 × 2 = \mathbf{2}$
	RHS = Multiply the unit's digits together
	i.e. $2 × 8 = \mathbf{16}$

Note: *The number of digits on RHS is always double the number of 0's in the base.*

Since, $2 + 8 = 10$, base is 10 and has one 0, so we get two digits on RHS (i.e. 16).

So, the final answer for $12 × 18 = \mathbf{216.}$

Example 5:   **49 × 41**

At unit's place, $9 + 1 = 10$

At ten's place, 4 is same

	LHS = $4 × (4 + 1) = 4 × 5 = \mathbf{20}$
4 9	**RHS** = $9 × 1 = 9$, i.e. **09**
4 1	(since, the number of digits on RHS = double
20 / 09	of the number of 0's in the base and since
	$9 + 1 = 10$, base 10 has one 0)

So, the final answer is $49 × 41 = \mathbf{2009.}$

Note: *This formula holds true in such cases also where unit's digits add upto 10 and the group on the left of unit's digit is same.*

Example 6:   **407 × 403**

At unit's place, $7 + 3 = 10$ and 40 is same on the left of units place.

4 0 7	**LHS** = $40 × (40 + 1) = 40 × 41 = \mathbf{1640}$
4 0 3	**RHS** = $7 × 3 = \mathbf{21}$
1640 / 21	

So, the final answer is $407 \times 403 = \mathbf{164021}$.

This method can also be extended in such cases where groups on RHS in both multiplicand and multiplier adds upto bases like 1000, 10000 and so on, and the rest of the left side is same.

Example 7:   **197 × 103**

In this case, 7 and 3 on unit's place add upto 10, but 19 and 10 are not same.

So, in such cases, 97+3 =100 can be taken as base and remaining 1 on hundred's place is same.

$$
\begin{array}{l}
1\ 9\ 7 \\
1\ 0\ 3 \\
\hline
2\ /\ 0291
\end{array}
$$

LHS $= 1 \times (1 + 1) = 1 \times 2 = \mathbf{2}$

RHS $= 97 \times 3 = \mathbf{0291}$

(RHS will have 4 digits as $97 + 3 = 100$ base has two 0's)

So, the final answer is $197 \times 103 = \mathbf{20291}$.

Some solved examples in straight steps:

Example 8:

76 × 74

$$
\begin{array}{r}
7\ 6 \\
\times\ 7\ 4 \\
\hline
(7 \times 8)\ /\ 6 \times 4 \\
56\ /\ 24
\end{array}
$$

So, the answer for
$197 \times 103 = \mathbf{5624}$

Example 9:

113 × 117

$$
\begin{array}{r}
1\ 1\ 3 \\
\times\ 1\ 1\ 7 \\
\hline
(11 \times 12)\ /\ 3 \times 7 \\
132\ /\ 21
\end{array}
$$

So, the answer is
$113 \times 117 = \mathbf{13221}$

Example 10:

992 × 998

$$
\begin{array}{r}
9\ 9\ 2 \\
\times\ 9\ 9\ 8 \\
\hline
(99 \times 100)\ /\ 2 \times 8 \\
9900\ /\ 16
\end{array}
$$

So, the answer is
$992 \times 998 = \mathbf{990016}$

Example 11:

1088 × 1012

$$
\begin{array}{r}
1\ 0\ 8\ 8 \\
\times\ 1\ 0\ 1\ 2 \\
\hline
(10 \times 11)\ /\ 88 \times 12 \\
110\ /\ 1056
\end{array}
$$

So, the answer is
$1088 \times 1012 = \mathbf{1101056}$

EXERCISE 10.2

Multiply the following:
1. 88 × 82   2. 123 × 127   3. 66 × 64   4. 101 × 109
5. 1002 × 1098

TYPE II: Squares of numbers near the Base

The formulae used are:

 (i) *All from 9 and the last from 10*

(ii) *Lesson by the deficiency and set the square of the deficiency.*

The above will be clearer with the following examples:

Squares of numbers below the base

The answer will come in 2 parts – LHS and RHS.

When the number is below the base, subtract its deficiency (or complement) from the number for LHS answer and for RHS, write the square of the deficiency,

i.e. **(number – deficiency) / (square of the deficiency).**

Example 12:   Find **96²**

Base close to 96 is 100, so deficiency from the base or its complement is 4.

> *Step 1:*
> **92 /**   For **LHS**, subtract the deficiency from the
>   number,
>   i.e. 96 – 4 = **92**

> *Step 2 :*
> **92 / 16**   For **RHS**, write the square of the deficiency,
>   i.e. 4² = **16**

So , the final answer is 96² = **9216**

Note: *Make sure that the number of digits on RHS is equal to the number of 0's in the base.*

Example 13:   Find **992²**

Base = 1000 and Deficiency = 8

992²   **LHS** = 992 – 8 = **984**

984 / 064   **RHS** = 8² = 64 = **064**

(Since, base 1000 has three 0's, so to make three digits on RHS, we write it as 064)

So, the final answer is 992² = **984064**

Example 14:   Find **89²**

Base = 100 and Deficiency = 11

89²   **LHS** = 89 – 11 = **78**

RHS = 11² = $_1$21

78 / $_1$21   (base is 100, so only 2 digits should be there in RHS)

So, the final answer is 89² = 78 / 21 = **7921**

Squares of the numbers above the base

When the number is above the base, add the surplus from the base to the number for LHS answer and for RHS, write the square of the surplus,

i.e. **(number + surplus) / (square of surplus).**

Example 15:   Find **104²**

Base = 100

Surplus from the base = 4

104²   **LHS** = add the surplus to the number

108 / 16   = 104 + 4 = **108**

RHS = square of the surplus

= 4² = **16**

So, the final answer is 104² = **10816**

Example 16:   Find **112²**

Base = 100 and surplus = 12

112²   **LHS** = 112 + 12 = **124**

              RHS = 12² = $\underset{1}{44}$

124 / $\underset{1}{44}$ (one is carried over to the left side, since base
              is 100, so only 2 digits should be there in RHS)

So, the final answer for 112² = **12544**

GENERAL GUIDELINES

1. The answer will come in two parts.
2. For LHS answer:
   i. If the number is below the base, subtract the deficiency from its base or its complement from the given number.
   ii. If the number is above the base, add the surplus from its base to the given number.
3. For RHS answer, write the square of the deficiency or the surplus.
4. Make sure that the number of digits in the RHS of the answer should be equal to the number of 0's in the base.

Some solved example in straight steps:

Example 17:   **97²**

Deficiency from the base 100 = 3

(97 – 3) / 3²

94 / 09

So, 97² = **9409**

Example 18: **9988²**

Deficiency from the base 10000 = 12

(9988 – 12) / 12²

9976 / 0144

So, 9988² = **99760144**

Example 19:   **111²**

Surplus from the base 100 = 11

(111 + 11) / 11²

122 / $\underset{1}{21}$

So, 111² = **12321**

Example 20: **1013²**

Surplus from the base 1000 = 13

(1013 + 13) / 13²

1026 / 169

So, 1013² = **1026169**

EXERCISE 10.3

Find the square of the following numbers:

1. 92^2 2. 1006^2 3. 102^2 4. 109^2

5. 995^2 6. 115^2 7. 9985^2 8. 999^2

9. 88^2 10. 1025^2

FINDING SQUARES IN ONE LINE

By using the formula *"dwanda yoga"* or duplex combination, we can find the square of any number, of any length, with ease in one line.

We have discussed earlier how to find squares of numbers ending with 5 and numbers near the base.

Now, we see a general method for finding square of any number. For that, we first need to understand the concept of **duplex** which is denoted by a 'D'.

(1) Duplex of a single digit 'a' is defined as the square of that digit, i.e.

$D(a) = a^2$
$D(3) = 3^2 = 9$
$D(4) = 4^2 = 16$

(2) Duplex of 2 digits number, say 'ab', is defined as twice the product of 2 digits, i.e.;

$D(ab) = 2ab$
$D(34) = 2 \times 3 \times 4 = 24$
$D(13) = 2 \times 1 \times 3 = 6$

(3) Duplex of 3 digits number, say 'abc', is defined as twice the product of 1st and 3rd digit, plus the square of 2nd digit, i.e.;

$D(abc) = (2 \times a \times c) + b^2$
$D(341) = (2 \times 3 \times 1) + 4^2 = 6 + 16 = 22$
$D(724) = (2 \times 7 \times 4) + 2^2 = 56 + 4 = 60$

(4) Duplex of 4 digits number, say 'abcd', is defined as twice the product of 1st and last digit, plus twice the product of 2nd and 3rd digit:

$D(abcd) = (2 \times a \times d) + (2 \times b \times c)$
$D(1346) = (2 \times 1 \times 6) + (2 \times 3 \times 4) = 12 + 24 = 36$
$D(7402) = (2 \times 7 \times 2) + (2 \times 4 \times 0) = 28$
$D(3842) = (2 \times 3 \times 2) + (2 \times 8 \times 4) = 12 + 64 = 76$

(5) Duplex of 5 digits number is twice the product of first and last digit, plus twice the product of 2nd and 4th digit plus square of the 3rd digit:

$$D(abcde) = (2 \times a \times e) + (2 \times b \times d) + c^2$$
$$D(12345) = (2 \times 1 \times 5) + (2 \times 2 \times 4) + 3^2 = 10 + 16 + 9 = 35$$
$$D(72804) = (2 \times 7 \times 4) + (2 \times 2 \times 0) + 8^2 = 56 + 0 + 64 = 120$$
$$D(35617) = (2 \times 3 \times 7) + (2 \times 5 \times 1) + 6^2 = 42 + 10 + 36 = 88$$

(6) Similarly, duplex of 6 digits number can be shown as:-

$$D(abcdef) = (2 \times a \times f) + (2 \times b \times e) + (2 \times c \times d)$$
$$D(320416) = (2 \times 3 \times 6) + (2 \times 2 \times 1) + (2 \times 0 \times 4) = 36 + 4 + 0 = 40$$

(7) Also duplex of 7 digits number can be extended as:

$$D(abcdefg) = (2 \times a \times g) + (2 \times b \times f) + (2 \times c \times e) + d^2$$
$$D(4216435) = (2 \times 4 \times 5) + (2 \times 2 \times 3) + (2 \times 1 \times 4) + 6^2$$
$$= 40 + 12 + 8 + 36 = 96$$

Summary of Duplex Computation		
1.	D (a)	$= a^2$
2.	D (ab)	$= 2 \times a \times b$
3.	D (abc)	$= (2 \times a \times c) + b^2$
4.	D(abcd)	$= (2 \times a \times d) + (2 \times b \times c)$
5.	D(abcde)	$= (2 \times a \times e) + (2 \times b \times d) + c^2$
6.	D(abcdef)	$= (2 \times a \times f) + (2 \times b \times e) + (2 \times c \times d)$
7.	D(abcdefg)	$= (2 \times a \times g) + (2 \times b \times f) + (2 \times c \times e) + d^2$

EXERCISE 11.1

Find the Duplex of the following numbers:

1. 4	**2.** 72	**3.** 86	**4.** 19
5. 254	**6.** 563	**7.** 2189	**8.** 1053
9. 21628	**10.** 45162		

Computation of Squares using Duplex

Using the duplex along with vertical and crosswise, we can find the square of any number.

Starting from right, we first find the duplex of right most digit, then at each step, while finding the duplex, keep on adding one more digit till all the digits get involved. Then we start leaving one digit at a time again from the right till we reach the left most digit.

Keep finding the duplex at each step and add them as we do in general multiplication.

If a number consists of n digits, its square must have 2n or 2n − 1 digits.

Square of 2 digits number

Since, we have to find square of 2–digit number, it means it involves 2×2 digit multiplication, so answer will come in 3 parts − RHS, middle part and LHS:

Square of 2 digit number can be found as:

$$(ab)^2 = D(a) / D(ab) / D(b)$$

Example 1: 38^2

$$(38)^2 = D(3) / D(38) / D(8)$$

38^2 *Step 1:*

/ / 4   **RHS** = Duplex of right most digit (i.e. 8)
   6           $D(8) = 8^2 = $ **4**
                                   6

38^2 *Step 2:*

/ 8 / 4   **Middle Part** = Duplex of both the digits of 38
  4   6 $D(38) = 2(3 \times 8) = $ **8**
                                       4

38^2 *Step 3:*

9 / 8 / 4   **LHS** = Duplex of left most digit (i.e. 3)
   4   6 $D(3) = 3^2 = $ **9**

As we go from right to left, retain 1 digit at each location and carry the surplus to the left. You shall see that this example had 2 digits, so the answer has 2(2) = 4 digits.

So, the answer is $38^2 = 9 / 8 / 4 = 9 / 4 / 4 = $ **1444**
                                  4   6   5

Example 2:

$$53^2 = D(5) / D(53) / D(3)$$
$$= 5^2 / 2(5 \times 3) / 3^2$$
$$= 25 / \underset{3}{0} / 9$$

Taking the carry over to the left, we get:

$$53^2 = \mathbf{2809} \text{ (2 digits in number, so 4 digits in its square)}.$$

Some more solved examples:

Example 3:

$$74^2 = D(7) / D(74) / D(4)$$
$$= 7^2 / 2(7 \times 4) / 4^2$$
$$= 49 / \underset{5}{6} / \underset{1}{6}$$
$$= \mathbf{5476}$$

Example 4:

$$86^2 = D(8) / D(86) / D(6)$$
$$= 8^2 / 2(8 \times 6) / 6^2$$
$$= 64 / \underset{9}{6} / \underset{3}{6}$$
$$= \mathbf{7396}$$

Example 5:

$$27^2 = D(2) / D(27) / D(7)$$
$$= 2^2 / 2(2 \times 7) / 7^2$$
$$= 4 / \underset{2}{8} / \underset{4}{9}$$
$$= \mathbf{729}$$

Example 6:

$$42^2 = D(4) / D(42) / D(2)$$
$$= 4^2 / 2(4 \times 2) / 2^2$$
$$= 16 / \underset{1}{6} / 4$$
$$= \mathbf{1764}$$

EXERCISE 11.2

Find the squares of the following numbers:

1. 52^2 2. 71^2 3. 36^2 4. 29^2

5. 89^2 6. 32^2 7. 92^2 8. 14^2

9. 67^2 10. 23^2

Square of 3 digits number

In a 3 – digit number, finding the square means, it involves 3×3 digit multiplication, so the answer comes in 5 steps.

$$(abc)^2 = D(a) / D(ab) / D(abc) / D(bc) / D(c)$$

__Example 7:__

     521^2

Step 1:

     5 2 1²

    / / / /**1**   Starting from right side, duplex of last digit, $D(1) = 1^2 = \mathbf{1}$

Step 2:

     5 2 1²

    / / /**4**/ 1   Duplex of two digits from the right, $D(21) = 2(2 \times 1) = \mathbf{4}$

Step 3:

     5 2 1²

   / /$\underset{1}{\mathbf{4}}$/ 4 / 1   Duplex of all 3 digits, $D(521) = 2(5 \times 1) + 2^2 = 10 + 4 = \underset{1}{\mathbf{4}}$

Step 4:

     5 2 1²

   /$\underset{2}{\mathbf{0}}$/ 4 / 4 / 1   Duplex of 2 digits from the left, $D(52) = 2(5 \times 2) = \underset{2}{\mathbf{0}}$

Step 5:

$$5\,2\,1^2$$

Duplex of left most digit,

$$D(5) = 5^2 = \mathbf{25}$$

$$25\,/\,\underset{2}{0}\,/\,\underset{1}{4}\,/\,4\,/\,1$$

Taking the carry over to the left, we get:

$$521^2 = \mathbf{271441}$$

Example 8:

$$314^2 \quad = D(3)\,/\,D(31)\,/\,D(314)\,/\,D(14)\,/\,D(4)$$

$$= 3^2\,/\,2(3{\times}1)\,/\,2(3{\times}4) + 1^2\,/\,2(1{\times}4)\,/\,4^2$$

$$= 9\,/\,6\,/\,\underset{2}{5}\,/\,8\,/\,\underset{1}{6}$$

$$= \mathbf{98596}$$

Example 9:

$$743^2 \quad = D(7)\,/\,D(74)\,/\,D(743)\,/\,D(43)\,/\,D(3)$$

$$= 7^2\,/\,2(7{\times}4)\,/\,2(7{\times}3) + 4^2\,/\,2(4{\times}3)\,/\,3^2$$

$$= 49\,/\,\underset{5}{6}\,/\,\underset{5}{8}\,/\,\underset{2}{4}\,/\,9$$

$$= \mathbf{552049}$$

Example 10:

$$629^2 \quad = D(6)\,/\,D(62)\,/\,D(629)\,/\,D(29)\,/\,D(9)$$

$$= 6^2\,/\,2(6{\times}2)\,/\,2(6{\times}2) + 2^2\,/\,2(2{\times}9)\;\;9^2$$

$$= 36\,/\,\underset{2}{4}\,/\,\underset{11}{2}\,/\,\underset{3}{6}\,/\,\underset{8}{1}$$

$$= \mathbf{395641}$$

Example 11:

$$426^2 \quad = D(4)\,/\,D(42)\,/\,D(426)\,/\,D(26)\,/\,D(6)$$

$$= 4^2\,/\,2(4{\times}2)\,/\,2(4{\times}6) + 2^2\,/\,2(2{\times}6)\,/\,6^2$$

$$= 16\,/\,\underset{1}{6}\,/\,\underset{5}{2}\,/\,\underset{2}{4}\,/\,\underset{3}{6}$$

$$= \mathbf{181476}$$

Instead of carrying over the digits in the end, they can also be directly carried over to their left at each step, as we have been doing in vertical and crosswise multiplication,

i.e. $426^2 = 18 \underset{2}{\,1\,} \underset{5}{\,4\,} \underset{2}{\,7\,} \underset{3}{\,6} = 181476$

This process can be extended to finding square of any number of digits.

Square of 4 digits number:

The answer will come in 7 steps as follows:

$(abcd)^2 = D(a) / D(ab) / D(abc) / D(abcd) / D(bcd) / D(cd) / D(d)$

Example 12:

$3425^2 = D(3) / D(34) / D(342) / D(3425) / D(425) / D(25) / D(5)$

$= 3^2 / 2(3\times4) / 2(3\times2) + 4^2 / 2(3\times5) + 2(4\times2) / 2(4\times5) + 2^2 / 2(2\times5) / 5^2$

$= 9 / \underset{2}{\,4\,} / \underset{2}{\,8\,} / \underset{4}{\,6\,} / \underset{4}{\,4\,} / \underset{2}{\,0\,} / \underset{2}{\,5}$

Taking the carry over to the left, we get:

$3425^2 = \mathbf{11730625}$

Square of 5 digits number:

The answer will come in 9 steps.

Example 13:

$12345^2 = D(1) / D(12) / D(123) / D(1234) / D(12345) / D(2345)/ D(345) \; D(45) \; D(5)$

$= 1^2/2(1\times2)/2(1\times3) + 2^2 /2(1\times4) + 2(2\times3) / 2(1\times5) + 2(2\times4) + 3^2$

$\quad 2(2\times5)+2(3\times4) / 2(3\times5) + 4^2 / 2(4\times5) / 5^2$

$= 1/4 / \underset{1}{\,0\,} / \underset{2}{\,0\,} / \underset{3}{\,5\,} / \underset{4}{\,4\,} / \underset{4}{\,6\,} / \underset{4}{\,0\,} / \underset{2}{\,5}$

Taking the carry over to the left, we get:

$12345^2 = \mathbf{152399025}$

GENERAL GUIDELINES:

1. Start from the right most digit and move towards left.
2. First find Duplex of right most digit.
3. Keep adding a digit at each step and find their duplex.
4. When all the digits get involved, start leaving digits from the right one at a time and continue till we reach the left most digit.
5. While writing the answer, put down one digit at a time and carry the surplus to the next digit to the left.

EXERCISE 11.3

Find the squares of the following numbers:

1. 251^2	2. 123^2	3. 434^2	4. 624^2
5. 821^2	6. 328^2	7. 4321^2	8. 2806^2
9. 23142^2	10. 10405^2		

A fraction has a number on top and a number on the bottom with a line between the two numbers. The number on the bottom of a fraction is called the *denominator* and that on top of a fraction is called the *numerator*.

e.g. in fraction $\dfrac{2}{7}$, 2 is the numerator and 7 is the denominator.

By the use of the formula, *vertically & crosswise*, the fractions can be easily added or subtracted in one line.

Computations of fractions can be divided into two categories:

1). When the denominators are relatively prime (i.e. they don't have any common factor other than one).

2). When the denominators are composite numbers (i.e. they have one or more common factors other than one).

CASE I : When the denominators are relatively prime

▌ADDITION OF FRACTIONS

Example 1:

$$\frac{2}{7} + \frac{1}{3}$$

Step 1: $\dfrac{2}{7} \diagdown\!\!\!\diagup \dfrac{1}{3}$ We cross multiply and add the result to get the **numerator**, i.e. $(2 \times 3) + (7 \times 1) = 6 + 7 = \mathbf{13}$

Step 2: $\dfrac{2}{7} \quad \dfrac{1}{3}$ We multiply the denominators to get the final **denominator**, i.e. $7 \times 3 = \mathbf{21}$

So, the answer is $\dfrac{2}{7} + \dfrac{1}{3} = \dfrac{13}{21}$

Example 2:

$$\frac{4}{9} + \frac{2}{11}$$

Numerator $= (4 \times 11) + (9 \times 2) = 44 + 18 = \mathbf{62}$

Denominator $= 9 \times 11 = \mathbf{99}$

So, the answer is $\dfrac{4}{9} + \dfrac{2}{11} = \dfrac{\mathbf{62}}{\mathbf{99}}$

Note: *Cross multiplication and addition can be done mentally also to get the answer in one step.*

SUBTRACTION OF FRACTIONS

Subtraction also involves the same steps except that we cross multiply and subtract rather than add.

Example 3:

$$\frac{4}{7} - \frac{1}{4}$$

Numerator $= (4 \times 4) - (7 \times 1) = 16 - 7 = \mathbf{9}$

Denominator $= 7 \times 4 = \mathbf{28}$

So, the answer is $\dfrac{4}{7} - \dfrac{1}{4} = \dfrac{\mathbf{9}}{\mathbf{28}}$

Example 4:

$$\frac{9}{11} - \frac{2}{3}$$

$$\frac{9}{11} - \frac{2}{3} = \frac{(9 \times 3) - (2 \times 11)}{11 \times 3} = \frac{27 - 22}{33} = \frac{5}{33}$$

So, the answer is $\dfrac{9}{11} - \dfrac{2}{3} = \dfrac{\mathbf{5}}{\mathbf{33}}$

Note: *While finding the numerator, in case of subtraction of fractions, the first number in subtraction will be, the product of numerator of first fraction and denominator of the second fraction,* *i.e. in case of* $\dfrac{9}{11}\diagdown\dfrac{2}{3}$

Numerator = (9×3) – (2×11) = 27 – 22 = 5

In case of addition, it doesn't matter which product is taken first.

ADDITION AND SUBTRACTION OF MIXED FRACTIONS

A mixed fraction has a whole number part and a fractional part, e.g.

$2\dfrac{3}{5}$ is a mixed number as it has a whole number 2, mixed with the

fraction $\dfrac{3}{5}$.

Example 5:

$$4\dfrac{1}{3} + 2\dfrac{3}{5}$$

In case of mixed fractions, add the whole parts and the fractional parts separately and then write them together as mixed fraction in the answer.

Step 1:   Add the **whole part**, i.e. $4 + 2 = 6$

Step 2:   Add the **fractional part** as before;

$$\dfrac{1}{3}+\dfrac{3}{5}=\dfrac{(1\times5)+(3\times3)}{3\times5}=\dfrac{14}{15}$$

So, $4\dfrac{1}{3}+2\dfrac{3}{5}=6\ \&\ \dfrac{14}{15}=6\dfrac{14}{15}$

So, the answer is $4\dfrac{1}{3}+2\dfrac{3}{5}=6\dfrac{14}{15}$

Example 6:

$$2\dfrac{3}{5}-1\dfrac{1}{2}$$

Step 1:   Dealing with the **whole part** first, it gives:

$2 - 1 = 1$

Step 2:   Subtracting the **fractional part** gives:

$$\frac{3}{5} - \frac{1}{2} = \frac{6-5}{10} = \frac{1}{10}$$

So, the answer is $2\frac{3}{5} - 1\frac{1}{2} = 1\frac{1}{10}$

Example 7:

$$5\frac{2}{5} - 2\frac{3}{7}$$

Step 1:   Dealing with the **whole part** first, it gives:

$$5 - 2 = 3$$

Step 2:   Subtracting the fractional part as before gives:

$$\frac{2}{5} - \frac{3}{7} = \frac{14-15}{35} = -\frac{1}{35} \text{ (i.e. } \frac{\overline{1}}{35})$$

$$5\frac{2}{5} - 2\frac{3}{7} = 3\frac{\overline{1}}{35}$$

Here, we get a negative number, but it is easily dealt with by taking $\frac{1}{35}$ from one of the whole ones.

i.e. $1 - \frac{1}{35} = \frac{34}{35}$

So, the final answer is $5\frac{2}{5} - 2\frac{3}{7} = 2\frac{34}{35}$

CASE II : When the denominators of 2 fractions are composite numbers (i.e. they have a common factor):

Example 8:

$$\frac{7}{12} + \frac{5}{18}$$

Step 1:

We take the highest common factor (HCF) of the denominators 12 and 18.

In this case it is 6 and divide the denominators 12 and 18 by 6. Put the numbers thus obtained 2 and 3 below 12 and 18 respectively as shown below:

$$\frac{7}{12} + \frac{5}{18}$$
$$(2) \quad (3)$$

Step 2:

For **numerator**, cross multiply using 2 and 3 as denominator rather than 12 and 18.

$$\frac{7}{12} + \frac{5}{18} = (7 \times 3) + (5 \times 2) = \mathbf{31} \text{ as numerator}$$
$$(2) \quad (3)$$

Step 3:

For **denominator** of the answer, cross multiply in the denominator either (12×3) or (18×2), both give 36 as the answer.

$$\frac{7}{12} + \frac{5}{18} \quad (12 \times 3) \text{ or } (18 \times 2) = \mathbf{36} \text{ as denominator}$$
$$(2) \quad (3)$$

So, the answer is $\dfrac{7}{12} + \dfrac{5}{18} = \dfrac{\mathbf{31}}{\mathbf{36}}$

Example 9:

$$\frac{\mathbf{5}}{\mathbf{18}} - \frac{\mathbf{1}}{\mathbf{27}}$$

HCF of 18 and 27 is 9

$$\frac{5}{18} - \frac{1}{27} = \frac{5}{18} - \frac{1}{27} = \frac{(5 \times 3) - (2 \times 1)}{(27 \times 2) \text{ or } (18 \times 3)} = \frac{15 - 2}{54} = \frac{13}{54}$$
$$\qquad\qquad\qquad (2) \quad (3)$$

So, the answer is $\dfrac{5}{18} - \dfrac{1}{27} = \dfrac{\mathbf{13}}{\mathbf{54}}$

Some more solved examples:

Example 10:

$$\frac{2}{5} + \frac{3}{7} = \frac{14 + 15}{35} = \frac{29}{35}$$

Example 11:

$$\frac{3}{8} + \frac{2}{9} = \frac{27 + 16}{72} = \frac{43}{72}$$

Example 12:

$$\frac{8}{9} - \frac{2}{7} = \frac{56 - 18}{63} = \frac{38}{63}$$

Example 13:

$$\frac{9}{13} - \frac{4}{7} = \frac{63 - 52}{91} = \frac{11}{91}$$

Example 14:

$$\frac{4}{35} + \frac{3}{14} = \frac{4}{35} + \frac{3}{14} = \frac{8 + 15}{70} = \frac{23}{70} \qquad \text{(HCF of 35 and 14 is 7)}$$
$$\quad (5) \quad (2)$$

Example 15:

$$\frac{7}{12} - \frac{1}{30} = \frac{7}{12} - \frac{1}{30} = \frac{35 - 2}{60} = \frac{33}{60} = \frac{11}{20} \text{ (HCF of 12 and 30 is 6)}$$
$$\quad (2) \quad (5)$$

Example 16:

$$4\frac{1}{2} + 3\frac{7}{9}$$

whole part = $4 + 3 = 7$

fractional part $= \dfrac{1}{2} + \dfrac{7}{9} = \dfrac{9+14}{18} = \dfrac{23}{18} = 1\dfrac{5}{18}$

So, $4\dfrac{1}{2} + 3\dfrac{7}{9} = 7 + 1\dfrac{5}{18} = 8\dfrac{5}{18}$

Example 17:

$$7\dfrac{1}{3} - 2\dfrac{1}{4}$$

whole part $= 7 - 2 = 5$

fractional part $= \dfrac{1}{3} - \dfrac{1}{4} = \dfrac{4-3}{12} = \dfrac{1}{12}$

So, $7\dfrac{1}{3} - 2\dfrac{1}{4} = 5 + \dfrac{1}{12} = 5\dfrac{1}{12}$

Example 18:

$$6\dfrac{1}{5} - 7\dfrac{1}{3}$$

whole part $= 6 - 7 = -1$

fractional part $= \dfrac{1}{5} - \dfrac{1}{3} = \dfrac{3-5}{15} = -\dfrac{2}{15}$

So, $6\dfrac{1}{5} - 7\dfrac{1}{3} = -1\dfrac{2}{15}$

EXERCISE 12.1

Add / Subtract the following fractions:

1. $\dfrac{3}{4} + \dfrac{2}{3}$ 2. $\dfrac{4}{5} + \dfrac{1}{8}$ 3. $\dfrac{2}{5} + \dfrac{2}{3}$ 4. $\dfrac{2}{15} - \dfrac{3}{7}$

5. $\dfrac{11}{12} - \dfrac{3}{7}$ 6. $\dfrac{1}{16} - \dfrac{7}{24}$ 7. $\dfrac{7}{12} + \dfrac{1}{9}$ 8. $\dfrac{2}{7} + \dfrac{1}{21}$

9. $2\dfrac{1}{3} + 1\dfrac{1}{5}$ 10. $4\dfrac{1}{4} - \dfrac{4}{21}$

COMPARING FRACTIONS

Sometimes we need to compare fractions or arrange them in order of their value.

Example 19:

Compare the fractions $\dfrac{2}{7}$ and $\dfrac{9}{11}$, find the larger one.

To compare the fractions $\dfrac{2}{7}$ and $\dfrac{9}{11}$, we cross multiply them, i.e. multiply the numerator of first fraction with the denominator of the second fraction and vice-versa. Then compare the two products, i.e.

$2 \times 11 = 22$ and $9 \times 7 = 63$

Since, $63 > 22$, so, $\dfrac{9}{11} > \dfrac{2}{7}$.

Example 20:

Arrange the fractions $\dfrac{7}{8}, \dfrac{2}{3}, \dfrac{5}{6}$ in ascending order:

Step 1:

First lets compare the 1ˢᵗ two fractions $\dfrac{7}{8}$ and $\dfrac{2}{3}$

By cross multiplying, we get: $7 \times 3 = 21$ and $2 \times 8 = 16$

Since, $21 > 16$, so $\dfrac{7}{8} > \dfrac{2}{3}$

Step 2:

Now comparing $\dfrac{2}{3}$ and $\dfrac{5}{6}$

By cross multiplying, we get: $2 \times 6 = 12$ and $5 \times 3 = 15$,

Since, $12 < 15$, so, $\dfrac{2}{3} < \dfrac{5}{6}$

We can conclude that $\dfrac{2}{3}$ is the smallest of 3 fractions.

Step 3:

Now compare $\dfrac{7}{8}$ and $\dfrac{5}{6}$

By cross multiplying, we get $7 \times 6 = 42$ and $5 \times 8 = 40$

Since, $42 > 40$, so $\dfrac{7}{8} > \dfrac{5}{6}$

So, the fractions in ascending order are $\dfrac{2}{3} < \dfrac{5}{6} < \dfrac{7}{8}$

Example 21:

Arrange the fractions $\dfrac{1}{3}, \dfrac{2}{7}, \dfrac{4}{9}$ in descending order:

Step 1:

Comparing $\dfrac{1}{3}$ and $\dfrac{2}{7}$ by cross multiplying:

$1 \times 7 = 7$ and $2 \times 3 = 6$

Since, $7 > 6$, so $\dfrac{1}{3} > \dfrac{2}{7}$

Step 2:

Now comparing $\dfrac{2}{7}$ and $\dfrac{4}{9}$, we get: $2 \times 9 = 18$ and $4 \times 7 = 28$

Since, $28 > 18$, so $\dfrac{4}{9} > \dfrac{2}{7}$

So, $\dfrac{2}{7}$ is the smallest of the three fractions.

Step 3:

Comparing $\dfrac{1}{3}$ and $\dfrac{4}{9}$, we get: $1 \times 9 = 9$ and $4 \times 3 = 12$

Since, $12 > 9$, so $\dfrac{4}{9} > \dfrac{1}{3}$

So, the fractions in the descending order are: $\dfrac{4}{9} > \dfrac{1}{3} > \dfrac{2}{7}$

EXERCISE 12.2

Arrange the following fractions in ascending order:

1. $\dfrac{2}{9}, \dfrac{1}{7}, \dfrac{6}{11}$

2. $\dfrac{3}{7}, \dfrac{2}{5}, \dfrac{5}{9}$

3. $\dfrac{1}{3}, \dfrac{2}{7}, \dfrac{8}{9}$

4. $\dfrac{8}{9}, \dfrac{9}{11}, \dfrac{11}{13}$

5. $\dfrac{4}{13}, \dfrac{6}{17}, \dfrac{3}{11}$

13 / DIVISION

We have seen in the previous chapters, various methods of multiplications for different patterns of numbers. There was base multiplication method for numbers near the base and there were some for general random numbers.

Similarly, in case of division also, we can categorize the methods into the following:

1. Division by numbers below the base.
2. Division by numbers above the base.
3. Division by any random number.

First of all, we need to understand four basic terms used in the division – divisor, dividend, quotient and remainder.

Let's take an example, say $4257 \div 8$

$$\text{Divisor} \longleftarrow 8 \mid 4257 \longrightarrow \text{Dividend}$$
$$532 / 1$$
$$\text{Quotient} \qquad \text{Remainder}$$

The number to be divided, i.e. 4257 is the *Dividend*. The number we are dividing by, i.e. 8 is the *Divisor*. The end result of the division, i.e. 532 is the *Quotient* and the number which remains undivided, i.e. 1 is the *Remainder*.

CASE I: Division by numbers below the base

We use the formula: *"All from nine and last from 10"*.

1) When the base is 10

Suppose the divisor is 9

We have seen that 9 is a special number in itself. So division by 9 is also very special and unique.

First let's see an example by general method and then we shall see how it is special for 9.

Example 1:   **231 ÷ 9**

Step 1:

Divide the dividend into two parts such that the number of digits in the right part (also called the remainder column) is equal to the number of 0's in the base of the divisor.

Since 9 is near the base 10 which has one 0, so put a vertical line one digit from the right of the dividend. The computation on the left side of the line will give the quotient of the answer and the right side will give the remainder of the answer.

Write the sum as shown with the divisor 9 to the left of the sum and its complement i.e. 1 below it.

Step 2:

Bring down the first digit of the dividend, i.e. 2 as it is, as the first quotient digit.

Step 3:

Multiply this quotient digit 2 with the complement of 9 (i.e. 1) to get **2** ($2 \times 1 = 2$) and write this **2** below the next digit of the dividend, i.e. below 3, as shown.

Step 4:

Add both the digits 3 and 2 in the second column to get **5** and bring this **5** down as the second quotient digit.

Step 5:

Again multiplying this quotient digit 5 with the complement of 9 (i.e.1) to get **5** ($5 \times 1 = 5$) and write this below the next digit of the dividend, i.e. below 1, which is to the right side of the vertical line.

Step 6:

```
9 | 2 3 | 1 |
1 |_____| 5↓
    2 5 | 6
```

Finally add the digit 1 and 5 in the right/ remainder column to get **6** as remainder.

So, the final answer is 231 ÷ 9 gives **25 as quotient**
and **6 as remainder**.

How division by 9 is special:

Since at each step when the quotient digit is multiplied by the complement of 9 (i.e.1), it will always be the quotient digit itself. So we can skip this multiplication step. We can directly add the quotient digit to the next digit of dividend to get next quotient digit.

Let's understand this better with the help of an example:

Example 2: 302 ÷ 9

Step 1:

```
9 | 3 0 | 2
  |_____|___
       |
```

Since nearest base to the divisor 9 is 10, which has one 0, put a vertical line in the dividend 1 digit from the right as shown.

Step 2:

```
9 | 3 0 | 2
  ↓_____|___
  3      |
```

Bring down **3** of the dividend as it is as the first quotient digit.

Step 3:

```
9 | 3 0 | 2
  |_3↓___|___
  3⁄3    |
```

Add the quotient digit 3 to the next dividend digit 0 to get **3** (3+0 = 3).

Bring this **3** down as next quotient digit.

Step 4:

```
9 | 3 0 | 2 |
  |_____|_3↓
  3 3 ⁄5
```

Again add this second quotient digit 3 to the next dividend digit 2 in the remainder column to get **5** (2+3 =5). Bring this **5** down as the remainder.

So, the final answer is 302 ÷ 9 gives **33 as quotient**
and **5 as remainder.**

Example 3:   **412 ÷ 9**

Step 1:

9 | 4 | 1 | 2
↓
4 |

Write the sum as shown and bring down **4** as first quotient digit.

Step 2:

9 | 4 | 1 | 2
  | 4↓|
4 5 |

Add this quotient digit, i.e. 4 to next dividend digit i.e. 1, to get **5** (i.e. 4+1 = 5)

Bring down this **5** as next quotient digit.

Step 3:

9 | 4 | 1 | 2 |
  | 4 | 5↓|
4 5 7

Add this 5 to next dividend digit 2 in the remainder column to get **7** as remainder (2+5 =7).

So, the final answer is 412 ÷ 9 gives **45 as quotient**
and **7 as remainder**.

Example 4:   **5123 ÷ 9**

Step 1:

9 | 5 1 2 | 3
↓
5 |

Write the sum as shown and bring down **5** as first quotient digit.

Step 2:

9 | 5 1 | 2 | 3
  | 5↓|
5 6 |

Add this 5 to next dividend digit i.e. 1, to get **6** (i.e. 5+1 = 6) and bring **6** down as next quotient digit.

Step 3:

9 | 5 1 2 | 3
  | 5 6↓|
5 6 8 |

Add this 6 to next dividend digit i.e. 2, to get **8** (i.e. 6+2 = 8) and bring **8** down as next quotient digit.

Step 4:

9 | 5 1 2 | 3 |
  | 5 6 8↓|
5 6 8 11

Add this 8 to next dividend digit i.e. 3 in the remainder column to get **11** (8+3 = 11) and bring this **11** down as the remainder.

The division gives the answer: 568 as quotient and 11 as remainder.

Step 5:   Since, there is 1 more 9 in remainder 11, so we

9 | 1 | 1| divide 11 by 9 once more to get 1 as quotient
  └─┤ 1↓   and 2 as remainder.
   1│2

Adding this quotient 1 to previously obtained
quotient 568, we get 569 as the final quotient
and 2 as final remainder.

So, the final answer is 5123 ÷ 9 gives (568+1) = **569 as quotient**

                                                       and **2 as remainder**.

GENERAL GUIDELINES (*for division by 9*):

1. Divide the dividend in 2 columns — quotient and remainder columns such that only 1 digit from the right of the dividend remains in the remainder column.

2. Bring down the first digit of the dividend as the first digit of the quotient.

3. Quotient digit obtained at each step is added to the next digit in the dividend to give the next digit of quotient.

4. The answer we get in quotient column is the quotient and that we get in remainder column is the remainder of the answer.

5. If the remainder is more than 9, then divide it again by 9. The quotient thus obtained is added to the already obtained quotient to get the final quotient and the remainder thus obtained is the final remainder.

Some more solved examples:

Example 5:   **1352 ÷ 9**

9 | 1 3 5 | 2
  └─┤ 1 4 | 9
    1 4 9 | 11

Dividing the remainder 11 again by 9, we get Q = 1 and R = 2:

So, the final answer is: **Quotient**   = 149 + 1 = **150**

                         Remainder = **2**

Example 6:   **5037 ÷ 9**

```
9 | 5 0 3 | 7
  |   5 5 | 8
  --------
    5 5 8 | 15
```

Dividing the remainder 15 by 9, we get, Q = 1 and R = 6

So, the final answer is: **Quotient** = 558 + 1 = **559**

                        Remainder = 6

Example 7:   **2372 ÷ 9**

```
9 | 2 3 7 | 2
  |   2 5 | 12
  --------
    2 5 2 | 14
        1
```

The first 1 in the 12 must be carried over to the 5, giving 262 as quotient and 14 as remainder. 14 when again divided by 9 gives 1 as quotient and 5 as remainder.

So, the final answer is: **Quotient** = 262 + 1 = **263**

                        Remainder = 5

Example 8:   **160 ÷ 9**

```
9 | 1 6 | 0
  |   1 | 7
  ------
    1 7 | 7
```

      Quotient = 17

      Remainder = 7

EXERCISE 13.1

Divide the following by 9 and write the quotient and the remainder:

1. 241 ÷ 9   **2.** 3022 ÷ 9   **3.** 6124 ÷ 9   **4.** 7012 ÷ 9

5. 11326 ÷ 9

2) When the base is 100

Since the base is 100, which has two 0's, so the dividend should be divided by a vertical line in 2 columns such that there are 2 digits on the right side of the line, which is also called the remainder column. The left side of the line will give the quotient of the answer.

Also, the number of digits to be placed under the dividend digits, at each step (after multiplication of quotient with the complement), should be equal to the number of 0's in the base of divisor.

Let's understand this better with the help of the following example:

***Example 9*:**   2403 ÷ 99

Step 1:

Write the sum as shown. Since, nearest base to 99 is 100 having two 0's, so there should be 2 digits in the remainder column.

Complement of 99 is 01 *(by all from 9 and last from 10)*, which is written below 99. Bring down the first digit **2** as the first quotient digit.

Step 2:

Now multiply this quotient digit 2 with complement of 99 (i.e. 01), to get **02** (2×01 = 02) and write this **02** below the next two dividend digits (4 and 0), as shown:

(02 as base is 100, so at each step, we will place 2 digits at a time.)

Step 3:

99 | 2 4 | 0 3
0 1 | 0 | 2
   2 **4** |

Add the number 4 and 0 in the second column to get **4** (4+0 =4) and write this **4** down as the second quotient digit.

Step 4:

Multiply this 4 with complement 01 to get **04** (4×01 = 04) and write it below the next two dividend digits (0 and 3) as shown.

Step 5:

```
9 9 | 2 4 | 0 3
0 1 |   0 | 2
    |     | 0 4
  ───────────
    2 4 | 2 7
```

Adding all the digits in the remainder column, we get **27** as remainder.

So, 2403 ÷ 99 gives **24 as quotient**
                     and **27 as remainder**.

Example 10: **2532 ÷ 89**

Step 1:

```
8 9 | 2 5 | 3 2
1 1 |
  ───────────
      2
```

Base = 100 and complement of 89 = 11

Write the sum as shown and bring down first digit **2** of the dividend as a first quotient digit.

Step 2:

```
8 9 | 2 5 | 3 2
1 1 |   2 2
  × 2
```

Multiplying this 2 by complement 11, we get **22** and write this **22** below next 2 dividend digits (5 and 3) as shown.

Step 3:

```
8 9 | 2 5 | 3 2
1 1 |   2 | 2
  ───────────
    2 7
```

Adding in the second column, we get **7** which we write as second quotient digit.

Step 4:

```
8 9 | 2 5 | 3 2
1 1 |  2 | 2
    |    | 7 7
  2 7 | 1 2 9
  ×
```

Multiplying this 7 by complement 11, we get **77** and write it below next 2 dividend digits (3 and 2) in the remainder column, as shown.

Adding all the digits in the remainder column, we get **129** as the remainder.

Step 5:

```
8 9 | 1 | 2 9
1 1 |   | 1 1
  ───────────
    1 | 4 0
```

Since, (remainder)129 > 89 (divisor), so we again divide it by 89 to get 1 as quotient digit and 40 as remainder.

So, the final answer is 2532 ÷ 89 gives
        (27 + 1) = **28 as quotient** and **40 as remainder.**

3) When the base is 1000

Since base is 1000, which has three 0's, so divide the dividend in 2 columns such that there are 3 digits in the right column, which gives the remainder.

Also, after multiplication of the quotient digit with the complement, three digits has to be placed at each step.

Example 11:   **13225 ÷ 888**

Step 1:

```
888 | 1 3 | 225
112 |  ↓  |
    |  1  |
```

Put a vertical line 3 digits from the right of dividend as shown and write the complement of 888 (i.e. 112) below it.

Bring down first digit **1** of dividend as first quotient digit.

Step 2:

```
888 | 1 3 | 2 2 5
112 |  1  | 1 2
  × | 1 4 |
```

Multiplying this 1 by complement 112, we get **112** and write this below the next three dividend digits as shown.

Add 3 and 1 in the second column to get **4** and write this **4** down as next quotient digit.

Step 3:

```
888 | 1 3 | 2 2 5
112 |  1  | 1 2
    |     | 4 4 8
  × | 1 4 |
```

Multiplying this 4 by complement 112, we get **448** and write this below the next three dividend digits as shown.

Step 4:

```
888 | 1 3 | 2 2 5
112 |  1  | 1 2
    |     | 4 4 8
    | 1 4 | 7 9 3
```

Add all the digits in the remainder column to get **793** as remainder.

So, 13225 ÷ 888 gives **14 as quotient**

and **793 as remainder**

GENERAL GUIDELINES

1. Divide the dividend into 2 parts such that the digits on the right side, i.e. the remainder side is equal to the number of 0's in the base.

2. Write the complement of the divisor below the divisor.

3. Bring down the first dividend digit and write it as the first quotient digit.

4. Multiply this quotient digit by the complement of the divisor and write it down below the next digits of the dividend (one digit in one column). Also the number of digits to be written at each step below the digits of dividend should be equal to the number of 0's in the base of divisor.

5. Only the digits of the next column are added to get the next quotient digit.

6. Then this quotient digit is again multiplied by the complement of divisor and written under the next digits of the dividend from the next column.

7. Addition of digits in each column in each step will give the new digit of the quotient.

8. We continue this till we have written a digit under the last digit of the dividend in the remainder side.

9. Add all the digits in the remainder column to get the remainder of the sum.

10. If the remainder is bigger than the divisor, we divide the remainder again by the divisor, and quotient thus obtained is added to the previously obtained quotient, to give the final quotient and the remainder thus obtained will be the final remainder.

Some more solved examples:

Example 12:

11023 ÷ 97

```
97 | 1 1 0 | 2 3
03 |   0 3 |
   |     0 | 3
   |       | 0 9
   |—————————————
     1 1 3 | 6 2
```

Q = 113
R = 62

Example 13:

2732 ÷ 99

```
99 | 2 7 | 3 2
01 |   0 | 2
   |     |   0 7
   |———————————
     2 7 | 5 9
```

Q = 27
R = 59

Example 14:

42301 ÷ 996

```
976 | 4 2 | 3 0 1
004 |   0 | 1 6
    |     | 0 0 8
    |———————————————
      4 2 | 4 6 9
```

Q = 42
R = 469

Example 15:

93678 ÷ 991

```
991 | 9 3 | 6 7 8
009 |   0 | 8 1
    |     | 0 2 7
    |———————————————
      9 3 | 1515
```

Dividing remainder 1515
again by 991, we get

```
991 | 1 | 5 1 5
009 |   | 0 0 9
    |——————————
      1 | 5 2 4
```

Q = 93+1 = 94
R = 524

Example 16:

39854 ÷ 9989

```
9989 | 3 | 9 8 5 4
0011 |   | 0 0 3 3
     |——————————————
       3 | 9 8 8 7
```

Q = 3
R = 9887

Example 17:

85743 ÷ 9899

```
9899 | 8 | 5 7 4 3
0101 |   | 0 8 0 8
     |——————————————
       8 | 6 5 5 1
```

Q = 8
R = 6551

Example 18:

$14367 \div 889$

$$
\begin{array}{c|c|c}
889 & 1\,4 & 3\,6\,7 \\
111 & 1 & 1\,1 \\
& & 5\,5\,5 \\
\hline
& 1\,5 & 1032
\end{array}
$$

On dividing the remainder 1032 again by 889,

we get Q = 1 and R = 143

So the final answer is:

Q = 15 + 1 = 16

R = 143

Example 19:

$113121 \div 8799$

$$
\begin{array}{c|c|c}
8799 & 1\,1 & 3\,1\,2\,1 \\
1201 & 1 & 2\,0\,1 \\
& & 2\,4\,0\,2 \\
\hline
& 1\,2 & 7\,5\,3\,3
\end{array}
$$

Q = 12
R = 7533

Example 20:

$307211 \div 898$

$$
\begin{array}{c|c|c}
898 & 3\,0\,7 & 2\,1\,1 \\
102 & 3\,0 & 6 \\
& 3 & 0\,6 \\
& & 1\,0\,2\,0 \\
\hline
& 3\,3\,0 & 1\,8\,9\,1 \\
& \;\;_1 &
\end{array}
$$

= 340 / 1891

On dividing 1891 again by 898, we get Q = 2 and

$$R = 1891 - (2 \times 898)$$

$$= 1891 - 1796 = 95$$

So, the final answer is :

Q = 340 + 2 = 342

R = 95

Example 21:

$917385 \div 985$

$$
\begin{array}{c|c|c}
985 & 9\,1\,7 & 3\,8\,5 \\
015 & 1\,3 & 5 \\
& 0 & 3\,0 \\
& & 1\,5\,0 \\
\hline
& 9\,2\,0 & 1\,3\,3\,5 \\
& \;\;_1 &
\end{array}
$$

= 930 / 1335

On dividing the remainder 1335 again by 985, we get:

Q = 1, R = 1335–985 = 350

So, the final answer is:

Q = 930 + 1 = 931

R = 350

EXERCISE 13.2

Divide the following and write the quotient and the remainder:

1.	2415 ÷ 99	**2.**	53064 ÷ 93
3.	45962 ÷ 93	**4.**	235897 ÷ 9898
5.	3572 ÷ 87	**6.**	112233 ÷ 9978
7.	9345626 ÷ 89996	**8.**	42051 ÷ 987
9.	837894 ÷ 9979	**10.**	73984 ÷ 978

CASE II: Division by numbers above the base

When we divide any number by a divisor just above the base, we make use of the formula *"Transpose and Apply"*. The working rule is the same as what we have been doing in 'below the base' except that in this case, we write the *surplus* of the divisor from the base beneath it, with a *negative* sign.

Also the multiplication of the quotient digit with the surplus performed at each step is written with the appropriate sign.

Let's understand it better with the help of an example:

1) When base is 10

We divide the dividend in the similar manner as we have done in case of divisor below the base.

Since, base is 10 which has one 0, divide the dividend by a vertical line in 2 columns such that there is 1 digit on the right side of the line, which is also called the remainder column. The left side of the line will give the quotient of the answer.

Example 22: **2449 ÷ 12**

Step 1:

```
1 2 | 2 4 4 | 9
  2 |   ↓    |
    |   2    |
```

Write the sum as shown with divisor 12 to the left of the dividend and the surplus of the divisor from the base, i.e. 2 below it with a negative sign.

Bring down the first dividend digit **2** as the first quotient digit.

Step 2:

$$1\;2\begin{array}{|cccc}2\;4\;4&9\\ \hline 2\;\;\;\overline{4}\\ \times\;\overline{2}\;\;0\end{array}$$

Multiply this 2 by $\overline{2}$ to get $\overline{4}$ and place this $\overline{4}$ just below the next dividend digit as shown.

Add 4 and $\overline{4}$ in the second column to get **0** and write it as the second quotient digit.

Step 3:

$$1\;2\begin{array}{|cccc}2\;4\;4&9\\ \hline 2\;\;\overline{4}\;0\\ \times\;2\;0\;4\end{array}$$

Multiply this 0 by $\overline{2}$ to get **0** and place this **0** below the next dividend digit 4, as shown:

Add 4 and 0 in the third column to get **4** as the third quotient digit.

Step 4:

$$1\;2\begin{array}{|cccc}2\;4\;4&9\\ \hline 2\;\;\overline{4}\;0\;\overline{8}\\ \times\;2\;0\;4\;1\end{array}$$

Multiply this 4 by $\overline{2}$ to get $\overline{8}$.

Place this $\overline{8}$ below the next dividend digit 9 in the remainder column.

Add 9 and $\overline{8}$ to get **1** as remainder.

So, 2449 ÷ 12 gives **204** as **quotient** and **1** as **remainder**.

Note: *Number of digits to be placed under the dividend digits at each step should always be equal to the number of 0's in the base of divisor.*

In the above base, when base is 10, and there is one 0 in it, so at each step, only one digit will be placed at a time.

Some more solved examples:

Example 23:

267 ÷ 11

$$11\begin{array}{|cc}2\;6&7\\ \overline{1}\;\;\;\overline{2}\\ \;\;\;\;\;\overline{4}\\ \hline 2\;4&3\end{array}$$

Q = 24
R = 3

Example 24:

25477 ÷ 12

$$12\begin{array}{|cccc}2\;5\;4\;7&7\\ \overline{2}\;\;\overline{4}\\ \;\;\;\;\overline{2}\\ \;\;\;\;\;\;\overline{4}\\ \;\;\;\;\;\;\;\;\overline{6}\\ \hline 2\;1\;2\;3&1\end{array}$$

Q = 2123
R = 1

Example 25:

39158 ÷ 13

```
13 | 3 9 1 5 | 8
 3 |   9     |
   |   0     |
   |   3     |
   |         | 6
   ─────────────
   3 0 1 2 | 2
```

Q = 3012
R = 2

Example 26:

29694 ÷ 14

```
14 | 2 9 6 9 | 4
 4 |   8     |
   |   4     |
   |   8     |
   |         | 4
   ─────────────
   2 1 2 1 | 0
```

Q = 2121
R = 0

2) When base is 100

Since base is 100, so we have 2 digits in the remainder column and there shall always be 2 digits placed at a time at each step.

Example 27:   1056 ÷ 103

Base = 100

Surplus of 103 from the base = 03

We will write this surplus 03 below the divisor with a negative sign and multiply accordingly.

Step 1:

```
103 | 1 0 | 5 6
 03 |     |
    | 1   |
```

Write the sum as shown with 2 digits from the right of dividend in the remainder column.

Bring down the first digit **1** of the dividend as it is as the first quotient digit.

Step 2:

Multiply this 1 with $\overline{03}$, i.e. $1 \times \overline{03} = \overline{03}$ and write this $\overline{03}$ below the next two dividend digits (0 and 5), as shown

Step 3:

Add the 0's of the second column and bring the sum **0** as the second quotient digit.

Now multiply this 0 by $\overline{03}$ to get **0** and place it below next two dividend digits (5 and 6) as shown.

Step 4:

Add all the digits in the remainder column to get the remainder as **26**.

So, 1056 ÷ 103 gives **10** as **quotient** and **26** as **remainder**.

Example 28: 25841 ÷ 112

Step 1:

$$112 \; \overline{\begin{array}{c} 2 \; 5 \; 8 \; 4 \; 1 \\ \hline 12 \end{array}} \begin{array}{c} \downarrow 2 \; 4 \\ \hline 2 \end{array}$$

Write the sum as shown.

Bring down first dividend digit **2** as first quotient digit.

Step 2:

$$112 \; \overline{\begin{array}{c} 2 \; 5 \; 8 \; 4 \; 1 \\ \hline 12 \end{array}} \begin{array}{c} \underline{2\,4} \\ \times \;\; 2 \end{array}$$

Multiply this quotient digit 2 by $\overline{12}$ to get $\overline{24}$ (i.e. $2 \times \overline{12} = \overline{24}$).

Write them below the next two digits of dividend (5 and 8), as shown.

Step 3:

$$112 \; \overline{\begin{array}{c} 2 \; 5 \; 8 \; 4 \; 1 \\ \hline 12 \end{array}} \begin{array}{c} 2 \; 4 \\ 3 \; \overline{6} \\ \times \; 2 \; 3 \end{array}$$

Add 5 and $\overline{2}$ in the second column to get 3, i.e. $5 + \overline{2} = 3$

Bring this **3** down as second quotient digit.

Multiply this quotient digit 3 by $\overline{12}$ to get $\overline{36}$, i.e. $3 \times \overline{12} = \overline{36}$.

Write them below next two dividend digits (8 and 4) as shown.

Step 4:

$$112 \begin{array}{|c c|c c} 2\ 5\ 8 & 4\ 1 \\ \overline{12} & 2\ 4 \\ & 3\overline{6} \\ & \overline{1}\,\overline{2} \end{array}$$

Add the numbers in the third column, i.e. 8 + $\overline{4}$ + $\overline{3}$ = **1**.

Bring this **1** down as the third quotient digit.

Multiply this quotient digit 1 by $\overline{12}$ to get $\overline{12}$, i.e. $1 \times \overline{12}$ = $\overline{12}$.

Write them below next two dividend digits (4 and 1) as shown.

Step 5:

$$112 \begin{array}{|c c|c c} 2\ 5\ 8 & 4\ 1 \\ \overline{12} & 2\ 4 \\ & 3\overline{6} \\ & \overline{1}\,\overline{2} \\ \hline 2\ 3\ 1 & 3\ 1 \end{array}$$

Add all the digits in the remainder column to get $\overline{31}$ as the remainder.

Step 6:   Since, the remainder cannot be negative, so we carry 1 from the quotient to the remainder side, which means adding the divisor once to the remainder, i.e. adding 112 (divisor) to $\overline{31}$ (remainder).

So, final **quotient** = 231 – 1 = **230**

final **remainder** = 112 + $\overline{31}$ = **81**

The same method is applicable when divisors are above other bases also.

***Some more solved examples*:**

***Example 29*:**

16453 ÷ 102

$$102 \begin{array}{|c c|c c} 1\ 6\ 4 & 5\ 3 \\ \overline{02} & 0\ \overline{2} \\ & \overline{1}\,\overline{2} \\ & \overline{0}\ \overline{2} \\ \hline 1\ 6\ 1 & 3\ 1 \end{array}$$

Q = 161
R = 31

***Example 30*:**

79999 ÷ 111

$$111 \begin{array}{|c c|c c} 7\ 9\ 9 & 9\ 9 \\ \overline{11} & 7\ 7 \\ & 2\ \overline{2} \\ & 0\ 0 \\ \hline 7\ 2\ 0 & 7\ 9 \end{array}$$

Q = 720
R = 79

Example 31:

321987 ÷ 1003

$$\begin{array}{c|cc|ccc}
1003 & 3 & 2 & 1 & 9 & 8 & 7 \\
\overline{003} & & \bar0 & \bar0 & 9 & & \\
 & & & \bar0 & \bar0 & 6 & \\
 & & & & \bar0 & \bar0 & 3 \\
\hline
 & 3 & 2 & 1 & 0 & 2 & 4
\end{array}$$

Q = 321
R = 024

Example 32:

13545 ÷ 1212

$$\begin{array}{c|cc|ccc}
1212 & 1 & 3 & 5 & 4 & 5 \\
\overline{212} & & \bar2 & \bar1 & \bar2 & \\
 & & & \bar2 & \bar1 & \bar2 \\
\hline
 & 1 & 1 & 2 & 1 & 3
\end{array}$$

Q = 11
R = 213

Example 33:

10121 ÷ 113

$$\begin{array}{c|ccc|cc}
113 & 1 & 0 & 1 & 2 & 1 \\
\overline{13} & & \bar1 & \bar3 & & \\
 & & & 1 & 3 & \\
 & & & & 1 & 3 \\
\hline
 & 1 & \bar1 & \bar1 & 6 & 4
\end{array}$$

Note: In this case, while adding the digits in second column, i.e. 0 and $\bar1$ gives $\bar1$, which is brought down as second quotient digit. Now this $\bar1$ when multiplied by $\bar1\,\bar3$ gives $\bar1 \times \bar1\,\bar3 = 13$ and in the next step also, we get 13.

Q = 1\bar1\bar1 = 100 – 11 = 89 *(all from nine and last from 10)*
R = 64

EXERCISE 13.3

Divide the following and write the quotient and the remainder:

1. 1238 ÷ 12
2. 120456 ÷ 1113
3. 12023 ÷ 13
4. 312607 ÷ 1123
5. 42095 ÷ 103
6. 3456 ÷ 1321
7. 598502 ÷ 11002
8. 133586 ÷ 1133
9. 24681 ÷ 111
10. 63421 ÷ 1006

Long Division in One Line
(The Crowning Glory)

Now we have come to the most amazing technique of division, applicable in all cases whatever may the dividend or divisor be.

This method is very easy to understand in which we get the answer of long divisions in just one line.

However, in this method, no matter how long the divisor is, we divide the dividend by only the first digit of the divisor, i.e. only by a single digit thereby making the whole process very easy.

That is why it is called *"the crowning gem of all"*.

The formula used here is *"on top of the flag"*.

Let's see the difference between the two methods:

$9186 \div 72$

Conventional Method

```
72)9186(127.583
   72
   198
   144
   546
   504
   420
   360
   600
   576
   240
   216
    24
```

Vedic Method

```
72|9 1 8 6 0 0 0
    2 5 5 7 4 3
  127.583
```

Long trial & error method   *Vedic One-Line method*

In the conventional method, a considerable amount of guesswork is required. At each step, an approximate quotient digit is guessed, which is then multiplied by the divisor and a remainder is computed. This is a slow and tedious procedure and as the number of digits increase in the divisor, the process becomes slower and time consuming.

But in Vedic Maths, no matter how long the divisor be, every division can be reduced to a division by a single digit in most cases or in some case, at the most upto two short digits like 12, 13, etc.

Let's understand this by solving the following by the vedic method.

Division of a number by a 2-digit divisor (with 0 remainder)

Example 1:   **9216 ÷ 72**

In this, we don't have to divide by 72, instead we write down only the first digit 7 in the divisor column and place 2 on the top of 7 'as flag' as shown below:

$$7^2$$

The entire division is done by 7.

Simple and alternate steps of division and subtraction are followed at each step until we reach at the required answer.

Format for writing the question is:

Divisor ^{flag} | Dividend
                  | Quotient / Remainder

Step 1:   Write the divisor as shown with 7 in the divisor
7^2 | 9 2 1 | 6   column and 2 on the top of it, as flag, i.e. 7^2

Write the dividend as shown with one digit from right end marked off by a slash for the remainder portion or decimal part of the an-swer.

(Remember that the number of digits on the right side of the slash = number of digits on the top of flag).

Step 2:   Division
7^2 | 9 2 1 | 6   Divide the first digit of the dividend, i.e. 9 by divisor
      $_2$ 7 to get **1** as the first quotient digit (Q_1) and **2** as the
   1   first remainder (R_1).

Put down 1 in the quotient column and place the remainder 2 before the next dividend digit 2, to form **22**, which is our next gross dividend (GD)

Subtraction

From this (GD) 22, subtract the product of flag digit 2 and first quotient digit 1, i.e. $22 - (2 \times 1) = 20$.

This 20 is our next net dividend (ND).

Step 3:

$7^2 \lfloor 9 \, 2 \, 1 \mid 6$
$\quad _{2 \, 6}$
$\quad 1 \, 2$

Division

Divide (ND) 20 by 7 to get **2** as next quotient digit (Q_2) and **6** as remainder (R_2).

Place (R_2) i.e. 6 before next dividend digit, i.e. 1 to get **61** as GD.

Subtraction

From (GD) 61, subtract the product of flag digit 2 and the second quotient digit 2, i.e. $61 - (2 \times 2) = 57$ (ND)

Step 4:

$7^2 \lfloor 9 \, 2 \, 1 \mid 6$
$\quad _{2 \, 6} \, _1$
$\quad 1 \, 2 \, 8$

Division

Divide (ND) 57 by 7 to get **8** as next quotient digit (Q_3) and **1** as remainder (R_3).

Place (R_3) i.e. 1 before next dividend digit, i.e. 6 to get **16** as GD.

Since, we have reached the slash, i.e. the place of decimal, so we put a decimal in the quotient at this point, i.e. after 8.

Subtraction

From (GD) 16, subtract the product of flag digit 2 and third quotient digit 8,

i.e. $16 - (2 \times 8) = 0$ (ND)

Further, when this 0 is multiplied by 7, the next quotient digit will be 0. Since, there are no further digits in dividend and we get the final difference as 0, this finishes the whole process of division of the above sum.

So, the final answer for $9216 \div 72$ is **Q = 128, R=0**

The amazing part of this division is that all of it is one-line mental arithmetic, in which, all the actual division is simply done by a simple single divisor 7. This rids us of all those long multiplications and subtractions which are not so easy to perform mentally.

Division of a number by a 2-digit divisor (with remainder)

Example 2: $10576 \div 83$

Step 1:

$8^3 | 1\ 0\ 5\ 7\ 6$

Write the sum as shown with the divisor 8^3 (3 on the top of the flag) in the divisor column and place a slash at one digit from the right of dividend (since there is 1 digit on the flag).

Step 2:

$8^3 | 1\ 0\ _2 5\ 7 | 6$

$\quad\ 1$

Divide 10 by 8 to get $Q_1 = 1$ and $R_1 = 2$

Place 2 before next dividend digit 5 to get **25** as GD

Now, (GD) 25 – (flag digit 3 × Q_1), i.e. 25 – (3×1) = 22 (ND)

Step 3:

$8^3 | 1\ 0\ _2 5\ _6 7 | 6$

$\quad\ 1\ 2$

Divide (ND) 22 by 8 to get $Q_2 = 2$ and $R_2 = 6$

Place 6 before next dividend digit 7 to get **67** as GD

Now, (GD) 67 – (flag digit 3 × Q_2), i.e. 67 – (3×2) = 61 (ND)

Step 4:

$8^3 | 1\ 0\ _2 5\ _6 7 |\ _5 6$

$\quad\ 1\ 2\ 7$

Divide (ND) 61 by 8 to get $Q_3 = 7$ and $R_3 = 5$

Place 5 before next dividend digit 6 to get **56** as GD

Now, (GD) 56 – (flag digit 3 × Q_3), i.e. 56 – (3×7) = 35 (ND)

Step 5:

$8^3 | 1\ 0\ _2 5\ _6 7 |\ _5 6\ _3 0$

$\quad\ 1\ 2\ 7.4$

Now we have reached the slash, so we put a decimal in the quotient. Divide (ND) 35 by 8 to get $Q_4 = 4$ and $R_4 = 3$

Place 3 before a 0 (which we have added to the dividend, as after decimal we can place as many 0's in the dividend).

So, we get GD as **30** and now, GD – (flag digit 3 × Q_4),

i.e. 30 – (3×4) = 18 (ND)

Step 6:

$$8^3 | 1 \; 0 \; \underset{2 \; 6}{5} \; \underset{5}{7} \; | \; \underset{3}{6} \; \underset{2}{0} \; 0$$
$$\overline{1 \; 2 \; 7 . \; 4 \; \mathbf{2}}$$

Divide (ND) 18 by 8 to get $Q_5 = \mathbf{2}$ and $R_5 = \mathbf{2}$

Place this (R_5) 2 before a 0 (added to the dividend, as before) to get **20** as GD and now, GD – (flag digit 3 × Q_5), i.e. 20 – (3×2) = 14 (ND)

Step 7:

$$8^3 | 1 \; 0 \; \underset{2 \; 6}{5} \; \underset{5}{7} \; | \; \underset{3}{6} \; \underset{2}{0} \; \underset{6}{0} \; 0$$
$$\overline{1 \; 2 \; 7 . \; 4 \; 2 \; \mathbf{1}}$$

Divide (ND) 14 by 8 to get $Q_6 = \mathbf{1}$ and $R_6 = \mathbf{6}$

The answer has now been arrived at upto 3 decimal places.

It can be carried out upto any desired level of accuracy.

So, the final answer upto 3 decimal places is:

$10576 \div 83 = \mathbf{127.421}$

Example 3:   **5312 ÷ 94**

Step 1:

$$9^4 | 5 \; 3 \; 1 | 2$$

Write the sum as shown with 9^4 (4 on top of the flag) in the divisor column.

Step 2:

$$9^4 | 5 \; 3 \; \underset{8}{1} \; | \; 2$$
$$\overline{5}$$

$53 \div 9 \Rightarrow Q_1 = \mathbf{5}, R_1 = \mathbf{8}$, this gives GD = **81**

(GD) – (flag 4 × Q_1) = 81 – (4×5) = 61 (ND)

Step 3:

$$9^4 | 5 \; 3 \; \underset{8}{1} \; | \; \underset{7}{2}$$
$$\overline{5 \; 6 .}$$

(ND) 61 ÷ 9 ⇒ $Q_2 = \mathbf{6}, R_2 = \mathbf{7}$, this gives GD = **72**,

(GD) – (flag 4 × Q_2) = 72 – (4×6) = 48 (ND)

Place the decimal in the quotient at this point.

Step 4:

$$9^4 | 5 \; 3 \; \underset{8}{1} \; | \; \underset{7}{2} \; \underset{3}{0} \; 0 \; 0$$
$$\overline{5 \; 6 . \; 5}$$

(ND) 48 ÷ 9 ⇒ $Q_3 = \mathbf{5}, R_3 = \mathbf{3}$, this gives GD = **30**,

(GD) – (flag 4 × Q_3) = 30 – (4×5) = 10 (ND)

Step 5:

$9^4 \overline{\smash{\big|}\, 53\,1 \underset{8\ \ 7\ \ 3\ \ 1}{\big|}\, 2\,0\ 00}$

$\ \ 5\,6.\,5\,1$

(ND) $10 \div 9 \Rightarrow Q_4 = 1$, $R_4 = 1$, this gives GD = **10**,

(GD) – (flag 4 × Q_4) = 10 – (4×1) = 6 (ND)

Step 6:

$9^4 \overline{\smash{\big|}\, 53\,1 \underset{8\ \ 7\ \ 3\ \ 1\ \ 6}{\big|}\, 2\,0\,0\,0}$

$\ \ 5\,6.\,5\,1\,\mathbf{0}$

(ND) $6 \div 9 \Rightarrow Q_5 = 0$, $R_5 = 6$, this gives GD = **60**,

(GD) – (flag 4 × Q_5) = 60 – (4×0) = 60 (ND)

Step 7:

$9^4 \overline{\smash{\big|}\, 53\,1 \underset{8\ \ 7\ \ 3\ \ 1\ \ 6}{\big|}\, 2\,0\,0\,0}$

$\ \ 5\,6.\,5\,1\,0\,\mathbf{6}$

(ND) $60 \div 9 \Rightarrow Q_6 = 6$, $R_6 = 6$.

So, the final answer is $5312 \div 94 = \mathbf{56.5106}$

Some more solved examples in one line:

Example 4:

682 ÷ 31

$3^1 \overline{\smash{\big|}\, 6\,8 \underset{0}{\big|}\, 2 \underset{0}{}}$

$\ \ 22.0$

Example 5:

70 ÷ 83

$8^3 \overline{\smash{\big|}\, 7 \underset{7\ \ 6\ \ 4\ \ 4}{\big|}\, 0\,0\,0\,0}$

$\ \ 0.\,8\,4\,3$

Example 6:

93562 ÷ 82

$8^2 \overline{\smash{\big|}\, 9\,3\,5\,6 \underset{1\ \ 3\ \ 1}{\big|}\, 2 \underset{0}{}}$

$\ \ 1\,1\,4\,1.\,0$

Example 7:

72688 ÷ 6

$6^1 \overline{\smash{\big|}\, 7\,2\,6\,8 \underset{1\ \ 5\ \ 1}{\big|}\, 8\,0\,0 \underset{3\ \ 1\ \ 4}{}}$

$\ \ 1\,1\,9\,1.\,6\,0\,6$

EXERCISE 14.1

Divide the following and give answers upto 3 decimal places.

1. 2296 ÷ 41   **2.** 5437 ÷ 82   **3.** 935 ÷ 73

4. 568 ÷ 62   **5.** 2568 ÷ 32   **6.** 67 ÷ 74

7. 432397 ÷ 83   **8.** 5934 ÷ 96   **9.** 9583 ÷ 56

10. 3322 ÷ 22

Division of a number by a 2-digit divisor (with adjustments)

Example 8:   **$87325 \div 76$**

Step 1:

$$7^6 \big| 8\,_17\,3\,2 \big| 5$$
$$\, 1$$

Write the sum as shown with 7^6 in the divisor column and a slash at one digit from the right side of the dividend.

$8 \div 7 \Rightarrow Q_1 = 1, R_1 = 1$, this gives GD = 17
GD − (flag 6 × Q_1) = 17 − (6×1) = 11 (ND)

Step 2:

$$7^6 \big| 8\,_17\,3\,_42 \big| 5$$
$$\, 1\ 1$$

(ND) 11 ÷ 7 ⇒ $Q_2 = 1, R_2 = 4$ to give GD as **43**
(GD) 43 − (6 × 1) = 37(ND)

Step 3:

$$7^6 \big| 8\,_17\,_43\,_{②}2 \big| 25$$
$$\, 1\ 1⑤$$

(ND) 37 ÷ 7 ⇒ $Q_3 = 5, R_3 = 2$ to give GD as 22, which is too small for the subtraction expected at the next step.
i.e. (GD) 22 − (6 × 5) = −8(ND)

We cannot move further with a negative net dividend, so first we have to make this positive.

So, now we modify the last step, by **reducing the quotient by 1** and thereby get a higher value of remainder. Thus giving a bigger GD.

$$7^6 \big| 8\,_17\,_43\,_92 \big| 2\ 5$$
$$\, 1\ 1\ 4$$

i.e. 37 ÷ 7 ⇒ $Q_3 = 4, R_3 = 9$ to give GD as **92**,
(GD) 92 − (6×4) = 68 (ND).

Note: The circled numbers signifies that an adjustment is required for those numbers.

Step 4:

$$7^6 \big| 8\,_17\,_43\,_92 \big| _55$$
$$\, 1\ 1\ 4\ 9.$$

(ND) 68 ÷ 7 ⇒ $Q_4 = 9, R_4 = 5$ to give GD as **55**,
(GD) 55 − (6 × 9) = 1 (ND).

Since, we have reached the slash, so we put a decimal at this place in the quotient.

Step 5:

$7^6\overline{\smash{)}8\,7\,3\,2}\,\underset{5\ \ 1}{|\,5\ 0}$ (ND) $1 \div 7 \Rightarrow Q_5 = 0$, $R_5 = 1$ to give GD as **10**,

$1\ 1\ 4\ 9\,.0$ (GD) $10 - (6 \times 0) = 10$ (ND).

Step 6:

$\cdot\,7^6\overline{\smash{)}8\,7\,3\,2}\,\underset{5\ \ 1\ \ 3}{|\,5\ 0\,0}$ (ND) $10 \div 7 \Rightarrow Q_6 = 1$, $R_6 = 3$ to give GD as **30**,

$1\ 1\ 4\ 9\,.0\,\textbf{1}$ (GD) $30 - (6 \times 1) = 24$ (ND).

Step 7:

$7^6\overline{\smash{)}8\,7\,3\,2}\,\underset{5\ \ 1\ \ 3\ \ 3}{|\,5\ 0\,0\,0}$ (ND) $27 \div 7 \Rightarrow Q_7 = 3$, $R_7 = 3$ to give GD as **30**,

$1\ 1\ 4\ 9\,.0\,1\,\textbf{3}$

So, the final answer upto 3 decimal places is:

$87325 \div 76 = \textbf{1149.013}$

So, we see that the vedic method of division has a **self-checking system** in itself. As soon as we get a negative net dividend, we make a correction at the previous step and thereby reduce the possibilities of making mistakes.

Example 9: **69878 ÷ 89**

Step 1:

$8^9\,\big|\,69\underset{5}{\,8}\,7\,\big|\,8$
$\underset{\textcircled{8}}{}$

$8^9\,\big|\,69\underset{13}{\,8}\,7\,\big|\,8$
7

$69 \div 8 \Rightarrow Q_1 = 8$, $R_1 = 5$, GD = **58**
This (GD) 58 will give a negative ND at the next step of subtraction. So after reducing Q_1 by 1, we get:
Final $Q_1 = 7$, $R_1 = 13$, GD = **138**
$138 - (9 \times 7) = 75$ (ND)

Step 2:

$8^9\,\big|\,69\underset{13}{\,8}\,\underset{\textcircled{3}}{\,7}\,\big|\,8$
$7\textcircled{9}$

$8^9\,\big|\,69\underset{13\ \ 11}{\,8}\,7\,\big|\,8$
$7\,8$

$75 \div 8 \Rightarrow Q_2 = 9$, $R_2 = 3$, GD = **37**
Again we will get negative at next step, so after adjustment:
Final $Q_2 = 8$, $R_2 = 11$, GD =**117**
$117 - (9 \times 8) = 45$ (ND)

Step 3:

$$8^9 \begin{array}{|c c c|c} 69 & 8 & 7 & 8 \\ & _{13} & _{11} & _5 \end{array}$$
$$\overline{\quad 7\ 8\ 5\ .\quad}$$

$45 \div 8 \Rightarrow Q_3 = 5, R_3 = 5, GD = 58$

Place decimal point in the quotient

$58 - (9 \times 5) = 13$ (ND)

Step 4:

$$8^9 \begin{array}{|c c c|c c} 69 & 8 & 7 & 8 & 0 \\ & _{13} & _{11} & _5 & _5 \end{array}$$
$$\overline{\quad 7\ 8\ 5\ .\ 1\quad}$$

$13 \div 8 \Rightarrow Q_4 = 1, R_4 = 5, GD = 50$

$50 - (9 \times 1) = 41$ (ND)

Step 5:

$$8^9 \begin{array}{|c c c|c c c} 69 & 8 & 7 & 8 & 0 & 0 \\ & _{13} & _{11} & _3 & _5 & _① \end{array}$$
$$\overline{\quad 7\ 8\ 5\ .\ 1\,⑤\quad}$$

$41 \div 8 \Rightarrow Q_5 = 5, R_5 = 1, GD = 10$

Again we will get negative after subtraction at next step.

So reducing 1 from quotient, we get:

$$8^9 \begin{array}{|c c c|c c c} 69 & 8 & 7 & 8 & 0 & 0 \\ & _{13} & _{11} & _{13} & _5 & _9 \end{array}$$
$$\overline{\quad 7\ 8\ 5\ .\ 1\ 4\quad}$$

Final $Q_5 = 4, R_5 = 9, GD = 90$

$90 - (9 \times 4) = 54$ (ND)

Step 6:

$$8^9 \begin{array}{|c c c|c c c c} 69 & 8 & 7 & 8 & 0 & 0 & 0 \\ & _{13} & _{11} & _{13} & _5 & _9 & _6 \end{array}$$
$$\overline{\quad 7\ 8\ 5\ .\ 1\ 4\ 6\quad}$$

$54 \div 8 \Rightarrow Q_6 = 6, R_6 = 6$

So, the final answer upto 3 decimal places is:

$69878 \div 89 = \mathbf{785.146}$

Some solved examples in one line:

Example 10:

56789 ÷ 37

$$3^7 \begin{array}{|c c c c|c c c} 5 & 6 & 7 & 8 & 9 & 0 & 0 \\ & _2 & _4 & _3 & _5 & _7 & _5 \end{array}$$
$$\overline{\quad 1\ 5\ 3\ 4\ .\ 8\ 3\ 7\quad}$$

Example 11:

72396 ÷ 45

$$4^5 \begin{array}{|c c c c|c c} 7 & 2 & 3 & 9 & 6 & 0 \\ & _3 & _3 & _3 & _7 & _4 \end{array}$$
$$\overline{\quad 1\ 6\ 0\ 8\ .\ 8\ 0\quad}$$

Example 12:

3748 ÷ 76

7^6 | 37̠4 | 8̠0̠0
      ₉   ₇ ₃ ₅

    4 9 .3 1 5

Example 13:

6894 ÷ 87

8^7 | 68̠9 | 4̠0̠0̠0
     ₁₂ ₈ ₅ ₄ ₄

    7 9 .2 4 1

EXERCISE 14.2

Divide the following and give answers upto 3 decimal places.

1.	536 ÷ 24	**2.**	8539 ÷ 73
3.	37 ÷ 83	**4.**	9382 ÷ 77
5.	47298 ÷ 64		

Division of a number by a 3-digit divisor

In this case also, we will divide the dividend by the first digit of divisor and rest of the digits are placed on the top of the flag. There is a slight modification in the subtraction; instead of multiplying previous quotient digit by the flag digit, here we cross multiply two immediately previous quotient digits with the two flagged digits. Though in the first step of subtraction, when there is only one digit in the quotient, we multiply it with the first flag digit only.

Let's understand it with the following example:

Example 14:   **25711 ÷ 724**

Step 1:

7^{24} | 2 5 7 | 1 1

Write the sum as shown with the divisor as 7^{24} (24 flagged on the top of 7) and place a slash at two digits from the right of the dividend to mark the decimal point place, (2 digits from the right because there are two digits on the flag).

Step 2:

$$7^{24} \underline{|25\,7_4|1\,1}$$
$$\qquad 3$$

$25 \div 7 \Rightarrow Q_1 = 3$, $R_1 = 4$, GD = **47**.

From (GD) 47, subtract the product of the first flag digit (2) and the first quotient digit (3). i.e. $47 - (2 \times 3) = 41$ (ND)

Since, we have only one digit in the quotient, so we will multiply it by only the first digit on the flag.

Step 3:

$$7^{24} \underline{|25\,7_4|11_6|}$$
$$\qquad 3\ 5.$$

(ND) $41 \div 7 \Rightarrow Q_2 = 5$, $R_2 = 6$, GD = **61**.

From (GD) 61, subtract the cross product of the two flag digits (2 and 4) and the two quotient digits (3 and 5)

$$\begin{matrix} 2 & & 4 \\ & \times & \\ 3 & & 5 \end{matrix}$$

cross product $= (2 \times 5) + (3 \times 4) = 10 + 12 = 22$.

(GD) $61 - 22 = 39$ (ND)

Step 4:

$$7^{24} \underline{|25\,7_4|1_6\,1_4|}$$
$$\qquad 3\ 5.\ 5$$

(ND) $39 \div 7 \Rightarrow Q_3 = 5$, $R_3 = 4$, GD = **41**

From (GD) 41, subtract the cross product of the two flag digits (2 and 4) and the last two quotient digits (5 and 5)

$$\begin{matrix} 2 & & 4 \\ & \times & \\ 5 & & 5 \end{matrix}$$

cross product $= (2 \times 5) + (5 \times 4) = 10 + 20 = 30$.

(GD) $41 - 30 = 11$ (ND)

Step 5:

$$7^{24} \underline{|25\,7_4|1_6\,1_4\,0_4|}$$
$$\qquad 3\ 5.\ 5\ 1$$

(ND) $11 \div 7 \Rightarrow Q_4 = 1$, $R_4 = 4$, GD = **40**

From (GD) 40, subtract the cross product of the two flag digits (2 and 4) and the last two quotient digits (5 and 1)

$$\begin{matrix} 2 & & 4 \\ & \times & \\ 5 & & 1 \end{matrix}$$

cross product $= (2 \times 1) + (5 \times 4) = 2 + 20 = 22$.

(GD) $40 - 22 = 18$ (ND)

Step 6:

7^{24} | 25.7 | $1\,1\,0\,0$ (ND) $18 \div 7 \Rightarrow Q_5 = 2,\ R_5 = 4,\ GD = 40$
　　　$_4$ $_6$ $_4$ $_4$ $_4$
　　　$3\,5.\,5\,1\,2$

So, the final answer upto 3 decimal places is:

　　$25711 \div 724 = \mathbf{35.512}$

Some more solved examples in one line:

Example 15:	*Example 16*:	*Example 17*:
85721 ÷ 632	**2837 ÷ 824**	**60712 ÷ 537**

6^{32} | $8\,5\,7$ | $2\,1\,0$ 　　　　8^{24} | 28 | $3\,7\,0\,0$ 　　　　5^{37} | $6\,0\,7$ | $1\,2\,0\,0$
　　$_2$ $_4$ 　$_6$ $_5$ $_5$ 　　　　　　　$_4$ $_5$ $_5$ $_2$ 　　　　　　$_1$ $_2$ 　$_2$ $_5$ $_6$ $_{10}$
　　$1\,3\,5\,.6\,3\,4$ 　　　　　　　　$3\,.4\,4\,3$ 　　　　　　　$1\,1\,3\,.0\,5\,7$

EXERCISE 14.3

Divide the following and give answers upto 3 decimal places.

1.	$2374 \div 712$	**2.**	$93647 \div 513$
3.	$586248 \div 942$	**4.**	$9124 \div 873$
5.	$8521 \div 614$		

Division of a number by a 4-digit divisor (with decimal in the dividend)

Here also, we divide the dividend with the first digit of the divisor and the rest three digits are placed on the top of the flag. Alternate division and subtraction steps are carried out until we reach the desired decimal places. The subtraction is done in the same manner by cross multiplication as just now explained *(but this time we shall apply 3×3 cross multiplication)*.

When the dividend already has a decimal, we place the slash at those many digits from the right of decimal as there are number of digits on the flag.

Example 18:   **7031.95 ÷ 8231**

Step 1:

8^{231} | 7 | 031.95

Write the sum as shown with divisor as 8^{231} (231 on flag).

Since, there is a decimal in the dividend and 3 digits on flag, we put a slash three digits from the right of decimal point as shown.

Step 2:

8^{231} | 7 |$_7$ 031.95
0.

$7 \div 8 \Rightarrow Q_1 = 0, R_1 = 7, GD = 70$.

Decimal point will come at the place of slash.

(GD) 70 – (first flagged digit × first quotient digit), i.e.

$$70 - (2 \times 0) = 70 \text{ (ND)}$$

Step 3:

8^{231} | 7 |$_7$ 0$_6$ 31.95
0.**8**

(ND) $70 \div 8 \Rightarrow Q_2 = 8, R_2 = 6, GD = 63$.

(GD) 63 – (cross product of the two flagged digit 23, and last two quotient digits 08), i.e.

$$\begin{array}{cc} 2 & 3 \\ 0 & 8 \end{array}$$

cross product = $(2 \times 8) + (0 \times 3) = 16$.

(GD) $63 - 16 = 47$ (ND).

Step 4:

8^{231} | 7 |$_7$ 0$_6$ 3$_7$ 1.95
0.8 **5**

(ND) $47 \div 8 \Rightarrow Q_3 = 5, R_3 = 7, GD = 71$

(GD) 71 – (cross product of the three flagged digit 231, and last three quotient digits 085), i.e.

$$\begin{array}{ccc} 2 & 3 & 1 \\ 0 & 8 & 5 \end{array}$$

cross product = $(2 \times 5) + (0 \times 1) + (3 \times 8) = 34$.

(GD) $71 - 34 = 37$ (ND)

Step 5:

8^{231} | 7 | 0 3 1 . 9 5   (ND) $37 \div 8 \Rightarrow Q_5 = 4, R_5 = 5, GD = 59$

          ₇ ₆ ₇ · ₅

          0.8 5 4

(GD) 59 – (cross product of three flagged digits 231 and last three quotient digits 854)

$$
\begin{array}{ccc}
2 & 3 & 1 \\
8 & 5 & 4
\end{array}
$$

cross product = $(2 \times 4) + (1 \times 8) + (3 \times 5) = 31$.

(GD) $59 - 31 = 28$ (ND)

Step 6:

8^{231} | 7 | 0 3 1 . 9 5   (ND) $28 \div 8 \Rightarrow Q_6 = 3, R_6 = 4, GD = 45$

          ₇ ₆ ₇ · ₅ ₄

          0.8 5 4 3

No need to calculate further as we have already reached upto 4 decimal places. Though it can be continued upto any desired level of accuracy.

Therefore, $7031.95 \div 8231 = \mathbf{0.8543}$

Example 19:   **73856 ÷ 1243**

In this case instead of taking the divisor as 1^{243}, we will take the divisor as 12^{43}, i.e. the actual divisor will be 12 and 43 on the flag.

If we take 1^{243} as divisor, we have to make many adjustments, as we will find alternate quotients and remainders at each step.

Step 1:

12^{43} | 738|56

In this case, write the sum as shown with divisor as **12⁴³** (43 on the flag). Place a slash two digits from the right of dividend as there are 2 digits on the flag.

Step 2:

12^{43} | 73 8 |56
          ①
          ⑥

$73 \div 12 \Rightarrow Q_1 = 6, R_1 = 1, GD = 18$.

This remainder will give negative result in subtraction step. So reduce 1 from Q_1.

12^{43} | 73 8 |56
          ₁₃
          5

Final $Q_1 = 5, R_1 = 13, GD = 138$.

(GD) $138 - (4 \times 5) = 118$ (ND)

Step 3:

$$12^{43} \underline{\big|73_{\,13}\,8_{\,|10}\,56}$$
$$5\,9.$$

(ND) $118 \div 12 \Rightarrow Q_2 = 9, R_2 = 10, GD = 105$.

Put decimal at the place of slash.

(GD) $105 -$ (cross product of 43 and 59), i.e.

$$\begin{matrix} 4 & 3 \\ & \times \\ 5 & 9 \end{matrix}$$

cross product $= (4 \times 9) + (5 \times 3) = 51$.

(GD) $105 - 51 = 54$ (ND).

Step 4:

$$12^{43} \underline{\big|73_{\,13}\,8_{\,|10}\,5_{\,6}\,6}$$
$$5\,9.\,4$$

(ND) $54 \div 12 \Rightarrow Q_3 = 4, R_3 = 6, GD = 66$

(GD) $66 -$ (cross product of 43 and 94), i.e.

$$\begin{matrix} 4 & 3 \\ & \times \\ 9 & 4 \end{matrix}$$

cross product $= (4 \times 4) + (9 \times 3) = 43$.

(GD) $66 - 43 = 23$ (ND)

Step 5:

$$12^{43} \underline{\big|73_{\,13}\,8_{\,|10}\,5_{\,6}\,6_{\,11}\,0}$$
$$5\,9.\,4\,1$$

(ND) $23 \div 12 \Rightarrow Q_4 = 1, R_4 = 11, GD = 110$

(GD) $10 -$ (cross product of 43 and 41)

$$\begin{matrix} 4 & 3 \\ & \times \\ 4 & 1 \end{matrix}$$

cross product $= (4 \times 1) + (4 \times 3) = 16$.

(GD) $110 - 16 = 94$ (ND)

Step 6:

$$12^{43} \underline{\big|73_{\,13}\,8_{\,|10}\,5_{\,6}\,6_{\,11}\,0_{\,10}\,0}$$
$$5\,9.\,4\,1\,7$$

(ND) $94 \div 12 \Rightarrow Q_5 = 7, R_5 = 10$

So, the final answer upto 3 decimal places is:

$73856 \div 1243 = \textbf{59.417}$

Try out yourself the same sum with 1^{243} as divisor, i.e. 1 as actual divisor and 243 on flag and see the difference.

Some more solved examples in one line:

Example 20:

23588 ÷ 7302

7^{302} | 23 | 5 8 8 0 0
⠀⠀⠀⠀⠀⠀2 2 1 3 5

3 . 2 3 0 3

Example 21:

49362 ÷ 1632

16^{32} | 49 3 | 6 2 0 0
⠀⠀⠀⠀⠀1 4 8 12 8

3 0 . 2 4 6

EXERCISE 14.4

Divide the following and give answers upto 3 decimal places.

1. 40025 ÷ 6213
2. 0.8673 ÷ 5239
3. 121034 ÷ 7238
4. 56897 ÷ 10362
5. 39.742 ÷ 4236

GENERAL GUIDELINES:

1. Irrespective of the number of digits in the divisor, our actual divisor is of one digit only or at the most, a short two-digit one like 12, 17 and so on which one can easily divide by, and the rest of the digits of the divisor are placed on top of that number.

2. Put a slash in the dividend in such a way that the right side of slash has same number of digits as on the flag. In case, the dividend has a decimal in it, then also we put the slash at those many digits from the right of decimal as there are number of the digits on the flag.

3. Divide the first digit of the dividend by the divisor and write the quotient in the quotient column and remainder is placed before the next dividend digit to give gross dividend (GD).

4. From this (GD), subtract the product of flag digit and the previous quotient digit to get net dividend (ND).

5. This (ND) is again divided by the divisor. Write the quotient obtained as the second digit of the answer and place the remainder before the next quotient digit. This process of division and subtraction continues till the desired decimal places. We put the decimal point in the quotient when we reach the slash.

6. The net dividend should always be positive. It found negative, adjustment should be made in the previous step by reducing the quotient and recalculating the remainder accordingly.

7. However long the divisor is, the method remains the same except that the quantities to be subtracted at each step need to be understood well which are explained below.

In the subtraction step:

(a) When there is a single flag digit, we subtract the product of last quotient digit and the flag digit at each step.

(b) When there are two flag digits, in the first step product of first flag digit and the first quotient digit is subtracted and from the second step onwards, cross product of two flag digits and last two quotient digits is subtracted.

(c) When there are three flag digits:

1st Step: product of first flag digit and first quotient digit

2nd Step: cross product of first two flag digits and first two quotient digits.

3rd Step: cross product of three flag digits and three quotient digits.

And this subtraction of cross product of 3×3 continues till desired decimal places.

8. This process can be extended to any number of digits in the divisor.

Example 22:

5362968527 ÷ 9213649875

Taking 9 as actual divisor and placing all other digits on flag, we get the answer in one line as shown below:

$$9^{213649875} \overline{\left| 5 \right| 3 \underset{8}{6} \underset{4}{2} \underset{3}{9} \underset{3}{68527}}$$
$$0.5821$$

The detailed steps are given below:

Step 1:

$$\frac{53}{9} \Rightarrow Q = 5, R = 8, GD = 86$$

(GD) 86 – (5×2) = 76(ND)

Step 2:

$$\frac{76}{9} \Rightarrow Q = 8, R = 4, GD = 42$$

(GD) 42 – [(2×8) + (1×5)] = 21(ND)

Step 3:

$$\frac{21}{9} \Rightarrow Q = 2, R = 3, GD = 39$$

39 – [(2×2) + (1×8) + (3×5)] = 39 – 27 = 12(ND)

Step 4:

$$\frac{12}{9} \Rightarrow Q = 1, R = 3$$

We have already reached upto 4 decimal places, so no need to go further.

So, the final answer upto 4 decimal places is:

$$\frac{5362968527}{9213649875} = \mathbf{0.5821}$$

Isn't it marvelous that such a big calculation which one can't think of even trying it once, and that can be calculated in a single line in such short time mentally.

That is why; this method is called the *"crowning gem of all."*

Some more solved examples in one line:

Example 23:

5378942 ÷ 812059

8^{12059} |53| 7 8 9 42
⌊ 5 3 4 3
‾‾‾‾‾‾‾‾‾‾
6. 6 2 4

Example 24:

.0235896 ÷ 72.3518

Removing decimal in the divisor we get:

235.896 ÷ 723518

7^{23518} ‖002 3 5. 8 96
⌊ 2 2 5 3
‾‾‾‾‾‾‾‾‾‾
0. 0 0 0 3 2

EXERCISE 14.5

Divide the following and give answers upto 3 decimal places:

1. 7382462 ÷ 82359619   **2.** 0.926 ÷ 14.85

3. 83.7425 ÷ 91654   **4.** 3972056 ÷ 7310568.965

5. 0.002369 ÷ 8.421

Square Roots in One Line

We have seen earlier how easy and fast it is to compute square of any number in one line using the Duplex method. The same can be applied to find the square root of any number, but in this case, we would be subtracting the duplex at each step as in straight division.

Before learning the technique to calculate square root of any random number, we will see how to find the square roots of exact squares which can be answered by mere observation only without the actual process of computation.

Square root of a perfect square

The formula used is *"mere observation"*.

To find the square root of a perfect square, first we need to know if the number is a perfect square or not.

For this, we check the following to know if a given number is a perfect square:

1. A perfect square ends in 0, 1, 4, 5, 6, 8, 9.
2. A number is not a perfect square if it ends in 2,3,7 or 8.
3. It should end in even no of 0's.
4. If the number ends with 6, then its second last digit should be odd.
5. If the number doesn't end with 6, then its second last digit should be even.
6. If the number is even, its last two digits should be divided by 4.

So, if a number is not according to the above conditions, then the number is not a perfect square.

To find the square root of any number, we need to study the squares of first 10 natural numbers:

Number	Square	Last digit of Square
1	1	1
2	4	4
3	9	9
4	16	6
5	25	5
6	36	6
7	49	9
8	64	4
9	81	1
10	100	00

By observing the last digit of the square mentioned above, we can easily see the possibilities of the last digit of its square root.

If a square ends in	Last digit of its Square Root will be
1	1 or 9
4	2 or 8
5	5
6	4 or 6
9	3 or 7
00	0

GENERAL GUIDELINES

1. Arrange the given number in 2 digits groups from right to left. A single digit (if any) left over at the left end is counted as a single group by itself.

2. The number of digits in the square root = the number of digit groups in the square.

3. So, if a given number has n digits, the square root will have n/2 digits if n is even, or (n+1)/2 digits if n is odd.

4. The first digit of the square root will be computed from the first group, i.e. the left most group. Consider the highest possible perfect square, less than or equal to the left most

group and compute its square root. Write it down as the first digit of the square root.

5. For the second digit of the square root, simply observe the last digit of the square and check from square of $1 - 9$, whoose square ends with the same digit. That will give 2 options, if the square does not end in 5 and 0.

6. So now we have two options for the final answer and we have to choose one. We find the square of the number ending in 5 between the two options of the answer.

7. By judging whether the given square is bigger or smaller than the square of the number ending in 5, we can choose the correct answer from the 2 options.

Let's understand this better by the following example:

Example 1:

Find the **square root of 3481**

Step 1:

34| 81

Divide the number in 2 digit groups from the right as shown. Since the square has 4 digits, so the square root will have $4/2 = 2$ digits.

Step 2:

| 34|81
5

The perfect square less than 34 is 25, so the first digit is the square root of 25, i.e. **5**.

Step 3:

| 34| 81
5**1** or 5**9**

Since the square ends in 1, so the last digit can be either 1 or 9. So, we have 2 options for the answer, either **51** or **59**.

Step 4:

Now, the number between 51 and 59, ending with 5 is 55. Finding the square of 55, we get:

$55^2 = (5 \times 6) / 5^2 = 3025$

Now, $3481 > 3025$,

so, $\sqrt{3481} > \sqrt{3025}$ (i.e. 55).

Therefore, out of two options, 51 and 59, square root of 3481 will be 59.

So, the square root of $3481 = $ **59**.

Some more solved examples:

Example 2:

Find the **square root of 4096**

$\sqrt{40|96}$

First digit = 6
Second digit = 4 or 6
So, 2 options are 64 or 66
We know $65^2 = 4225$
Since, 4096 < 4225

So, $\sqrt{4096} < \sqrt{4225}$ (65)

So, the square root of 4096 is **64**

Example 3:

Find the **square root of 784**

$\sqrt{7|84}$

First digit = 2
Second digit = 2 and 8
So, 2 options are 22 or 28
We know, $25^2 = 625$
Since, 784 > 625

So, $\sqrt{784} > \sqrt{625}$ (25)

So, the square root of 784 is **28**

EXERCISE 15.1

Find the square roots of the following perfect squares by mere observation only:

1.	6889	**2.**	8281	**3.**	5476	**4.**	4624
5.	576	**6.**	961	**7.**	1369	**8.**	3249
9.	2116	**10.**	2704				

The above method is easy to apply when the square is a perfect square and it is a four digit number. For squares of more than four digits and also imperfect squares, we use the general method.

Square root of any random number

Now, we will learn how to find square roots of any random number upto as many decimal places as we want.

This method is the same as that of straight division, but with a slight difference:

1. The divisor in this case is always the double of the first digit of the square root.

2. Instead of subtracting the product of flag digit and the previous quotient digit, the duplex of the second digit onwards of the answer is subtracted from the gross dividend at each step.

Let's understand it with the following example:

Example 4:

Find the **square root of 1369** *(perfect square)*

Step 1:

13: 69   The number has 4 digits. So square root will have 4/2 = 2 digits. Make groups of 2 digits, starting from the right. We get 13 as the first group on the left, so we place a colon after 13 as shown.

Step 2:

$$6 \overline{\left| \begin{array}{l} 13: \ 69 \\ _4 \end{array} \right.}$$
$$3:$$

By observing the first group 13, we find the highest perfect square less than 13 is 9 and square root of 9 is **3**. So write this 3 as the first digit of the square root. Place a colon after it.

Difference of 9 from 13 is 4. Place this remainder 4 before the next dividend digit 6 to get **46** as gross dividend (GD).

Double the first digit of square root, i.e. 3 to get **6** and write it as the divisor.

Step 3:

$$6 \overline{\left| \begin{array}{l} 13: \ 6 \ 9 \\ _4 \ _4 \end{array} \right.}$$
$$3: \ 7.$$

Divide (GD) 46 by divisor 6 to get **7** as quotient and **4** as remainder.

Write **7** as second digit of answer and place (R) **4** before next dividend digit, i.e. 9 to get GD as **49**.

Since, we have computed 2 digits in the answer, which is the required number of digits, so we put a decimal in the quotient after 7.

Step 4:

$$6 \overline{\left| \begin{array}{l} 13: \ 6 \ 9 \\ _4 \ _4 \end{array} \right.}$$
$$3:7. \ \mathbf{0}$$

From (GD) 49, subtract the duplex of second digit, i.e. $49 - (\text{duplex of } 7) = 49 - 7^2 = \mathbf{0}$ (ND)

(ND) $0 \div 6$, gives **0** as quotient and 0 as remainder.

So, the final answer is: square root of 1369 = **37**.

Note: *We put a colon, after the first digit of the square root. At each step, we subtract the Duplex of all the digits after the colon from the corresponding gross dividend to get next net dividend and then the process of division and subtraction continues.*

Example 5:

Find the **square root of 58347** *(imperfect square)*

Step 1:

| 5: 8347

The number has 5 digits. So, square root will have $\dfrac{(5+1)}{2} = 3$ digits.

Make groups of 2 digits, starting from the right. We get our first group as 5, place a colon after it.

Step 2:

4	5: _1_8347
2:

The highest possible perfect square less than 5 is 4, square root of 4 is **2**.

Write **2** as first digit of the square root, place a colon after 2.

Double it: $2 \times 2 = 4$ (Divisor), $5 - 2^2 = 1$ (Remainder),

So, Gross Dividend (GD) = **18**.

Step 3:

4	5: _1_8 _2_347
2: 4

(GD) $18 \div 4 \Rightarrow Q = 4, R = 2, GD = 23$

Step 4:

4	5: _1_8 _2_3 _3_47
2: 4 **1.**

(GD) 23 – (Duplex of 4) = $23 - 4^2 = 23 - 16 = 7$(ND)

(ND) $7 \div 4 \Rightarrow Q = 1, R = 3, GD = 34$

Since, we have computed upto 3 digits, which is the required number of digits, we put a decimal point here.

Step 5:

4	5: _1_8 _2_3 _3_4 _6_7
2: 4 1.**5**

(GD) $34 - D(41) = 34 - 2(4 \times 1) = 26$(ND)

(ND) $26 \div 4 \Rightarrow Q = 6, R = 2, GD = 27$

(GD) $27 - D(416) = 27 - [(2 \times 4 \times 6) + 1^2] = 27 - 49 = -22$

To make it positive, we reduce Q by 1

So (ND) $26 \div 4 \Rightarrow Q = 5, R = 6, GD = 67$

(GD) $67 - D(415) = 67 - [(2 \times 4 \times 5) + 1^2] = 67 - 41 = 26$(ND)

Step 6:

$4|5: 8\ 3\ 4\ 7\ 0$
$\quad\ \ {}_{1\ 2\ 3\ 6\ 6}$
$2: 4\ 1.\ 5\ 5$

(ND) $26 \div 4 \Rightarrow Q = 6, R = 2, GD = 20$

(GD) $20 - D(4156)$ will give a negative answer.

So, reducing the Q by 1, we get

(ND) $26 \div 4 \Rightarrow Q = 5, R = 6, GD = 60$

(GD) $60 - D(4155) = 60 - [(2\times4\times5) + 2(1\times5)]$

$\quad\quad\quad = 60 - 50 = 10(ND)$

Step 7:

$4|5: 8\ 3\ 4\ 7\ 0\ 0$
$\quad\ \ {}_{1\ 2\ 3\ 6\ 6\ 6}$
$2: 4\ 1.\ 5\ 5\ \mathbf{1}$

(ND) $10 \div 4 \Rightarrow Q = 2, R = 2, GD = 20$

(GD) $20 - D(41552) = 20 - [2(4\times2) + 2(1\times5) + 5^2]$

$\quad\quad\quad\quad\quad = 20 - 31 = -11$

So, reducing the Q by 1, we get

(ND) $10 \div 4 \Rightarrow Q = 1, R = 6, GD = 60$

(GD) $60 - D(41551) = 60 - [(2\times4\times1) + 2(1\times5) + 5^2]$

$\quad\quad\quad\quad\quad = 60 - 43 = 17(ND)$

We have already got the answer upto 3 decimal places, so no need to go any further.

So, the final answer is: square root of 58347 = **241.551**

Square root of an imperfect square having decimals

Example 6:

Find the **square root of 8342.564**

Step 1:

$|83: 42.564$

When there is a decimal in a number, only the digits on the left of the decimal, i.e. the digits in the integral part are considered for the number of digits in square root.

Since there are 4 digits on the left of the decimal, so square root will have $4/2 = 2$ digits. So, the decimal in the answer will come after 2 digits. Also considering the integral part of decimal, we get 83 as our first group. Put a colon after 83.

Step 2:

$18 | 83:_2 42.564$
$\quad 9:$

Observing first group 83, we get the first digit of square root as **9** and R = 83 – 81 = **2**, GD = **24**.

Double of 9 = **18** = Divisor

Put a colon after 9.

Step 3:

$18 | 83:_2\ _6 4\ 2.564$
$\quad 9: \mathbf{1.}$

(GD) 24 ÷ 18 ⇒ Q = **1**, R = **6**, GD = **62**

Since, we have got 2 digits in the answer, so put a decimal point after 1.

(GD) $62 - D(1) = 62 - 1^2 = 61$ (ND)

Step 4:

$18 | 83:_2\ _6 4\ 2._7 564$
$\quad 9: \mathbf{1.\ 3}$

(ND) 61 ÷ 18 ⇒ Q = **3**, R = **7**, GD = **75**

(GD) $75 - D(13) = 75 - 2(1 \times 3) = 69$ (ND)

Step 5:

$18 | 83:_2\ _6 4\ 2._7 5._{15} 64$
$\quad 9: \mathbf{1.\ 3\ 3}$

(ND) 69 ÷ 18 ⇒ Q = **3**, R = **15**, GD = **156**

(GD) $156 - D(133) = 156 - [2(1 \times 3) + 3^2]$

$\quad = 156 - 15 = 141$ (ND)

Step 6:

$18 | 83:_2\ _6 4\ 2._7 5._{15} 6._{15} 4$
$\quad 9: \mathbf{1.\ 3\ 3\ 7}$

(ND) 141 ÷ 18 ⇒ Q = **7**, R = **15**, GD = **154**

So, the square root of 8342.564 upto 3 decimal places is **91.337**

Example 7:

Find the **square root of 0.05374**

When the number has only decimal part, the decimal point comes at the beginning of the answer and we make groups starting from the right of decimal point.

Step 1:

$4 | 0.05:_1 374$
$\quad \mathbf{0.\ 2:}$

Put the decimal point at the beginning of the answer. From observation we see our first group after decimal is 05. Put a colon after it. Also the first digit of the square root is **2**. Put a colon after it. Double it to get **4** as divisor.

$R = 5 - 2^2 = 5 - 4 = 1$, GD = **13**

Step 2:

$4\underline{\lvert 0.05: 3\ 74}$
${}_{1}\ {}_{1}$
$\overline{0.\ 2:\ 3}$

(GD) $13 \div 4 \Rightarrow Q = 3, R = 1, GD = 17$
(GD) $17 - D(3) = 17 - 3^2 = 17 - 9 = 8$ (ND)

Step 3:

$4\underline{\lvert 0.05: 3\ 7\ 4}$
${}_{1}\ {}_{1}\ {}_{4}$
$\overline{0.\ 2:\ 3\ 1}$

(ND) $8 \div 4 \Rightarrow Q = 2, R = 0, GD = 04$
But (GD) $04 - D(32) =$ negative answer
So, reducing 1 from quotient, we get:
$Q = 1, R = 4, GD = 44$
(GD) $44 - D(31) = 44 - 2(3 \times 1) = 38$ (ND)

Step 4:

$4\underline{\lvert 0.05: 3\ 7\ 4\ 0}$
${}_{1}\ {}_{1}\ {}_{4}\ {}_{6}$
$\overline{0.\ 2:\ 3\ 1\ 8}$

(ND) $38 \div 4 \Rightarrow Q = 9, R = 2, GD = 20$
But (GD) $20 - D(319) =$ negative answer
So, reducing 1 from quotient, we get:
$Q = 8, R = 6, GD = 60$

So, the square root of 0.05374 upto 4 decimal places is **0.2318**

So, we see how easy it is to find square root of any number with the same ease even if the number is a perfect square or imperfect or even with decimals.

Some solved examples:

Example 8:

$\sqrt{2304}$

$8\underline{\lvert 23:\ 0\ 4}$
${}_{7}\ {}_{6}$
$\overline{4:\ 8.0}$

Answer = 48

Example 9:

$\sqrt{57842}$

$4\underline{\lvert 5:\ 7\ 8\ 4\ 2\ 0\ 0}$
${}_{1}\ {}_{1}\ {}_{2}\ {}_{4}\ {}_{2}\ {}_{8}$
$\overline{2: 40.503}$

Answer = 240.503

Example 10:

$\sqrt{28.356}$

$10\underline{\lvert 28:.\ 3\ 5\ 6}$
${}_{3}\ {}_{3}\ {}_{6}$
$\overline{5:.325}$

Answer = 5.325

Example 11:

$\sqrt{37}$

$12\underline{\lvert 37:\ 0\ \ 0\ \ 0\ \ 0}$
${}_{1}\ {}_{10}\ {}_{4}\ {}_{16}$
$\overline{6:.0\ 8\ 2}$

Answer = 6.082

EXERCISE 15.2

Find the square roots of the following numbers:

1. 519841   2. 28   3. 1387   4. 4917

5. 262144   6. 835396   7. 71023   8. 7501.71

9. 296.5   10. 5042

GENERAL GUIDELINES:

1. Make 2 digit pairs starting from the right of the number. A single digit (if any) left over at the left end is counted as a single group by itself.

2. If the number has n digits, square root will have n/2 digits, if n is even, and (n+1)/2, if n is odd.

3. The first digit of the square root can be found by observing the first pair of the number. Place a colon after it so as to separate it from the other coming up answer digits.

4. Double the first digit of the square root and place it as divisor in the divisor column. Since, the first digit will always be a single digit , never more than 9, so our divisor will never be more than 18. Thus making the whole process of computation very easy.

5. Subtract the square of the first digit from the left most group and place the remainder before the next dividend digit. This is our Gross Dividend (GD).

6. Now, follow the alternate division and subtraction steps. Divide this gross dividend by the divisor and write the quotient digit as second answer digit and place the remainder before the next dividend to get next GD.

7. From this GD obtained, subtract the duplex of second answer digit to get Net Dividend (ND).

8. Again, divide this ND by the divisor and write the quotient digit as third answer digit and place the remainder before the next dividend digit to get the next GD.

9. At each step, the duplex of all the digits starting from the second digit of the square root to the column of computation is subtracted from the corresponding GD to get the next ND which is further divided by the divisor to get the next digit of the square root and

remainder thus obtained is placed before next digit of the dividend to get next GD.

10. At any step, if we get a negative ND, we go back to the previous step, reduce the quotient accordingly to increase the remainder and make the ND positive to proceed further.

11. This process continues till the ND becomes 0 and no more digits are left in the number for computation or when we have reached the desired level of accuracy, i.e. required number of decimal places.

12. Place the decimal point after the required digit from the left which is equal to the number of digit groups.

CHAPTER 16

Cube Roots at a Glance

Computation of the cube root of a number by the traditional method is a very long and time consuming process. By using a simple Vedic Mathematics formula – *"mere observation"*, the answer can be given in only 2–3 seconds, in one look without actually performing any computation.

Concept of Cube Root

When a number is multiplied by itself twice, we get the cube of the number,

e.g. Cube of $2 = 2 \times 2 \times 2 = 8$

Finding cuberoot is just the reciprocal procedure of calculating a cube. It is actually finding the number which has been twice multiplied by itself to obtain the cube.

So, if 8 is the cube of 2, 2 is the cube root of 8. If 27 is the cube of 3, 3 is the cube root of 27.

Let's find the cube root of 373248 by both conventional and vedic method:

Conventional Method

2	373248
2	186624
2	93312
2	46656
2	23328
2	11664
2	5832
2	2916
2	1458
3	729

3	729
3	243
3	81
3	27
3	9
	3

Vedic Method

By observation only

373248

= 72

Cube root $= 2 \times 2 \times 2 \times 3 \times 3 = 72$

Cube root of **perfect cubes** can be found out in the same manner as we have found square roots of perfect squares.

Let's first see and study the cubes of first 10 natural numbers:

Number	Cube	Last digit of Cube
1	1	1
2	8	8
3	27	7
4	64	4
5	125	5
6	216	6
7	343	3
8	512	2
9	729	9
10	1000	0

We can see that each cube has a unique ending digit, so finding the last digit of the cube root is even simpler than finding the last digit of the square root where we have to choose from two options.

The following chart of last digit of cube roots can be made:

If a cube ends in	Last digit of its cube root will be
1	1
2	8
3	7
4	4
5	5
6	6
7	3
8	2
9	9
0	0

From the above table, we can conclude that:

1. If a cube ends in 1, 4, 5, 6 and 9, their corresponding cube root also ends with the same digit.

2. If a cube ends with 2, its cube root ends with its complement 8 and vice-versa.

3. Similarly, cube of 3 ends with 7 and cube of 7 ends with 3.

GENERAL GUIDELINES

1. Divide the number in 2 groups by putting a slash after 3 digits from the right of the number.

2. First digit of the cube root can be found by mere observation of the first group in the number. Consider the perfect cube smaller than or equal to the first group and compute its cube root. Write it down as the first digit of the required cube root.

3. By looking at the last digit of the cube, we can find out the last digit or the second digit of the cube root.

Note: *This method of finding cube roots is possible only for perfect cubes with a maximum of six digits.*

Let's understand it by the following example:

Example 1:

Find the **cube root of 79507**

Step 1:

79| 507   Put a slash, 3 digits from the right of the number.

Step 2:

79| 507   Considering the first group 79, perfect cube
  ↙   smaller than it is 64 and cube root of 64 is 4.
4
                 So, first digit of required cube root is **4.**

Step 3:

79| 507   Last digit of the cube is 7, so the cube root must
   ↙   end in 3.
 4 3
                 So, the last digit of the required cube root is **3.**

So, cube root of 79507 is **43.**

Example 2:

Find the **cube root of 636056**

Step 1:

636| 056   Put a slash, 3 digits from the right of the number.

Step 2:

636| 056   Perfect cube smaller than the first group 636 is

8   512 and cube root of 512 is 8.

So, the first digit of the cube root is **8**.

Step 3:

636 | 056   Number ends in 6, so the last digit is **6**.

8 6

So, the cube root of 636056 is **86**.

Some more solved examples in one step:

Example 3:   *Example 4*:

Find the **cube root of 21952**   Find the **cube root of 531441**

21 | 952   531 | 441

2 8   8 1

So, $\sqrt[3]{21952} = 28$ So, $\sqrt[3]{531441} = 81$

EXERCISE 16.1

Find the cube roots of the following perfect cubes:

1. 175616	**2.** 2197	**3.** 59319	**4.** 681472
5. 857375	**6.** 474552	**7.** 97336	**8.** 250047
9. 4913	**10.** 2744		

Cubes

Cubes of 2 digit numbers *(proportionately)*

Let us consider a two digit number, say 'ab'.

To find the cube of a given number 'ab', we can take the help of the following formula:

$$(a + b)^3 = a^3 + 3a^2b + 3ab^2 + b^3$$

If we split the second term $3a^2b$ as $(a^2b + 2a^2b)$ and the third term $3ab^2$ as $(ab^2 + 2ab^2)$, we can write the formula as:

$$(a + b)^3 = a^3 + a^2b \quad + ab^2 + b^3$$
$$+ 2\,a^2\,b + 2ab^2$$
$$\overline{a^3 + 3a^2\,b \; + 3ab^2 + b^3}$$

In the first row, we notice that the first term is a^3

$$\text{the second term } a^2\,b = a^3 \times \frac{b}{a}$$

$$\text{the third term } ab^2 \quad = a^2b \times \frac{b}{a}$$

$$\text{the fourth term } b^3 \quad = ab^2 \times \frac{b}{a}$$

Thus, each of the second, third and fourth term can be computed from its previous term by multiplying it by the common ratio (b/a).

So, all we have to compute is a^3 and the ratio (b/a). Once it is done, we can derive all the remaining terms easily. Write the four terms in four columns in a row. Second term and third terms are then doubled and written below their corresponding terms. Then we just add from the right most column and keep writing one digit at a time below each column and take the carry over, if any, to the next column. The process continues till we reach the left most column.

Let's understand it better with the following example:

Example 1:　　Find the **cube of 12**

Here, a = 1, b = 2, ratio $\dfrac{b}{a} = \dfrac{2}{1} = 2$

Step 1:

1 2 4 8

The first four terms of the first row are:

1st term = a^3 = 1^3 = **1**

2nd term = a^2b = 1st term $\times \dfrac{b}{a}$ = 1×2 = **2**

3rd term = ab^2 = 2nd term $\times \dfrac{b}{a}$ = 2×2 = **4**

4th term = b^3 = 3rd term $\times \dfrac{b}{a}$ = 4×2 = **8**

The four terms are written in four columns as shown.

Step 2:

1 2 4 8
　　4 8

For the second row, double the second and third term:

2×2 = **4**

4×2 = **8**

Write them below 2 and 4 respectively as shown.

Step 3:

1 2 4 8
　　4 8
―――――――
1 7 $\underset{1}{2}$ 8

Add the terms in each column and write one digit at a time and carry over the digit, if any, to the next column as shown:

At unit's place 8 = **8**

At ten's place (4+8) = $\underset{1}{\textbf{2}}$ (1 is carried over)

At hundred's place (2+4) = **6**

　　　　　6 + 1(carry) = **7**

At thousand's place 1 = **1**

So, 12^3 = **1728**.

Example 2:   Find the **cube of 23**

Here, a = 2, b = 3, ratio $\dfrac{b}{a} = \dfrac{3}{2}$

Step 1:

8 12 18 27

The first four terms can be computed as below:

1st term = a^3 = 2^3 = **8**

2nd term = a^2b = $8 \times \dfrac{3}{2}$ = **12**

3rd term = ab^2 = $12 \times \dfrac{3}{2}$ = **18**

4th term = b^3 = $18 \times \dfrac{3}{2}$ = **27**

Step 2:

8 12 18 27

   24 36

Double the second and third terms:

$12 \times 2 =$ **24**

$18 \times 2 =$ **36**

Write them below 12 and 18 respectively as shown.

Step 3:

8 12 18 27

  24 36

————————

12 $_4$1 $_5$6 $_2$7

Add in each column starting from the right term, write one digit at a time:

unit's digit = 27 = $_2$7 (2 is carried over)

ten's digit = 18 + 36 + 2 (carry) = $_5$6 (5 is carried over)

hundred's digit = 12 + 24 + 5(carry) = $_4$1 (4 is carried over)

thousand's digit = 8 + 4(carry) = **12**

So, $23^3 =$ **12167**.

Example 3:   Find the **cube of 74**

Here, a = 7, b = 4, ratio $\dfrac{b}{a} = \dfrac{4}{7}$

Step 1:

343 196 112 64

The first four terms can be computed as below:

1st term = a^3 = 7^3 = **343**

2nd term = a^2b = $343 \times \dfrac{4}{7}$ = **196**

3rd term = ab^2 = $196 \times \dfrac{4}{7}$ = **112**

4th term = b^3 = $112 \times \dfrac{4}{7}$ = **64**

Step 2:

343 196 112 64
     392 224

Double the second and third terms:

196×2 = **392**

112×2 = **224**

Write them below the corresponding terms.

Step 3:

343 196 112 64
   392 224
_____

405   **2**$_{62}$ **2**$_{34}$ **4**$_6$

Starting from the most right column add them:

1. $64 = \mathbf{4}_6$
2. $112 + 224 + 6(\text{carry}) = \mathbf{2}_{34}$
3. $196 + 392 + 34(\text{carry}) = \mathbf{2}_{62}$
4. $343 + 62(\text{carry}) = \mathbf{405}$

So, 74^3 = **405224.**

GENERAL GUIDELINES

1. For finding the cube of any number 'ab', first find the cube of a, i.e. a^3 and the ratio of b/a.

2. We write four terms in the first row in four columns.
   - First term = the cube of the first digit a, i.e. a^3
   - Second term = First term × ratio b/a,

     i.e. $a^3 \times b/a = a^2b$
   - Third term = second term × ratio b/a,

     i.e. $a^2b \times b/a = ab^2$

- Fourth term = third term ab^2 × ratio b/a,

  i.e. $ab^2 \times b/a = b^3$

It is also equal to the cube of the second digit 'b'.

3. For the second row, we double the middle two terms and write them below the second and third terms respectively.

4. We add starting from the right most column and put down one digit at a time and carry over the other digits if any to the next column. The process continues till we reach the left most column.

Some more solved examples:

Example 4:

Find the **cube of 38**

$a = 3, b = 8$, ratio $\dfrac{b}{a} = \dfrac{8}{3}$

$a^3 \quad a^2b \quad ab^2 \quad b^3$

27 72 192 512

    144 384

———————————

54 $_{27}$8 $_{62}$7 $_{51}$2

So, $38^3 = $ **54872**

Example 5:

Find the **cube of 52**

$a = 5, b = 2$, ratio $\dfrac{b}{a} = \dfrac{2}{5}$

$a^3 \quad a^2b \quad ab^2 \quad b^3$

125 50 20 8

   100 40

———————————

140 $_{15}$6 $_{6}$0 8

So, $52^3 = $ **140608**

Example 6:

Find the **cube of 11**

$a = 1, b = 1$, ratio $\dfrac{b}{a} = 1$

1 1 1 1

  2 2

———————————

1 3 3 1

So, $11^3 = $ **1331**

Example 7:

Find the **cube of 89**

$a = 8, b = 9$, ratio $\dfrac{b}{a} = \dfrac{9}{8}$

512 576 648 729

    1152 1296

———————————

704 $_{192}$9 $_{201}$6 $_{72}$9

So, $89^3 = $ **704969**

EXERCISE 17.1

Find the cubes of the following numbers:

1.	26^3	**2.**	31^3	**3.**	45^3	**4.**	71^3
5.	37^3	**6.**	82^3	**7.**	93^3	**8.**	19^3
9.	54^3	**10.**	68^3				

Cubes of numbers near the Base

Cubes of numbers near the base can be found in one line only, no matter how big the number is. The method is very much similar to what we have used while computing the squares of numbers near the base.

CASE I: Cubes of numbers above the Base

Example 8:

Find the **cube of 104**

104 is 4 more than 100.

The answer will come in 3 parts — left part, middle part and the right part.

Step 1:

112 / /   For **LHS**:

Add twice the excess to the number, i.e. $104 + (2 \times 4) = \textbf{112}$

Step 2:

112 / **48** /   **Middle** part:

Multiply the square of the excess by 3, i.e. $3 \times (4)^2 = \textbf{48}$

Step 3:

112 / 48 / **64**   For **RHS**:

Write the cube of the excess in the number, i.e. $4^3 = \textbf{64}$

So, $104^3 = \textbf{1124864}$.

Note: *The number of digits in the middle part and the right part of the answer is equal to the 0's in the base. Since, in this case, base is 100, so there should be two digits in the middle and the right part.*

Example 9:

Find the **cube of 109**

Excess from the base 100 = 9

Step 1:

127 / /   LHS = 109 + twice of excess
                                            = 109 + (2×9) = 109 + 18 = **127**

Step 2:   **Middle part** = 3 × (square of excess)

127 / ₂43 /   = 3 × 9² = **243**

                                           (since base is 100, so only 2 digits in
                                           the middle part)

Step 3:   RHS = cube of excess = 9³ = **729**

127 / ₂43 / ₇29   (since base is 100, so only 2 digits in
                                           RHS)

Carrying over the digits to the left, we get the answer as:

        109³ = **1295029.**

Example 10:

Find the **cube of 1008**

Excess from the base 1000 = 8

                                           LHS = 1008 + (2×8) = **1024**

1024 / 192 / 512   **Middle part** = 3 × 8² = **192**

                                           RHS = 8³ = **512**

(Since, base is 1000, so three digits in the middle and right part)

So, the answer for 1008³ = **1024192512.**

Example 11:

Find the **cube of 112**

Excess from the base 100 = 12

                                           LHS = 112 + (2×12) = **136**

136 / 32 / 28   **Middle part** = 3 × 12² = ₄**32**
     ₄   ₁₇

                                           RHS = 12³ = ₁₇**28**

Carrying over the digits to the left, we get the answer as:

$112^3 = \textbf{1404928.}$

CASE II: Cubes of numbers below the Base

Example 12:

Find the **cube of 97**

97 is 3 less than its base 100.

So, deficiency is –3.

Answer will come in 3 parts — left, middle and right part.

The middle part and the right part will have two digits only, since base is 100.

Step 1:

91 / /

For **LHS** answer, add double the deficiency to the number 97,

i.e. $97 + (-3 \times 2) = 97 - 6 = \textbf{91}$

Step 2:

91 / **27** /

For **middle** part, multiplying the square of the deficiency by 3, i.e. $3 \times (-3)^2 = \textbf{27}$

Step 3:

91 / 27 / $\overline{\textbf{27}}$

For **RHS** answer, write the cube of the deficiency of the number,

i.e. $(-3)^3 = -27 = \overline{\textbf{27}}$

Step 4:

91 / 26 / (100 – 27)

91 / 26 / 73

To make the RHS positive, we reduce 1 in the middle part and carry it over to the RHS to take the complement of 27.

So, $97^3 = \textbf{912673.}$

Example 13:   Find the **cube of 9989**

9989 is 11 less than it base 10000.

So, deficiency is –11.

Step 1:

9967 / /

$$LHS = 9989 + (-11 \times 2)$$
$$= 9989 - 22 = 9967$$

Step 2:

9967 / **0363** /

Middle part $= 3 \times (-11)^2 = 0363$

(Since, base 10000 has four 0's, so middle part will have four digits)

Step 3:

9967 / 0363 / $\overline{1331}$

RHS = cube of $(-11) = (-11)^3$

$$= 1\ 1\ 1\ 1 \qquad \text{(cubing process)}$$
$$\underline{\ \ 2\ 2}$$
$$1\ 3\ 3\ 1$$

$$= -1331$$

Step 4:

9967 / 0362 / 8669

To convert RHS from negative to positive, we reduce 1 in the middle part and write the complement of 1331.

So, $9989^3 = $ **996703628669.**

GENERAL GUIDELINES

1. When a number is near a particular base, we find its deficiency or excess from that base.

2. We get our answer in 3 parts – LHS, middle, RHS.

3. For LHS answer, we add twice the deficiency/ excess to the number itself.

4. For middle part, multiply the square of deficiency/ excess by 3.

5. For RHS answer, write the cube of excess/ deficiency of the number from the base.

6. In case, we get the RHS answer as negative in finding cubes of numbers below the base, to make it positive, write the complement of it and reduce 1 from the middle part.

Some more solved examples:

Example 14:

Find the **cube of 113**

$113+2(13) / 3 \times 13^2 / 13^3$

139 / 07 / 97
      5   21

So, $113^3 = \mathbf{1442897}$

Example 15:

Find the **cube of 10012**

$10012+(2\times12) / 3\times12^2 12 / 12^3$

10036 / 0432 / 1728

So, $10012^3 = \mathbf{1003604321728}$

Example 16:

Find the **cube of 984**

Deficiency = –16

$984+2(-16) / 3 \times(-16)^2 / -16^3$

952 / 768 / $\overline{_4096}$

952 / 764 / $\overline{096}$
952 / 763 / 904
So, $984^3 = \mathbf{952763904}$

Example 17:

Find the **cube of 9996**

Deficiency = –4

$9996+(2\times-4) / 3\times(-4)^2 / -4^3$

9988 / 0048 / $\overline{0064}$

9988/0047/9936

So, $9996^3 = \mathbf{998800479936}$

Now, you can yourself compare the two methods as shown below:

Conventional Method	*Vedic Method*
9996³	**9996³**
9996	9988 / 0048 / $\overline{0064}$
×9996	**998800479936**
59976	
89964×	*Fast one line method*
89964××	
89964×××	
99920016	
99920016	
× 9996	
599520096	
899280144×	
899280144××	
89928014×××	
998800479936	*Long many steps method*

EXERCISE 17.2

Find the cubes of the following numbers:

1.	91^3	**2.**	85^3	**3.**	103^3	**4.**	1006^3
5.	998^3	**6.**	99^3	**7.**	102^3	**8.**	10004^3
9.	10011^3	**10.**	9992^3				

Magic Division

You have learnt the technique to divide any given number by any divisor, in just one line. But there are some additional techniques which serve as the fastest method of division where you can write the answers straightaway as if you already knew the answer!

These techniques are useful in dividing fractional numbers where:

(1) The dividend is less than the divisor.

(2) The divisor is a small 2-3 digit number.

(3) The divisor ends in either 9, 8, 1 or 2.

Other divisors ending in 3,4,5,6 and 7 can be converted to such divisors by multiplying them with a suitable number.

For this, the given fraction is initially converted into another supporting fraction called *"Auxiliary Fraction"*. The formula used is *"by one more than one before"* In this Method, actual big denominators are converted into small, more comfortable denominators and the whole division is carried out by this new divisor by a very unique procedure. This makes the whole process very easy and it seems the answer is computed like a magic.

If we compare the two methods – the conventional one and the Vedic one-sight method – nothing would be left to say.

Vedic Method:

$$\frac{1}{19} = 0.\overset{\bullet}{0}5263157894736842\overset{\bullet}{1}$$

Conventional Method:

19) 100(0.052631578

   95

    50

    38

   120

   114

     60

     57

    30

    19

   110

    95

   150

   133

    170

    152

     180

Let's understand the technique better with the following example:

CASE I: When the divisor ends in 9

Lets first consider the case where the divisor ends in 9, e.g. 19, 39, 69, 119, etc.

__Example 1__: **Convert the fraction** $\dfrac{1}{19}$ **to its decimal form.**

Step 1:

Convert the fraction $\dfrac{1}{19}$ to its auxiliary fraction (A.F.) as shown:

Add 1 to the denominator 19 to make it 20 and remove 0 from it by putting a decimal in the numerator as shown:

A.F. of $\dfrac{1}{19} = \dfrac{1}{19+1} = \dfrac{1}{20} = \dfrac{\mathbf{0.1}}{\mathbf{2}}$

This new fraction $\dfrac{0.1}{2}$ is called the Auxiliary Fraction (A.F.) of $\dfrac{1}{19}$

which will help to find the answer in a very easy and unique way. Now we will carry on step by step division by taking the divisor as 2 instead of 19.

Step 2:

Divide 0.1 by 2. This will be a slightly different kind of division as $\dfrac{0.1}{2}$ is an auxiliary fraction, not the original one.

Put the decimal point first and divide numerator 1 by denominator 2, i.e. $1 \div 2 \Rightarrow Q = 0, R = 1$.

Write $Q = 0$ after the decimal point in the answer line and place $R=1$ before the quotient 0 as shown. Reminder quotient taken together gives our first Gross Dividend (GD) as **10**.

$$\frac{0.1}{2} = 0.{}_1 0$$

Step 3:

Now divide 10 by 2, i.e.

$$10 \div 2 \Rightarrow Q = 5, R = 0$$

Write 5 as the next quotient digit and place 0 before 5 as shown to give **05** as next gross dividend.

$$\frac{0.1}{2} = 0.{}_1 0{}_0 5$$

Step 4:

Divide 05 by 2, i.e.

$$5 \div 2 \Rightarrow Q = 2, R = 1$$

Write 2 as the next quotient digit and place 1 before 2 as shown to give **12** as the next gross dividend

$$\frac{0.1}{2} = 0.{}_1 0{}_0 5{}_1 2$$

Step 5:

Now $12 \div 2 \Rightarrow Q = 6, R = 0$

Write 6 as next quotient digit and place 0 before 6 to give next gross dividend as **06**.

$$\frac{0.1}{2} = 0.{}_1 0{}_0 5{}_1 2{}_0 6$$

The process can be continued upto any level of accuracy.

Finding the answer upto 18 recurring places, we get:

$$\frac{1}{19} = \frac{0.1}{2} \text{ (A.F.)} = 0._1 0_0 5_1 2_0 6_0 3_1 1_1 5_1 7_1 8_0 9_4 0_7 1_3 6_0 8_0 4_0 21$$

Discarding all the remainders, we get the final answer as:

$$\frac{1}{19} = 0.\overset{\bullet}{0}5263157894736842\overset{\bullet}{1}$$

(the dots on 0 and 1 means that the whole number is recurring)

Example 2: **Convert the fraction $\dfrac{14}{79}$ to its decimal form (upto 8 decimal places).**

Step 1:

Convert the fraction $\dfrac{14}{79}$ to its auxiliary fraction, as shown:

$$\text{A.F. of } \frac{14}{79} = \frac{14}{80} = \frac{1.4}{8}$$

Step 2:

Divide 1.4 by 8, put the decimal point first

$$14 \div 8 \Rightarrow Q = 1, R = 6, GD = 61$$

Write Q = 1 after the decimal in the answer line and place R= 6 before 1 as shown to get gross dividend (GD) as 61.

$$\frac{1.4}{8} = 0._6 1$$

Step 3:

Divide 61 by 8, i.e.

$$61 \div 8 \Rightarrow Q = 7, R = 5, GD = 57$$

$$\frac{1.4}{8} = 0._6 1_5 7$$

Step 4:

$$57 \div 8 \Rightarrow Q = 7, R = 1, GD = 17$$

$$\frac{1.4}{8} = 0._6 1_5 7_1 7$$

Step 5:

$$17 \div 8 \Rightarrow Q = 2, R = 1, GD = 12$$

$$\frac{1.4}{8} = 0._6 1_5 7_1 7_1 \mathbf{2}$$

The final answer upto 8 decimal places is:

$$\frac{14}{79} = \frac{1.4}{8} \text{ (A.F.)} = 0._6 1_5 7_1 7_1 2_4 1_1 5_7 1_7 8$$

$$\frac{14}{79} = \mathbf{0.17721518}$$

Some solved examples in straight steps:

Example 3:

Convert $\dfrac{68}{129}$ to its decimal form.

$$\frac{68}{129} = \frac{68}{130} = \frac{6.8}{13} \text{ (A.F.)}$$

$$\frac{6.8}{13} = 0._3 5_9 2_1 7_4 1_2 3_{10} 1_{10} 7_3 8$$

So, the final answer upto 8 decimal places for

$$\frac{68}{129} = \mathbf{0.52713178}$$

Example 4:

Convert $\dfrac{18}{49}$ to its decimal form.

$$\frac{18}{49} = \frac{18}{50} = \frac{1.8}{5} \text{ (A.F.)}$$

$$\frac{1.8}{5} = 0._3 3_3 6_1 7_2 3_3 4_4 6_1 9_4 3$$

So, the final answer upto 8 decimal places for

$$\frac{18}{49} = \mathbf{0.36734693}$$

Isn't it like tossing off one digit after the other mentally as if you already knew the answer. This process of computing the answer just takes the time you require to write the answer. That is why I call it *Magical Division*.

EXERCISE 18.1

Convert the following fractions to decimals upto 8 decimal places:

1. $\dfrac{52}{99}$ 2. $\dfrac{35}{119}$ 3. $\dfrac{26}{39}$ 4. $\dfrac{6}{19}$ 5. $\dfrac{24}{29}$

We can also apply this technique to divisors that end in 8, 7, 6, etc. but with a slight change.

Lets first consider the cases where denominator / divisor ends in 8, e.g. 18, 28, 38, 88, 128, etc.

CASE 2: When the divisor ends in 8

The steps are almost the same except that since divisor ends in 8, which is one less than 9, so at each step, after division, the quotient thus obtained is one time added to get the gross dividend and then further divided by the denominator of A.F.

Lets understand it with the following example:

Example 5: **Convert the fraction $\dfrac{9}{38}$ to its decimal form:**

Step 1:

To find the auxiliary fraction of $\dfrac{9}{38}$, add 2 to the denominator to get 40, where 0 is further removed by placing a decimal in the numerator as shown.

$$\text{A.F. of } \frac{9}{38} = \frac{9}{38+2} = \frac{9}{40} = \frac{0.9}{4}$$

Step 2:

The first step will be the same as in case of divisor ending in 9, put the decimal point, then divide 9 by 4, i.e.

$$9 \div 4 \Rightarrow Q = 2, R = 1$$

Our gross dividend comes out to be 12 (remainder quotient), but since divisor 38 ends in 8 which is 1 less than 9, so one time quotient digit (2) will be added to 12 to get the final gross dividend and then further divide by 4.

i.e. Gross Dividend (GD) = Remainder Quotient (12) + Quotient (2) = 14

$$\frac{0.9}{4} = 0.{}_{1}2^{+2}$$

Step 3:

$$14 \div 4 \Rightarrow Q = 3, R = 2$$

GD = Remainder Quotient (23) + Quotient (3) = 26

$$\frac{0.9}{4} = 0.{}_{1}2_{2}3^{+3}$$

Step 4:

$$26 \div 4 \Rightarrow Q = 6, R = 2$$

GD = Remainder Quotient (26) + Quotient (6) = 32

$$\frac{0.9}{4} = 0.{}_{1}2_{2}3_{2}6^{+6}$$

The process is continued upto any level of accuracy.

The final answer upto 8 decimal places is:

$$\frac{9}{38} = \frac{9}{40} = \frac{0.9}{4} = 0.{}_{1}2^{+2}{}_{2}3^{+3}{}_{2}6^{+6}{}_{0}8^{+8}{}_{0}4^{+4}{}_{0}2^{+2}{}_{0}1^{+1}{}_{2}0^{+0} = \mathbf{0.23684210}$$

***Example 6*: Convert the fraction $\dfrac{57}{138}$ to its decimal form.**

$$\text{A.F.} = \frac{57}{140} = \frac{5.7}{14}$$

$$\frac{5.7}{14} = 0.{}_{1}4^{+4}{}_{4}1^{+1}{}_{0}3^{+3}{}_{6}0^{+0}{}_{4}4^{+4}{}_{0}3^{+3}{}_{10}4^{+4}{}_{10}7^{+7}$$

$$\frac{57}{138} = \mathbf{0.41304347}$$

EXERCISE 18.2

Convert the following fractions to decimals upto 8 decimal places:

1. $\dfrac{13}{38}$ 2. $\dfrac{63}{88}$ 3. $\dfrac{5}{28}$ 4. $\dfrac{71}{78}$ 5. $\dfrac{29}{118}$

CASE 3: When the divisor ends in 1

Let us consider the cases where denominator ends in 1, e.g. 21, 31, 51, 121, etc.

Example 7: **Convert the fraction** $\dfrac{8}{21}$ **to its decimal form.**

Step 1:

In this case, to get A.F. of $\dfrac{8}{21}$, subtract 1 from both numerator and denominator i.e. $\dfrac{8-1}{21-1}$ to get $\dfrac{7}{20}$ and replace 0 in the denominator by putting decimal in the numerator. So, we get $\dfrac{0.7}{2}$ as A.F.

A.F. of $\dfrac{8}{21}$ $\Rightarrow$ $\dfrac{8-1}{21-1} = \dfrac{7}{20} = \dfrac{\mathbf{0.7}}{\mathbf{2}}$

Step 2:

After putting the decimal point, divide 7 by 2, i.e.

$7 \div 2 \Rightarrow Q_1 = 3, R = 1$

Write $Q_1 = 3$ after the decimal and $R = 1$ before the quotient as done earlier,

$\dfrac{0.7}{2} = 0._1 3$

Step 3:

Now there is a slight change here. Instead of taking the remainder quotient, i.e. 13, as the gross dividend, we will take the remainder (9 – quotient) as the gross dividend. So subtract $Q_1 = 3$ from 9, i.e. $9 - 3 = 6$ and write this **6** on the top of Q_1 as shown:

Now we take next gross dividend as **16** not 13.

$\dfrac{0.7}{2} = 0._1 3^6 \qquad\qquad$ **Remainder** $\qquad (9 - Q_1)$

Step 4:

$16 \div 2 \Rightarrow Q_2 = 8, R = 0$

Subtract $Q_2 = 8$ from 9, i.e. $9 - 8 = 1$ and write this **1** on the top of Q_2.

Next gross dividend is **01**, not 08

$$\frac{0.7}{2} = 0.\,3^6_{\,1}\,8^1_{\,0}$$

Step 5:

$01 \div 2 \Rightarrow Q_3 = 0, R = 1$

Gross dividend $= 1\,(9 - 0) = \mathbf{19}$, not 10

$$\frac{0.7}{2} = 0.\,3^6_{\,1}\,8^1_{\,0}\,0^9_{\,1}$$

Step 6:

$19 \div 2 \Rightarrow Q_4 = 9, R = 1$

Gross dividend $= 1\,(9 - 9) = \mathbf{10}$, not 19

$$\frac{0.7}{2} = 0.\,3^6_{\,1}\,8^1_{\,0}\,0^9_{\,1}\,9^0_{\,1}$$

Continuing the procedure, we get the final answer upto 8 decimal places as

$$\frac{0.7}{2} = 0.\,3^6_{\,1}\,8^1_{\,0}\,0^9_{\,1}\,9^0_{\,1}\,5^4_{\,0}\,2^7_{\,0}\,3^6_{\,1}\,8^1_{\,0}$$

So, $\dfrac{8}{21} = \dfrac{0.7}{2}$ (A.F.) $= \mathbf{0.\dot{3}8095\dot{2}}$

Example 8: Convert the fraction $\dfrac{7}{61}$ to its decimal form.

Step 1:

$$\text{A.F.} = \frac{7-1}{61-1} = \frac{6}{60} = \frac{0.6}{6}$$

Step 2:

$$0.\,1^8_{\,0}$$

$$6 \div 6 \Rightarrow Q_1 = 1, R = 0$$

$$\text{GD} = 0\,(9 - Q_1) = 0\,(9 - 1) = \mathbf{08}$$

Step 3:

$$0.\ \underset{0}{1}{}^{8}\ \underset{2}{1}{}^{8} \qquad\qquad 08 \div 6 \Rightarrow Q_2 = 1,\ R = 2$$
$$GD = 2\,(9 - Q_2) = 2\,(9 - 1) = \mathbf{28}$$

Step 4:

$$0.\ \underset{0}{1}{}^{8}\ \underset{2}{1}{}^{8}\ \underset{4}{4}{}^{5} \qquad\qquad 28 \div 6 \Rightarrow Q_3 = 4,\ R = 4$$
$$GD = 4\,(9 - Q_3) = 4\,(9 - 4) = \mathbf{45}$$

Step 5:

$$0.\ \underset{0}{1}{}^{8}\ \underset{2}{1}{}^{8}\ \underset{4}{4}{}^{5}\ \underset{3}{7}{}^{2} \qquad\qquad 45 \div 6 \Rightarrow Q_4 = 7,\ R = 3$$
$$GD = 3\,(9 - Q_4) = 3\,(9 - 7) = \mathbf{32}$$

Continuing the procedure, we get the final answer upto 8 decimal places as

$$\frac{0.6}{6} = 0.\ \underset{0}{1}{}^{8}\ \underset{2}{1}{}^{8}\ \underset{4}{4}{}^{5}\ \underset{3}{7}{}^{2}\ \underset{2}{5}{}^{4}\ \underset{0}{4}{}^{5}\ \underset{5}{0}{}^{9}\ \underset{5}{9}{}^{0}$$

So, $\dfrac{7}{61} = \mathbf{0.11475409}$

__Example 9__: **Convert the fraction** $\dfrac{9}{121}$ **to its decimal form.**

$$A.F. = \frac{9 - 1}{121 - 1} = \frac{8}{120} = \frac{0.8}{12}$$

$$\frac{0.8}{12} = 0.\ \underset{8}{0}{}^{9}\ \underset{5}{7}{}^{2}\ \underset{4}{4}{}^{5}\ \underset{9}{3}{}^{6}\ \underset{0}{8}{}^{1}\ \underset{1}{0}{}^{9}\ \underset{7}{1}{}^{8}\ \underset{6}{6}{}^{3}$$

So, $\dfrac{9}{121} = \mathbf{0.07438016}.$

__Example 10__: **Convert the fraction** $\dfrac{14}{91}$ **to its decimal form.**

$$A.F. = \frac{14 - 1}{91 - 1} = \frac{13}{90} = \frac{1.3}{9}$$

$$\frac{1.3}{9} = 0.\ \underset{4}{1}{}^{8}\ \underset{3}{5}{}^{4}\ \underset{7}{3}{}^{6}\ \underset{4}{8}{}^{1}\ \underset{5}{4}{}^{5}\ \underset{1}{6}{}^{3}\ \underset{4}{1}{}^{8}$$

So $\dfrac{14}{91} = \mathbf{0.1538461}$

EXERCISE 18.3

Convert the following fractions to decimals upto 8 decimal places:

1. $\dfrac{4}{31}$ 2. $\dfrac{8}{51}$ 3. $\dfrac{19}{51}$ 4. $\dfrac{16}{31}$ 5. $\dfrac{19}{161}$

CASE 4: When the divisor ends in 2

The whole process remains the same as in case of divisor ending in 1, except that while converting the fraction into it's A.F., we subtract 2 from the denominator. Also while computing the gross dividend at each step, we double the quotient digit before subtracting it from 9 and then it is further divided by the denominator of the A.F.

Let's understand it by the following example:

Example 11: **Convert the fraction $\dfrac{7}{32}$ to its decimal form:**

Step 1:

$$A.F. = \frac{7-1}{32-2} = \frac{6}{30} = \frac{\mathbf{0.6}}{\mathbf{3}}$$

Step 2:

Putting the decimal point first, divide 6 by 3, i.e.

$$\frac{6}{3} \Rightarrow Q_1 = 2, R = \mathbf{0}$$

Double the quotient digit 2 to get 4 and subtract it from 9, i.e. $9 - 4 = \mathbf{5}$ and write this 5 on the top of Q_1 as shown:

$$GD = 0\,(9 - 2Q_1) = 0\,(9 - 4) = \mathbf{05}$$

$$\frac{0.6}{3} = 0.\,2^{5}_{\;0}$$

Step 3:

$$05 \div 3 \Rightarrow Q_2 = 1, R = \mathbf{2}$$
$$GD = 2\,(9 - 2Q_2) = 2(9 - 2) = \mathbf{27}$$
$$\frac{0.6}{3} = 0.\,2^{5}_{\;0}\,1^{7}_{\;2}$$

Step 4:

$$27 \div 3 \Rightarrow Q_3 = 9, R = \mathbf{0}$$
$$GD = 0\,(9 - 2Q_3) = 0(9 - 18) = 0\,\overline{9}$$

To make it positive, we reduce the quotient by 1, so that

$Q_3 = 8$, $R = 3$

Now GD $= 3 (9 - 2Q_3) = 3 (9 - 16) = 3\overline{7} = 30 - 7 = 23$

$$\frac{0.6}{3} = 0.\,2\,\underset{0}{{}}\,1\,\underset{2}{{}^5}\,8\,\underset{3}{{}^7}\,\overline{7}$$

Continuing the process, we get the final answer as

$$\frac{0.6}{3} = 0.\,2\,\underset{0}{{}}\,1\,\underset{2}{{}^5}\,8\,\underset{3}{{}^7}\,7\,\underset{2}{{}^{\overline{7}}}\,5\,\underset{0}{{}^{\overline{5}}}\,{}^{\overline{1}}$$

$$\frac{7}{32} = \mathbf{0.21875}$$

The above example can also be computed by multiplying the whole fraction by 4, i.e. $\dfrac{7}{32} \times \dfrac{4}{4} = \dfrac{28}{128}$ and then can be calculated in the same way as in divisor ending in 8, taking it's A.F. as $\dfrac{2.8}{13}$.

Example 12: **Convert the fraction $\dfrac{9}{52}$ to its decimal form:**

A.F. $= \dfrac{9-1}{52-2} = \dfrac{8}{50} = \dfrac{0.8}{5}$

$$\frac{0.8}{5} = 0.\,1\,\underset{3}{{}}\,7\,\underset{2}{{}^{\overline{5}}}\,3\,\underset{0}{{}^3}\,0\,\underset{3}{{}^9}\,7\,\underset{4}{{}^{\overline{5}}}\,6\,\underset{5}{{}^{\overline{3}}}\,9\,\underset{2}{{}^9}\,\underset{1}{2}$$

$$\frac{9}{52} = \mathbf{0.17307692}$$

EXERCISE 18.4

Convert the following fractions to decimals upto 5 decimal places:

1. $\dfrac{5}{22}$ 2. $\dfrac{3}{32}$ 3. $\dfrac{5}{112}$ 4. $\dfrac{9}{82}$ 5. $\dfrac{}{62}$

CASE 5: When the divisor ends in 3, 4, 6 and 7

Multiply the numerator and denominator of the fraction by a suitable number so as to convert the denominator to a digit ending in either 1, 2, 8 or 9.

Let's take some examples to understand this:

Example 13: **Convert the fraction $\dfrac{7}{23}$ to its decimal form:**

Multiplying the numerator and denominator by 3, we get the fraction as

$$\frac{7}{23} \times \frac{3}{3} = \frac{21}{69}$$

A.F. of $\dfrac{21}{69} = \dfrac{2.1}{7}$

$$\frac{2.1}{7} = 0.\,3_0\,0_3\,4_2\,3_3\,4_5\,7_5\,8_1\,2_4$$

So, $\dfrac{7}{23} = \mathbf{0.30434782}$

Example 14: **Convert the fraction $\dfrac{4}{17}$ to its decimal form:**

In this case, we can either multiply the numerator and denominator of the fraction by 7, thus making the denominator ending in 9 or we can multiply them by 3, thus making the denominator ending in 1. Both ways the answer will be same.

When Multiplied by 7

$$\frac{4}{17} \times \frac{7}{7} = \frac{28}{119}$$

A.F. $= \dfrac{28}{120} = \dfrac{2.8}{12}$

$$= 0.\,2_4\,3_6\,5_3\,2_{11}\,9_4\,4_1\,1_2\,1_9$$

$$\frac{4}{17} = \mathbf{0.23529411}$$

When multiplied by 3

$$\frac{4}{17} \times \frac{3}{3} = \frac{12}{51}$$

A.F. $= \dfrac{12-1}{51-1} = \dfrac{11}{50} = \dfrac{1.1}{5}$

$$= 0.\,2_1^7\,3_2^6\,5_1^4\,2_4^7\,9_2^0\,4_0^5\,1_0^8\,1_3^8$$

$$\frac{4}{17} = \mathbf{0.23529411}$$

So, we enjoy the flexibility of using any method in Vedic Maths.

Example 15: **Convert the fraction $\dfrac{5}{56}$ to its decimal form.**

Multiplying the numerator and denominator by 2, we get

$$\frac{5}{56} \times \frac{2}{2} = \frac{10}{112}$$

Since, the divisor is ending in 2, so subtract 1 from numerator and 2 from denominator to get the A.F.

$$\text{A.F. of } \frac{10}{112} = \frac{10-1}{12-2} = \frac{9}{110} = \frac{0.9}{11}$$

$$\text{A.F.} = \frac{0.9}{11} = 0.\,0^9\,\overline{8}^7\,\overline{9}^9\,2^5\,\overline{8}^7\,\overline{5}^1\,\overline{7}^5\,1$$

So, $\dfrac{5}{56} = \mathbf{0.08928571}$

The above explanation can be summarized in the following table:

S. No.	Divisor Ending with	Example	Multiplied By	Resulting Fraction	Auxiliary Fractions	Computation Process	Answer in Decimal Form
1.	2	$\dfrac{7}{22}$	4	$\dfrac{28}{88}$	$\dfrac{2.8}{9}$	$0.\underset{1}{3}\underset{7}{1}\underset{0}{8}\underset{7}{1}\underset{0}{8}\underset{7}{1}$	$0.3\dot{1}\dot{8}$
2.	3	$\dfrac{6}{23}$	3	$\dfrac{18}{69}$	$\dfrac{1.8}{7}$	$0.\underset{4}{2}\underset{0}{6}\underset{6}{0}\underset{4}{8}\underset{6}{6}\underset{3}{9}\underset{4}{5}\underset{3}{6}$	0.26086956
			7	$\dfrac{42}{161}$	$\dfrac{4.1}{16}$	$0.\underset{9}{2}^{7}\underset{1}{6}^{3}\underset{13}{0}^{9}\underset{11}{8}^{1}\underset{15}{6}^{3}\underset{9}{9}^{0}\underset{10}{5}^{4}\underset{8}{6}^{3}$	
3.	4	$\dfrac{7}{54}$	2	$\dfrac{14}{108}$	$\dfrac{1.4}{11}$	$0.\underset{3}{1}\underset{10}{2}\underset{5}{9}\underset{2}{6}\underset{10}{2}\underset{5}{9}\underset{2}{6}\underset{10}{2}$	$0.\dot{1}29\dot{6}$
4.	6	$\dfrac{5}{26}$	2	$\dfrac{10}{52}$	$\dfrac{0.9}{5}$	$0.\underset{4}{1}^{7}\underset{2}{9}^{9}\underset{1}{2}^{5}\underset{0}{3}^{3}\underset{3}{0}^{9}\underset{4}{7}^{5}\underset{5}{6}^{7}\underset{2}{9}$	$0.\dot{1}92307\dot{6}$
5.	7	$\dfrac{4}{27}$	3	$\dfrac{12}{81}$	$\dfrac{1.1}{8}$	$0.\underset{3}{1}^{8}\underset{6}{4}^{5}\underset{1}{8}^{1}\underset{3}{1}^{8}$	$0.\dot{1}4\dot{8}$
			7	$\dfrac{28}{189}$	$\dfrac{2.8}{19}$	$0.\underset{9}{1}\underset{15}{4}\underset{2}{8}\underset{9}{1}$	

EXERCISE 19.5

Convert the following fractions to decimals upto 8 decimal places:

1. $\dfrac{7}{27}$ 2. $\dfrac{4}{13}$ 3. $\dfrac{37}{47}$ 4. $\dfrac{11}{26}$ 5. $\dfrac{9}{16}$

GENERAL GUIDELINES

1. Find the auxiliary fraction (A.F.) of the original fraction by adding 1 to the denominator. Remove 0 from the denominator by placing a decimal point in the numerator at the appropriate position.

2. Carry out a step-by-step division by using the new divisor. Divide the numerator by the denominator of the A.F. The quotient obtained is written after the decimal with remainder if any to be placed before it to get the next gross dividend.

3. At each step, we divide the gross dividend by the new divisor, i.e. the denominator of the A.F. and write the quotient thus obtained as the next answer digit and remainder is placed before that answer digit.

4. The answer can be computed to any desired level of accuracy.

These are the general guidelines, but there are small difference in finding out A.F. and computing their gross dividend at each step when the divisors ends in different numbers like 9, 8, 1 or 2.

These differences can be summarized as below:

S.No.	When divisor Ends in	Finding A.F.	Example	Finding Gross Dividend (GD)
1.	9	Add 1 to the denominator	$\dfrac{7}{19}$ $\dfrac{7}{19+1}=\dfrac{7}{20}=\dfrac{0.7}{2}$	(Remainder Quotient) taken together
2.	8	Add 2 to the denominator	$\dfrac{7}{18}$ $\dfrac{7}{18+2}=\dfrac{7}{20}=\dfrac{0.7}{2}$	(Remainder Quotient) + Quotient
3.	1	Subtract 1 from both numerator and denominator	$\dfrac{7}{51}$ $\dfrac{7-1}{51-1}=\dfrac{6}{50}=\dfrac{0.6}{5}$	Remainder (9 – Quotient)
4.	2	Subtract 1 from the numerator and 2 from the denominator	$\dfrac{7}{52}$ $\dfrac{7-1}{52-2}=\dfrac{6}{50}=\dfrac{0.6}{5}$	Remainder [9 – (2 × Quotient)]

Note: If the numerators are same, A.F. of divisors ending in 9 and 8 are same, also for divisors ending in 1 and 2 are same, but computing gross dividend in each case is different which makes the answers altogether different.

19 Check Divisibility By Prime Number

Now, we shall learn a very interesting way of determining the divisibility of a certain given number, however long it may be, by a given divisor without actually dividing it!

The current modern maths system taught in schools deals with the method of checking divisibility of any number by simple numbers like 2, 3, 4, 5, 6, 7, 8, 9, 10, 11, 18, 22 and so on. A summary of those is given below:

Number Being Tested	Test
2	The last figure should be 0 or even
3	The sum of all digits should be divisible by 3
4	Two figure number on the end should be divisible by 4
5	The last figure should be 0 or 5
6	The number should be divisible by 2 and 3
8	Three figure number on the end should be divisible by 8
9	The sum of all digits should be divisible by 9
10	The last figure should be 0
11	The difference between the sum of digits in odd position and the sum of digits in even position should be 0 or 11 or multiple of 11
12	The number should be divisible by 3 and 4
15	The number should be divisible by 3 and 5
18	The number should be divisible by 2 and 9

When testing for divisibility by higher divisors, write the number as the product of factors which are relatively prime and check the divisibility individually by those factors.

But, what if we have to check divisibility of any given number by other prime numbers, like 7, 13, 17, 19, 23, 29, 31, 41, 53, 139, 179 and so on. There is no other option left in modern maths to check divisibility by such numbers except going through the whole division process itself.

This is where Vedic Maths provides a very unique concept of '*Osculators*' which can easily determine the divisibility by such prime numbers without actual division.

Osculators are categorized into 2 main types:

1.   Positive Osculators – when the given divisor ends in 9.

2.   Negative Osculators – when the given divisor ends in 1.

Positive Osculators:

Osculator of a number is considered positive when the number ends in 9. The formula used to find the osculator is "*one more than the one before*", i.e. increase the digit(s) before 9 by 1 and take that as the osculator of the number.

For example, Osculator of 29 is 3 because the digit before 9 of 29 is 2 and one more than 2 is 3.

Similarly, osculator of 49 is 5 because the digit before 9 in this number is 4 and one more than 4 is 5.

This can be explained in this way also.

Osculator of a number ending in 9 can simply be found by dropping the last digit 9 and increasing the previous digit by 1. E.g. for 59, drop 9 and increase 5 by one, to get 6. So the osculator of 59 is 6.

If the given number does not end in 9, but in 1, 3 or 7, we multiply it by 9, 3 or 7 respectively, to convert it to a number which ends in 9 and then compute its osculator.

For example, if the number is 13, to obtain a 9 in the end, multiply 13 by 3 to get 39.

Now by dropping 9 and increasing the previous digit 3 by 1, we get 4 as the osculator of 13, i.e. $13 \times 3 = 39$, which gives 4 as the osculator.

EXERCISE 19.1
Give the positive osculators of the following numbers:

1. 7	**2.** 89	**3.** 129	**4.** 43	**5.** 37
6. 31	**7.** 69	**8.** 139	**9.** 23	**10.** 99

Once the osculator of a number is computed, the whole process of checking the divisibility becomes very simple, and the process by which osculator serves this purpose is technically called "*osculation*".

Osculation:

Osculation involves multiplying the last digit of a number by the osculator and adding the product to the previous digit. We keep doing this till we reach to a number that we already know is divisible by the given divisor.

Lets understand this better with the following examples:

Example 1:

Check if 98 is divisible by 7.

Step 1:

First compute the osculator of 7 as
$7 \times 7 = 49$
So, Osculator = 5

Step 2:

Multiply the last digit of the number, i.e. 8 by the osculator 5, add the product 40 to the previous digit 9 and write the total 49 below the previous digit as shown:

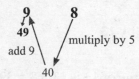

Since, 49 is divisible by 7, so **98 is divisible by 7**.

Note: *If the end result of the osculation is the divisor itself or a multiple of the divisor or a repetition of a previous result, then the given number is divisible by the given divisor.*

Example 2:

Check if 437 is divisible by 19.

Step 1:

Compute the **osculator** of 19 as **2**.

Step 2:

4   3   7

17

Multiply the last digit 7 by the osculator 2, add the resulting product 14 to previous digit 3 to get 17.

$$(7 \times 2) + 3 \, (previous\ digit)$$

(last digit)   *(osculator)*

$$= 14 + 3 = 17$$

Write the total **17** below the previous digit 3 as shown.

Step 3:

4   3   7

19   17

Since, 17 is a two digit number, so osculate it first by 2 and then add the result to 4 (previous digit), i.e.

$$[(7 \times 2) + 1] + 4 \, (previous\ digit) = 15 + 4 = 19$$
(osculation of 17)

Write **19** below 4 as shown.

Since, the end result 19 is the divisor itself, so **437 is divisible by 19.**

Example 3:

Check if 27426 is divisible by 13

Step 1:

Osculator of 13 is $13 \times 3 = 39 = 4$

Step 2:

2   7   4   2   6

           26

Multiply the last digit 6 by osculator 4 and add the product 24 to the previous digit 2 to get 26.

$(6 \times 4) + 2$ *(previous digit)* $= 24 + 2 = \mathbf{26}$

last digit   *osculator*

Write the resulting total **26** below 2 as shown.

Step 3:

2   7   4   2   6

       30   26

Osculate 26 by 4 and add the result to the previous digit 4 .

i.e. $[(6 \times 4) + 2]$ +   4

    (Osculation of 26)   *(Previous digit)*

$= 26 + 4 = \mathbf{30}$.

Write **30** below 4 as shown.

Step 4:

2   7   4   2   6

   10   30   26

Osculate 30 by 4 and add the result to the previous digit 7.

i.e. $[(0 \times 4) + 3]$ +   7

    (Osculation of 30)   *(Previous digit)*

$= 3 + 7 = \mathbf{10}$.

Write **10** below 7 as shown.

Step 5:

2   7   4   2   6

3   10   30   26

Osculate 10 by 4 and add the result to the previous digit 2 to get the final result.

i.e. $[(0 \times 4) + 1]$ +   2

    (Osculation of 10)   *(Previous digit)*

$= 1 + 2 = \mathbf{3}$.

Write **3** below 2 as shown.

Since, the final result of osculation, i.e. 3 is not divisible by 13, so 27426 is not **divisible by 13**.

**Example 4**:

Check if 191573 is divisible by 59.

Osculator of 59 is 6

1	9	1	5	7	3
59	**49**	**46**	**37**	**25**	

Step 1: $(3 \times 6) + 7$_(previous digit)_ $= 18 + 7 = $ **25**

↙ Last digit   ↘ Osculator

Step 2: $[(5 \times 6) + 2] + 5$ _(previous digit)_ $= 32 + 5 = $ **37**

(_osculation of 25_)

Step 3: $[(7 \times 6) + 3] + 1$_(previous digit)_ $= 45 + 1 = $ **46**

(_osculation of 37_)

Step 4: $[(6 \times 6) + 4] + 9$ _(previous digit)_ $= 40 + 9 = $ **49**

(_osculation of 46_)

Step 5: $[(9 \times 6) + 4] + 1$_(previous digit)_ $= 58 + 1 = $ **59**

(_osculation of 49_)

Since, the osculation result 59 is the divisor itself, so **191573 is also divisible by 59**.

Some more examples in straight steps:
Check the divisibility of:

**Example 5**:

32886 by 29

Osculator of 29 = 3

3	2	8	8	6
29	28	28	26	

Since, 29 is the divisor itself

So, **32886 is divisible by 29**.

**Example 6**:

115328 by 53

Osculator of 53 is $= 53 \times 3 = 159$
$= 16$

1	1	5	3	2	8
53	43	102	16	130	

Since, 53 is the divisor itself

So, **115328 is divisible by 53**.

Example 7:

63094821 by 79

Osculator of 79 = 8

$$\left\{\begin{array}{ccccccc} 6 & 3 & 0 & 9 & 4 & 8 & 2 & 1 \\ 13 & 70 & 38 & 64 & 76 & 9 & 10 \end{array}\right\}$$

Since, 13 is not divisible by 79,

So, **63094821 is not divisible by 79.**

Example 8:

93148 by 17

Osculator of 17 is 17 × 7 = 119 = 12

$$\left\{\begin{array}{ccccc} 9 & 3 & 1 & 4 & 8 \\ 82 & 16 & 11 & 100 \end{array}\right\}$$

Since, 82 is not divisible by 17,

So, **93148 is not divisible by 17.**

EXERCISE 19.2

Osculate the following numbers and test the divisibility of:

1. 2774 by 19   **2.** 5332 by 49   **3.** 14061 by 43

4. 21947 by 17   **5.** 83742821 by 69

Negative Osculators:

Osculator of a number is considered negative when the number ends in 1.

To get negative osculator, just drop 1 and the remaining number is taken as the osculator, e.g., Osculaor of 21 is 2, 41 is 4, 81 is 8 and 131 is 13.

If the given number ends in 3, 7 or 9, we multiply it by 7, 3 or 9 respectively, to convert it to a number which ends in 1 and then drop the 1 and find the negative osculator.

e.g. If the number is 67, to obtain 1 in the end, multiply 67 by 3 to get 201. Now by dropping 1, we get the negative osculator of 67 as 20, i.e. 67 × 3 = 201, which gives 20 as the osculator.

Similarly, negative osculator of 23 is 16 (23 × 7 = 161)

EXERCISE 19.3

Give the negative osculators of the following numbers:

1. 41   **2.** 7   **3.** 17   **4.** 71   **5.** 47

6. 37   **7.** 81   **8.** 111   **9.** 121   **10.** 13

Note: *It is called the negative osculator because it is not the process of addition, as in the case of positive osculator, but of subtraction leftwards.*

Lets understand it by the following example.

Example 9:

Check divisibility of 84651 by 21

Step 1:

Compute the **osculator** of 21 as **2**.

Step 2:

$8\ \bar{4}6\bar{5}1$

Mark all alternative digits from the second last digit (leftwards) as negative by placing a bar on the top as shown.

Step 3:

$8\ \bar{4}\ 6\ \bar{5}\ 1$

$\bar{3}$

Multiply the last digit of the number, i.e. 1 by negative osculator 2 and add the product 2 to the previous digit $\bar{5}$ to get $\bar{3}$.

$$(1\ \times\ 2) + \bar{5}\ \text{\textit{(previous digit)}} = \bar{3}$$

last digit   osculator

Write $\bar{3}$ below $\bar{5}$ as shown

Step 4:

$8\ \bar{4}\ 6\ \bar{5}\ 1$

$0\ \bar{3}$

Multiply this $\bar{3}$ by the osculator 2 and add the product $\bar{6}$ to the previous digit 6 to get 0.

Write 0 below 6 as shown;

$$(\bar{3} \times 2) + 6\ \text{\textit{(previous digit)}}\ = 0$$

Step 5:

$8\ \bar{4}\ 6\ \bar{5}\ 1$

$\bar{4}\ 0\ \bar{3}$

Multiply this 0 by the osculator 2 and add the product 0 to the previous digit $\bar{4}$ to get $\bar{4}$.

$$(0 \times 2) + \bar{4}\ \text{\textit{(previous digit)}} = \bar{4}$$

Step 6:

8 $\bar{4}$ 6 $\bar{5}$ 1   Multiply this $\bar{4}$ by the osculator 2 and add

0 $\bar{4}$ 0 $\bar{3}$ the product $\bar{8}$ to the previous digit 8 to get 0.

$$(\bar{4} \times 2) + 8 \ \textit{(previous digit)} = \mathbf{0}$$

Since, the result of osculation is 0, so **84651 is divisible by 21.**

If the result of osculation by a negative osculator is 0 or the divisor itself or the multiple of divisor, then that given number is divisible by the given divisor.

Example 10:

Check the divisibility of 58321 by 27

Step1:

Osculator of $27 = 27 \times 3 = 81$

So, **Osculator is 8.**

Step 2:

Mark the alternate digits from second last digit as negative by placing a bar on the top of the digits as shown:

5 $\bar{8}$ 3 $\bar{2}$ 1

Step 3:

Osculate the number by osculator 8 as shown below:

5 $\bar{8}$ 3 $\bar{2}$ 1

$\overline{35}$ $\bar{5}$ 51 6

(a)   (1   ×   8) + $\bar{2}$ *(previous digit)* = **6**
         last digit   osculator

(b) $(6 \times 8) + 3 = \mathbf{51}$

(c)   First osculate 51 by 8 and then add previous digit $\bar{8}$ to it, i.e

$$(1 \times 8 - 5) + \bar{8} \ \textit{(previous digit)} = \bar{5}$$
osculation of 51

(d) $(\bar{5} \times 8) + 5 \ \textit{(previous digit)} = \overline{35}$

Since, –35 is not divisible by 27.

So, **58321 is not divisible by 27.**

Some examples in straight steps:

Check the divisibility of:

Example 11: **43721 by 51**

The osculator of 51= 5

$$\left\{ \begin{array}{ccccc} 4 & \overline{3} & 7 & \overline{2} & 1 \\ 29 & 5 & 22 & 3 & \end{array} \right\}$$

29 is not divisible by 51,

So, **43721 is not divisible by 51.**

Example 12: **404395 by 31**

The osculator of 31 = 3

$$\left\{ \begin{array}{cccccc} \overline{4} & 0 & \overline{4} & 3 & \overline{9} & 5 \\ 31 & 9 & 3 & 21 & 6 & \end{array} \right\}$$

— 31 is divisible by 31,

So, **404395 is divisible by 31**.

Example 13: **442165 by 47**

47 × 3 = 141

So, osculator of 47 = 14

$$\left\{ \begin{array}{cccccc} \overline{4} & 4 & \overline{2} & 1 & \overline{6} & 5 \\ 14 & 102 & 7 & 51 & 64 & \end{array} \right\}$$

14 is not divisible by 47,

So, **442165 is not divisible by 47**

Example 14: **38573 by 17**

17 × 3 = 51

So, osculator of 17 = 5.

$$\left\{ \begin{array}{ccccc} 3 & \overline{8} & 5 & \overline{7} & 3 \\ 17 & 13 & 45 & 8 & \end{array} \right\}$$

17 is divisible by 17,

So, **38573 is divisible by 17**.

EXERCISE 19.4

Osculate the following numbers using negative osculators and test the divisibility of:

1. 6603 by 31   **2.** 11234 by 41   **3.** 42731 by 13

4. 79641 by 81   **5.** 59597 by 61

Note: *When the divisor number ends with 9, always take the positive osculator and when its ends with 1, take the negative osculator.*

But when it ends with 3 or 7, the number can be converted to a number ending in either 9 or 1 by a suitable multiplication. In few cases, osculating by both positive and negative osculators are equally simple, but in some cases, osculation with one type of osculator is much simpler than the other one.

Example 15:

Check the divisibility of 24836 by 7 *(using both the osculators)*

Positive Osculator:

osculator is $7 \times 7 = 49 = 5$

$$\begin{Bmatrix} 2 & 4 & 8 & 3 & 6 \\ 35 & 36 & 26 & 33 & \end{Bmatrix}$$

Since, 35 is divisible by 7

So, **24836 is divisible by 7**.

Negative Osculator:

osculator is $7 \times 3 = 21 = 2$

$$\begin{Bmatrix} 2 & \bar{4} & 8 & \bar{3} & 6 \\ 14 & 6 & 26 & 9 & \end{Bmatrix}$$

Since, 14 is divisible by 7.

So, **24836 is divisible by 7**.

In the above example, we saw that the positive osculator of 7 is 5 and the negative osculator of 7 is 2 and by both ways, osculation is equally easy.

Now, consider the following example:

Example 16:

Check the divisibility of 83785 by 23 *(using both the osculators)*

Positive Osculator:

osculator is $23 \times 3 = 69 = 7$

$$\begin{Bmatrix} 8 & 3 & 7 & 8 & 5 \\ 10 & 20 & 32 & 43 & \end{Bmatrix}$$

Since, 10 is not divisible by 23, so, 83785 **is not divisible by 23**.

Negative Osculator:

osculator is $23 \times 7 = 161 = 16$

$$\begin{Bmatrix} 8 & \bar{3} & 7 & \bar{8} & 5 \\ 102 & 26 & 32 & 72 & \end{Bmatrix}$$

On further osculating 102 by 16, we get the result as 22.
Since, 22 is not divisible by 23, so, 83785 **is not divisible by 23**.

In this case, osculating with the positive osculator is much simpler as compared to the negative osculator.

Note: *It has been observed that mostly numbers ending in 7 should be multiplied by 3, to get a number ending in 1, and those ending in 3 should be multiplied by 3, to get a number ending in 9, to facilitate smaller osculators.*

GENERAL GUIDELINES:

1. To check if the given number is divisible by any prime number, find the osculator of that prime number first. Osculator of a number is considered positive if number ends in 9 and negative, if it ends in 1. The procedure of finding the osculator is summarized in the table below:

S.No.	Divisor ending with	Procedure	Example	Osculator (Type)
1.	9	Drop 9 and add 1 to the previous digit	49	5 (positive)
2.	1	Drop 1 and remaining number is the osculator	41	4 (negative)
3.	3	Multiply by 3	$23 \times 3 = 69$	9 (positive)
		Multiply by 7	$23 \times 7 = 161$	16 (negative)
4.	7	Multiply by 3	$17 \times 3 = 51$	5 (negative)
		Multiply by 7	$17 \times 3 = 119$	12 (positive)

2. After finding the osculator, multiply the last digit of the dividend by the osculator and add the product to the digit prior to the last digit and write the sum below that previous digit.

3. (a) If the sum is a single digit, again multiply by osculator and add the product to the previous digit and continue doing it till we reach to a number that we already know is divisible by the given number.

    (b) If the sum is a two digit number, first osculate that number by the osculator and then add it to the previous digit and then continue.

4. In case of negative osculator, the process remains the same except that the alternate digits from the second last digit in the dividend are marked as negative. The steps are done according to the signs.

500 Years Calendar

Now, let's learn an amazing technique of mastering 500 years. calendar on your fingertips, i.e. using this technique, you can instantly tell the day on which any particular date of a given year falls.

You can amaze your friends and relatives by telling the day on which they were born on hearing their birth dates in less than 5 seconds. The technique is very useful in competitive exams, where questions related to dates and ages are to be answered.

Calculating the day of any particular date

If we observe any date, there are 4 main things – *date, month, century and year*. Each of these has different codes. The sum of all these codes helps in determining the day of the week on which any given date falls.

Let's understand it by the following example:

Example 1:

Find the day of 23rd May, 1992.

For Date: Divide the date by 7. Write the remainder as the code of the date.

$$23 \div 7 \text{ gives 2 as remainder}$$

So, code for date (23) is **2**.

For Month: Each month has a unique code. Below is the table showing codes for all 12 months.

Table 1: Months Codes

Month	Code
January	1
February	4
March	4
April	0
May	2
June	5
July	0
August	3
September	6
October	1
November	4
December	6

Code for May month = **2**

Table 2: Centuries Codes

Century	Code
1600's	6
1700's	4
1800's	2
1900's	0
2000's	6 or – 1
2100's	4

Code for century 1900 = **0**.

Table 3: Years Codes

YEAR	CODE	YEAR	CODE	YEAR	CODE	YEAR	CODE
01	1	26	4	51	0	76	4
02	2	27	5	52	2	77`	5
03	3	28	0	53	3	78	6
04	5	29	1	54	4	79	0
05	6	30	2	55	5	80	2
06	0	31	3	56	0	81	3
07	1	32	5	57	1	82	4
08	3	33	6	58	2	83	5
09	4	34	0	59	3	84	0
10	5	35	1	60	5	85	1
11	6	36	3	61	6	86	2
12	1	37	4	62	0	87	3
13	2	38	5	63	1	88	5
14	3	39	6	64	3	89	6
15	4	40	1	65	4	90	0
16	6	41	2	66	5	91	1
17	0	42	3	67	6	92	3
18	1	43	4	68	1	93	4
19	2	44	6	69	2	94	5
20	4	45	0	70	3	95	6
21	5	46	1	71	4	96	1
22	6	47	2	72	6	97	2
23	0	48	4	73	0	98	3
24	2	49	5	74	1	99	4
25	3	50	6	75	2		

Code for the year 92 = **3**.

Adding all the codes together, we get:

2	+	2	+	0	+	3	= 7
(date)		(month)		(century)		(year)	

This final sum 7 will tell the day of the week. Each day has its own code as shown in the table below:

Table 4:

Day	Code
Sunday	1
Monday	2
Tuesday	3
Wednesday	4
Thursday	5
Friday	6
Saturday	0 and 7

Since, 7 corresponds to Saturday, so the day on 23rd May, 1992 was **Saturday**.

Some more examples:

Find days on which the following dates fall:

***Example 2*:**

28th March, 1980

Date = 28 ÷ 7 gives Remainder = **0**

Month = March = **4** *(refer table 1)*

Year = 1980 = 0 + 2 = **2** *(refers tables 2 and 3)*

Adding all, we get 0 + 4 + 2 = **6**.

6 is the code corresponding to Friday.

So, 28th March, 1980 was a **Friday**.

***Example 3*:**

5th April, 2010

Date = 5 ÷ 7 gives Remainder = **5**

Month = April = 0

Year = 2010 = 6 + 5 = **11**

Total = 5 + 0 + 11 = 16

Again 16 ÷ 7 gives Remainder = **2**

2 stands for **Monday**.

Note: *When the final total is more than 7, divide it again by 7 and the remainder thus obtained corresponds to the code of the day.*

Example 4: 18th Nov, 1984

Date = 18 ÷ 7 gives Remainder = **4**

Month = Nov = **4**

Year = 1984 = 0 + 0 = **0**

Total = 4 + 4 + 0 = 8

Again 8 ÷ 7 gives Remainder = **1**

1 stands for **Sunday**.

Example 5: 15th August, 1947

1 + 3 + 0 + 2 = **6**

6 stands for **Friday**.

Example 6: 25th Oct., 1958

4 + 1 + 0 + 2 = **7**

7 stands for **Saturday**.

SPECIAL CASE

If the given year is a Leap year and the months are January or February, then reduce 1 day from the day calculated.

Example 7: 23rd Feb., 1976

2 + 4 + 0 + 4 = 10

10 ÷ 7 gives remainder as 3 and 3 stands for Tuesday.

Ideally the day should be Tuesday, but 1976 is a leap year, so as per the rule for calculating the day in the leap year in the month of January and February, we reduce one day, i.e. instead of Tuesday, the day would be Monday.

So, 23rd Feb, 1976 was a **Monday**.

Note: *As soon as you hear the months of January and February, immediately check if it is a leap year (if the given year is divisible by 4, it means its a leap year). If it is, then reduce one day from the day calculated.*

If the year is leap year, but months are from March to December, then no need for any adjustment. We make adjustment only in the months of January and February.

How to calculate year codes

Instead of referring to the table, there is a method to calculate the code for the year.

Let's find the code for the year 98:

Step 1:

Divide the year by 4
$98 \div 4$ gives Q = 24, R = 2

Step 2:

Ignore the remainder and add the quotient obtained to the year, i.e.
24 + 98 = 122

Step 3:

Divide this 122 by 7 and take the remainder obtained as code, i.e.
$122 \div 7$ gives Q = 17, R = **3**

Remainder **3** is the **code for the year 98.**

Another Method for calculating year codes

Using the fact that calendar codes repeat themselves after every 28 years, we can subtract maximum multiples of 28 (84, 56 or 28) from the given year. Divide the number obtained by 4 and add the quotient to that number itself, i.e. if the year is 98, subtracting 84 (multiple of 28) from it, we get:

98 – 84 = 14

$14 \div 4$ gives 3 as quotientSo, 14 + 3 = 17

Divide 17 by 7 and find its remainder, i.e. 3.

So, 3 is the code for 98.

This method of first subtracting the multiple of 28 from the given year, facilitates smaller number to work on, thus faster calculation.

EXERCISE 20.1

Find the day of the following dates:

1. 8th Nov., 1956   **2.** 19th Nov., 2005   **3.** 2nd Oct., 1869

4. 3rd Jan., 1984   **5.** 7th April, 2008

Some more solved examples:

Example 8:

Shiv was born on the first Monday of March 1952. Then on which date was he born?

Lets first find the day of 1st March, 1952

$$1^{st} \text{ March, } 1952$$
$$1 + 4 + 0 + 2 = 6$$

6 suggests the day is Friday.

If 1st March, 1952 was Friday, that means date on 1st Monday of March, 1952 was 4th March.

So, Shiv was born on 4th March, 1952.

Example 9:

What day of the week was 8th September, 1783?

$$8^{th} \text{ Sept. } 1783$$
$$1 + 6 + 4 + 5 = 16$$
$$16 \div 7 \text{ gives 2 as remainder}$$

2 suggests Monday.

So, 8th September, 1783 was Monday.

Example 10:

How many times will Esha's birthday fall on Monday in the year 2001 and 2002, if she was born on the 19th April?

Let's first find the day of 19th April, 2001

$$5 + 0 - 1 + 1 = 5 \text{ (Thursday)}$$

So, 19th April, 2002 would be Friday.

So, Esha's birthday will not fall on Monday in either of the year 2001 and 2002.

EXERCISE 20.2

1. Which of the following is true?

   (a) 21st February, 2001 is a Saturday.

   (b) 27th February, 1999 is a Saturday.

   (c) 23rd February, 2002 is a Sunday.

   (d) 22nd February, 1998 is a Saturday.

2. Rita is younger than Pinki by less than 7 days. Rita's birthday is on 12th October. Find Pinki's birth date, if her birthday falls on Sunday in the year 2006.

   (a) 9th October

   (b) 15th October

   (c) 16th October

   (d) 8th October

PART II :

ALGEBRA

ALGEBRAIC MULTIPLICATION

In chapter 9, we learn to multiply any two random numbers. In this chapter, we will learn how vedic maths is helpful in finding answers to multiplication of algebraic expressions; like binomials and trinomials in just one line, as compared to conventional maths where we usually do it in 4–5 steps.

For example: (x + 3) (4x − 7)

Conventional Method

$(x + 3) (4x − 7)$
$= x (4x − 7) + 3(4x − 7)$
$= [x × 4x + x × (−7)] + [3 × 4x + 3 × (−7)]$
$= (4x^2 − 7x) + (12x − 21)$
$= 4x^2 − 7x + 12x − 21$
$= 4x^2 + 5x − 21$
(5 − steps method)

Vedic Method

$(x + 3) (4x − 7)$
$4x^2 + 5x − 21$

(mental one −line method)

Formula used in vedic maths is *"vertically & crosswise"*.

Let's understand it with the help of following examples:

Example 1: **(x + 2) (3x + 4)**

Step 1:

$$\begin{array}{r} x + 2 \\ 3x + 4 \\ \hline 8 \end{array}$$

Write one binomial under the other as shown. Multiply vertically the digits in the right hand column, i.e. $2 × 4 = 8$

Step 2:

$$\begin{array}{r} x + 2 \\ 3x + 4 \\ \hline 10x + 8 \end{array}$$

Multiply crosswise and add the products, i.e. $(4 × x) + (2 × 3x) = 4x + 6x = 10x$

Step 3:

$$\begin{array}{r} x + 2 \\ 3x + 4 \\ \hline 3x^2 + 10x + 8 \end{array}$$

Multiply vertically in the left hand column, i.e. $x × 3x = 3x^2$

So, $(x + 2) (3x + 4) = 3x^2 + 10x + 8$

Since there is no carry over required in algebraic multiplication, so we can start multiplying from L.H.S. also.

Example 2: $(4x + 3)(x - 5)$

Step 1:

$$\begin{array}{r} 4x \; + \; 3 \\ \times \; x \; - \; 5 \\ \hline 4x^2 \end{array}$$

Multiply vertically in the left hand column, i.e. $4x \times x = \mathbf{4x^2}$

Step 2:

$$\begin{array}{r} 4x \; + \; 3 \\ \times \; x \; - \; 5 \\ \hline 4x^2 - 17x \end{array}$$

Multiply crosswise and add the products, i.e. $[4x \times (-5)] + [3 \times x] = -20x + 3x = \mathbf{-17x}$

Step 3:

$$\begin{array}{r} 4x \; + \; 3 \\ \times \; x \; - \; 5 \\ \hline 4x^2 - 17x - 15 \end{array}$$

Multiply vertically in the right hand column, i.e. $3 \times (-5) = \mathbf{-15}$

So, $(4x + 3)(x - 5) = 4x^2 - 17x - 15$

Note: While multiplying vertically or crosswise, terms will be multiplied along with their signs (+ or –) and calculations will be done accordingly.

Example 3: $(4x + 3y)(2x + y)$

$$\begin{array}{r} 4x \; + \; 3y \\ \times \; 2x \; + \; y \\ \hline 8x^2 + 10xy + 3y^2 \end{array}$$

Vertically left: $4x \times 2x = \mathbf{8x^2}$

Crosswise: $(4x \times y) + (2x \times 3y)$
$$= 4xy + 6xy = 10xy$$

Vertically right: $3y \times y = 3y^2$

Example 4: $(x - y)(3x - 2y)$

$$\begin{array}{r} x \; - \; y \\ \times \; 3x \; - \; 2y \\ \hline 3x^2 - 5xy + 2y^2 \end{array}$$

Vertically left: $x \times 3x = 3x^2$

Crosswise: $x(-2y) + 3x(-y)$
$$= -2xy - 3xy = -5xy$$

Vertically right: $-y \times (-2y) = 2y^2$

Example 5:   **(2x + 5) (3x – 2)**

$$2x \;+\; 5$$
$$\underline{\times \;\; 3x \;-\; 2}$$
$$6x^2 + 11x - 10$$

Vertically left: $2x \times 3x = 6x^2$

Crosswise: $2x(-2) + 3x(5)$
$$= -4x + 15x = 11x$$

Vertically right: $5 \times (-2) = -10$

Note: Though the steps are shown to make you understand the process involved, but with practice the answer can be found mentally step after step & directly written in one line.

EXERCISE 21.1

Multiply the following:

1. $(x + 1)(x + 2)$ 2. $(2x - 3)(5x + 4)$
3. $(x + 8)(3x + 11)$ 4. $(x - y)(2x - 3y)$
5. $(4a - 3b)(a + b)$ 6. $(7x + 3y)(2x + 7y)$
7. $(2x - 3y)(5x + 8y)$ 8. $(3x + 4y)(2x - 7y)$
9. $(2x + 3y)(2x + 5y)$ 10. $(9x - 7y)(2x - 3y)$

Alternate Method: *(first by the first and last by the last)*

Instead of writing one binomial under another, we can directly give the answer by doing the following steps:

Example 6:   **(x + 3) (2x + 5)**

Step 1:

$(x + 3)(2x + 5)$ Multiply 1st term of 1st binomial with 1st term of 2nd binomial, i.e. $x \times 2x = 2x^2$

Step 2:

$(x + 3)(2x + 5)$ Multiply the extreme terms and the middle terms together and add them, i.e.
$$3(2x) + 5(x) = 6x + 5x = 11x$$

Step 3:

$(x + 3)(2x + 5)$ Multiply second terms of both binomial together, i.e. $3 \times 5 = 15$

So, $(x + 3)(2x + 5) = 2x^2 + 11x + 15$

The steps can be shown as:

Step 1   Step 3

$$(x + 3)\ (2x + 5)$$

$+$

Step 2

Example 7:   **$(2x + 3)\ (x - 1)$**

Step 1   Step 3   **_Step 1:_** $2x \times x = 2x^2$

$$(2x + 3)\ (x - 1)$$

$+$ **_Step 2:_** $(3 \times x) + (2 \times x - 1) = x$

Step 2   **_Step 3:_** $3 \times (-1) = -3$

So, $(2x + 3)\ (x - 1) = 2x^2 + x - 3$

EXERCISE 21.2

Multiply the following:

1. $(4x–5y)\ (3x–2y)$ 2. $(4x–3y)\ (2x+3y)$

3. $(7x–3y)\ (4x–8y)$ 4. $(17x+3y)\ (2x–7y)$

5. $(11a–2b)\ (3a–9b)$ 6. $(3p–2q)\ (7p–8q)$

7. $(7m+4n)\ (5m–7n)$ 8. $(3x–5y)\ (6x+2y)$

9. $(x+3)\ (x+4)$ 10. $(a+2b)\ (3a+b)$

Similarly we can extend this method for multiplication of **two trinomials** also using (3×3) vertical and crosswise multiplication *(as done in chapter 9)*.

Example 8: $(2x^2 + x + 3)\ (3x^2 + 2x + 4)$

$$\begin{array}{r} 2x^2 + x + 3 \\ \times\ \ 3x^2 + 2x + 4 \\ \hline 6x^4 + 7x^3 + 19x^2 + 10x + 12 \end{array}$$

Step 1: Write one trinomial under the other as shown.

Multiply vertically on the left, i.e. $2x^2 \times 3x^2 = 6x^4$

Step 2: Multiply crosswise in the first two columns and add the products, i.e. $(2x^2 \times 2x) + (3x^2 \times x) = 4x^3 + 3x^3 = 7x^3$

Step 3: Multiply crosswise in the left and right columns and vertically in the middle column and add all the three products, i.e. $(2x^2 \times 4) + (3x^2 \times 3) + (x \times 2x)$
$= 8x^2 + 9x^2 + 2x^2 = \mathbf{19x^2}$

Step 4: Multiply crosswise in the second and last column and add the products, i.e.
$(2x \times 3) + (x \times 4) = 6x + 4x = \mathbf{10x}$

Step 5: Multiply vertically on the right, i.e. $3 \times 4 = \mathbf{12}$

So, $(2x^2 + x + 3)(3x^2 + 2x + 4) = \mathbf{6x^4 + 7x^3 + 19x^2 + 10x + 12}$

If and when a power of x is absent, it should be given a zero coefficient and steps should be carried on exactly as before.

Example 9: $\qquad (x^2 + 3x + 4)(2x^2 + 7)$

$$\begin{array}{r} x^2 + \quad 3x \ + \ 4 \\ \times \quad 2x^2 + \quad 0x \ + \ 7 \\ \hline 2x^4 + 6x^3 + 15x^2 + 21x + 28 \end{array}$$

Step 1:
$x^2 \times 2x^2 = 2x^4$

Step 2:
$(x^2 \times 0x) + (3x \times 2x^2)$
$= 0 + 6x^3 = 6x^3$

Step 3:
$(x^2 \times 7) + (2x^2 \times 4) + (3x \times 0x)$
$= 7x^2 + 8x^2 + 0 = 15x^2$

Step 4:
$(3x \times 7) + (0x \times 4) = 21x + 0 = 21x$

Step 5:
$4 \times 7 = 28$

So, $(x^2 + 3x + 4)(2x^2 + 7) = 2x^4 + 6x^3 + 15x^2 + 21x + 28$

EXERCISE 21.3

Multiply the following:

1. $(2x^2 + x + 3)(3x^2 + 2x + 4)$
2. $(x^2 - x + 5)(2x^2 + 3x - 2)$
3. $(2x^2 + 2x + 3)(5x^2 + 5x + 1)$
4. $(x^2 + 6x - 3)(2x^2 + 3x + 4)$
5. $(2x^2 + 2xy + 3y^2)(x^2 + 5xy + y^2)$

FACTORIZING QUADRATIC EXPRESSIONS

In the last chapter, we learn to multiply the two binomials in one line to get a quadratic expression, i.e. $(x + 3)(4x + 1) = 4x^2 + 13x + 3$.

Now we will see the reverse process of converting a quadratic expression, like $4x^2 + 13x + 3$, into its binomial factors, i.e. $(x + 3)(4x + 1)$. This process is called factorizing the quadratic.

In general, when we have to factorize any algebraic expression of the type $ax^2 + bx + c$, we find two numbers p and q such that:

p+q = b and **pq = ac**

For example: Let a quadratic expression be $x^2 + 5x + 6$, then factorizing it by the **conventional method**, we get

$$x^2 + 5x + 6$$
$$x^2 + (2+3)x + 6$$
$$x^2 + 2x + 3x + 6$$
$$x(x + 2) + 3(x + 2)$$
$$(x + 2)(x + 3)$$

Though it is a lengthy process, but when coefficient of x^2 is 1, as in the above case, answer can be given mentally also, immediately after splitting the middle term.

But when the first coefficient of quadratic expression is not 1, e.g. $6x^2 + 23x + 7$, one has to do all the steps to work out the answer as shown below:

$$6x^2 + 23x + 7$$
$$6x^2 + (21+2)x + 7$$
$$6x^2 + 21x + 2x + 7$$
$$3x(2x + 7) + 1(2x + 7)$$
$$(2x + 7)(3x + 1)$$

However, by **vedic method**, this factorization can also be done mentally in one go with the help of two formulae –

- *Proportionately*
- *First by the first and last by the last*

Let's understand them by the following example:

Example 1:   Factorize $x^2 + 9x + 18$

Step 1:
Look at the coefficients in the quadratic $x^2 + 9x + 18$, i.e. 1, 9 and 18.

Step 2:
Split the middle coefficient, i.e. 9 into two parts, say 3 and 6, such that $3 + 6 = 9$ and $3 \times 6 = 18$, as shown below:

$$1x^2 + 9x + 18$$

$$(3 + 6)$$

Now observe that the ratio of the first coefficient (i.e.1) to the first part (i.e.3) of the middle coefficient is 1:3, and the ratio of the second part (i.e.6) of the middle coefficient to the last coefficient (i.e.18) is 6:18. Both the ratios are equal as shown below:

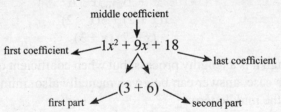

first coefficient : first part = second part : last coefficient
$$1 : 3 = 6 : 18$$

This ratio (1:3) gives us the coefficients of one of the factors as $(1x + 3)$ or $(x + 3)$.

Step 3:

To find the second factor,
(a) Divide the first term of the quadratic (x^2) by the first term of the first factor (x).

(b) Divide the last term of the quadratic (18) by the last term of the first factor (3).

i.e. quadratic $= x^2 + 9x + 18$

first factor $\quad = (x + 3)$

second factor $= \dfrac{x^2}{x} + \dfrac{18}{3} = x + 6$

Note: The middle coefficient 9 could also have been split as 6+3

$$1x^2 + 9x + 18$$

$$1:6 \quad 3:18$$

This ratio 1:6 gives the first factor as $(x + 6)$ and on dividing

gives the second factor as $\dfrac{x^2}{x} + \dfrac{18}{6} = (x + 3)$

So, the order of the parts does not affect the final answer.

So, $x^2 + 9x + 18 = (x + 3)(x + 6)$

Example 2: $\qquad$ **$6x^2 + 11x + 3$**

Step 1:

Coefficients are 6, 11 and 3.

Split the middle coefficient 11 into 9 and 2, so as to obtain two equal ratios.

$$6x^2 + 11x + 3$$

$$9 \quad 2$$

$$6:9 = 2:3$$

This ratio (2:3) gives the first factor as $(2x + 3)$

Step 2:

Quadratic $= 6x^2 + 11x + 3$

First factor $= (2x + 3)$

Second factor $= \dfrac{6x^2}{2x} + \dfrac{3}{3} = (3x + 1)$

So, $6x^2 + 11x + 3 = (2x + 3)(3x + 1)$

Example 3: $8x^2 - 22x + 5$

Step 1:

Splitting middle coefficient (–22), we get

$8x^2 - 22x + 5$

$8 : -20 \quad -2 : 5$

Ratio = $2 : -5$

First factor = $(2x - 5)$

Step 2:

Second factor = $\dfrac{8x^2}{2x} + \dfrac{5}{-5} = (4x - 1)$

So, $8x^2 - 22x + 5 = (2x - 5)(4x - 1)$

Note: With little practice of splitting in mind, you will be able to work out the factors mentally & directly write the answer as shown in given solved examples.

Example 4: $4x^2 + 12x + 5$

               10   2   *Ratio* = $2 : 5$

        $(2x + 5)(2x + 1)$

Example 5: $3x^2 - 7x + 2$

           –6   –1   *Ratio* = $1 : -2$

       $(x - 2)(3x - 1)$

Example 6: $12x^2 + 13x - 4$

          –3   +16   *Ratio* = $4 : -1$

      $(4x - 1)(3x + 4)$

COMPARISON

Vedic Method	*Conventional Method*

$7x^2 + 19xy - 6y^2$ $7x^2 + 19xy - 6y^2$

   21 –2 $7x^2 + (21 - 2)xy - 6y^2$

$(x + 3y)(7x - 2y)$ $7x^2 + 21xy - 2xy - 6y^2$

                                   $7x(x + 3y) - 2y(x + 3y)$

                                   $(x + 3y)(7x - 2y)$

You have to split the middle coefficient in both methods, but after the splitting part, vedic method is shorter and straight as compared to the conventional method.

Some more solved examples:

Example 7:

$$3x^2 + 13x - 30 = (x + 6)(3x - 5)$$

     18 , –5

Example 8:

$$12x^2 + 5x - 2 = (3x + 2)(4x - 1)$$

     8 , –3

Example 9:

$$6x^2 + 13x + 6 = (2x + 3)(3x + 2)$$

     9 , 4

Example 10:

$$12x^2 - 16xy - 3y^2 = (2x - 3y)(6x + y)$$

     –18 , +2

Example 11:

$$2a^2 + 9ab + 10b^2 = (a + 2b)(2a + 5b)$$

     4 , 5

Checking of Factorization

This checking method is the same as digit sum checking method, as done in *chapter 6*.

We apply the formula, *"The product of the sum of the coefficients in the factors is equal to the sum of the coefficients in the product"*.

Example 12:

$$(x + 2)(x + 3) = x^2 + 5x + 6$$
$$(1 + 2)(1 + 3) = 1 + 5 + 6$$
$$3 \times 4 = 12$$
$$12 = 12$$

Thus, we can say that the factorization is correct.

EXERCISE 22.1

Factorize the following:

1. $x^2 + 6x + 5$
2. $x^2 + 5x + 6$
3. $x^2 + 7x + 12$
4. $x^2 - 8x + 12$
5. $4x^2 + 12x + 9$
6. $2x^2 - 11x + 15$
7. $5x^2 + 24xy - 5y^2$
8. $3x^2 - 14xy + 8y^2$
9. $2x^2 - 7xy + 6y^2$
10. $x^2 - xy - 6y^2$

FACTORIZATION OF HARDER QUADRATICS

When we have to factorize the homogenous quadratics like

$2x^2 + 3y^2 + 21z^2 + 7xy + 16yz + 17zx$, then finding the ratios of the coefficients of the various powers of various variables is quite difficult and the whole process is cumbersome. But vedic sub sutra *"By Alternate Elimination and Retention"* removes the whole difficulty and makes the factorization of a quadratic of this type as easy and simple as we have learnt earlier in case of simple quadratic.

The procedure can be understood by the following example:

Example 13:

$$2x^2 + 3y^2 + 21z^2 + 7xy + 16yz + 17zx$$

Step 1:

    (a) We first eliminate z by putting $z=0$ and retain only x and y, so we get the expression (E_1) as:

$$\text{when } z=0, \ E_1 = 2x^2 + 7xy + 3y^2$$

    (b) Factorizing the resulting quadratic, we get the factors as:

$$2x^2 + 7xy + 3y^2 = (x + 3y)(2x + y)$$

Step 2:

    Similarly, now eliminate y and retain only x and z and factorize the resulting quadratic in x and z; i.e.

$$\text{when } y = 0, \text{ we get } E_2 = 2x^2 + 17zx + 21z^2$$
$$\text{and factors as } (x + 7z)(2x + 3z)$$

Step 3:

    With these two sets of factors, we fill in the gaps which we ourselves have created by eliminating z and y respectively and we get the real factors of the given expression as shown below:

First set of factors $= (x + 3y)(2x + y)$

Second set of factors $= (x + 7z)(2x + 3z)$

Filling in the gaps, we get $(x + 3y + 7z)(2x + y + 3z)$

Example 14:

$$2x^2 + 3y^2 - z^2 + 5xy - 2yz - xz$$

when $z = 0$, expression $(E_1) = 2x^2 + 5xy + 3y^2$

$$= (x + y)(2x + 3y)$$

when $y = 0$, expression $(E_2) = 2x^2 - xz - z^2$

$$= (x - z)(2x + z)$$

∴ Filling in the gaps, we get the final factors as:

$$(x + y - z)(2x + 3y + z)$$

Note: We could also get one set of factors by eliminating x and retaining only y and z. That would not, however have any effect on the final answer.

Let's understand it by eliminating x instead of z in the above example only:

$$2x^2 + 3y^2 - z^2 + 5xy - 2yz - xz$$

when $x = 0$, expression $(E_1) = 3y^2 - 2yz - z^2$

$$= (y - z)(3y + z)$$

when $y = 0$, expression $(E_2) = 2x^2 - xz - z^2$

$$= (x - z)(2x + z)$$

∴ Filling in the gaps, we get the final factors as:

$$(x + y - z)(2x + 3y + z)$$

So, when 3 variables x, y, z are there, only two eliminations will help out finding the factors of the given quadratic, thus making the whole procedure short and simple.

EXERCISE 22.2

Factorize the following:

1. $x^2 + 2y^2 + 3xy + 2xz + 3yz + z^2$

2. $x^2 - y^2 - 2yz - z^2$

3. $2x^2 + 2y^2 + 5xy + 7xz + 5yz + 3z^2$

4. $3x^2 + y^2 - 2z^2 - 4xy - xz - yz$

5. $2x^2 + 6y^2 + 3z^2 + 7xy + 11yz + 7zx$

▌APPLICATION IN WORD PROBLEMS

Q1. Divide 12 into two parts such that the sum of their squares is 74.

Solution:

Let the required parts be x and $(12 - x)$

Then, $x^2 + (12 - x)^2 = 74$

$$x^2 + 144 + x^2 - 24x = 74$$
$$2x^2 - 24x + 70 = 0$$
$$x^2 - 12x + 35 = 0$$
$$(x - 7)(x - 5) = 0$$
$$x = 7, 5$$

So, required **parts are 7 and 5**.

Q2. The age of a man is twice the square of the age of his son. Eight years hence, the age of the man will be 4 years more than three times the age of his son. Find their present ages.

Solution:
Let the present age of son be x years
Then the present age of father is $(2x^2)$ years
$$2x^2 + 8 = 3(x + 8) + 4$$
$$2x^2 + 8 = 3x + 24 + 4$$
$$2x^2 - 3x - 20 = 0$$
$$(x - 4)(2x + 5) = 0$$
$$x = 4, \frac{-5}{2}$$

$\therefore x = 4$ *(as age cannot be negative)*
$\therefore$ Son's present age is 4 years
and Father's age is $(2 \times 4^2) = 32$ years

Q3. The hypotenuse of a right-angled triangle is 6cm more than twice the shortest side. If the third side is 2cm less than the hypotenuse, find the sides of the triangle.

Solution:
Let the shortest side of the triangle be x cm
Then, the hypotenuse $= (2x + 6)$ cm
and the third side $= (2x + 6) - 2 = (2x + 4)$cm

By Pythagoras' Theorem, we have
$$(2x + 6)^2 = (2x + 4)^2 + x^2$$
$$4x^2 + 24x + 36 = 4x^2 + 16x + 16 + x^2$$
$$x^2 - 8x - 20 = 0$$
$$(x - 10)(x + 2) = 0$$
$$x = 10, -2$$
$\therefore x = 10$ *(since, side of a triangle is never negative)*
Thus, **shortest side** $= 10$cm
   hypotenuse $= (2 \times 10 + 6) = 26$cm
   third side $= 24$cm

LINEAR EQUATIONS IN ONE VARIABLE

Vedic mathematics provides us with many simple formulae for solving different types of equations. Instead of going through long process of opening brackets, doing multiplications, changing sides and then finding the solution of an equation, answer can be directly computed in one line using these simple formulae.

The formula used is *"Transpose and apply"*.

Though the applications of this formula are numerous and splendidly useful, here we will learn its application in four major common types of equations:

TYPE – I:

When the equation is of type:

$$ax + b = cx + d$$

where, a and c are coefficients of x,

and b and d are independent terms, then x can be equated as follows:

$$x = \frac{d-b}{a-c}$$

Example 1:

$$\underset{a \quad\; b \quad\; c \quad\; d}{2x + 3 = x + 9}$$

$$x = \frac{9-3}{2-1} = 6$$

Example 2:

$$17x - 13 = 13x + 3$$

$$x = \frac{3-(-13)}{17-13} = \frac{16}{4} = 4$$

EXERCISE 23.1

Solve the following:

1. $6x - 5 = 3x + 10$

2. $2x + 6 = 3x - 2$

3. $10x + 1 = 25 - 2x$

4. $3y - 4 = 2y + 1$

5. $2x + 7 = 18 - 9x$

TYPE – II:

$$(x + a)(x + b) = (x + c)(x + d)$$
$$x^2 + ax + bx - cx - dx = cd - ab$$
$$x(a + b - c - d) = cd - ab$$
$$x = \frac{cd - ab}{a + b - c - d}$$

Mostly the student will go through this long process needlessly, but with practice, one should be able to assimilate and assume the whole of this and do it all mentally in a single operation as:

$$x = \frac{cd - ab}{a + b - c - d}$$

Example 3:

$$\underset{a}{(x + 2)}\underset{b}{(x + 5)} = \underset{c}{(x + 1)}\underset{d}{(x + 4)}$$

then, $x = \dfrac{1 \times 4 - 2 \times 5}{2 + 5 - 1 - 4} = \dfrac{4 - 10}{2} = \dfrac{-6}{2} = -3$

Some more solved examples:

Example 4:

$$(x + 1)(x + 2) = (x - 3)(x - 4)$$

$$x = \frac{12 - 2}{1 + 2 + 3 + 4} = \frac{10}{10} = 1$$

Example 5:

$$(x + 7)(x + 9) = (x - 8)(x - 11)$$

$$x = \frac{88 - 63}{7 + 9 + 8 + 11} = \frac{25}{35} = \frac{5}{7}$$

Example 6:

$$(x - 6)(x + 7) = (x + 3)(x - 11)$$

$$x \frac{-33 + 42}{-6 + 7 - 3 + 11} = \frac{9}{9} = 1$$

EXERCISE 23.2

Solve the following:

1. $(x - 3)(x - 5) = (x - 2)(x - 4)$

2. $(x + 4)(x - 2) = (x - 4)(x + 1)$

3. $(x - 10)(x - 12) = (x - 1)(x - 20)$

4. $(x - 5)(x + 2) = (x + 3)(x + 1)$

5. $(x - 8)(x + 5) = (x - 1)(x - 2)$

TYPE – III:

$$\frac{ax + b}{cx + d} = \frac{p}{q}$$

After all the cross multiplication and transpositions, we get:

$$x = \frac{pd - bq}{aq - cp}$$

Example 7:

$$\frac{x - 5}{3x + 2} = \frac{2}{23}$$

$$x = \frac{4 + 115}{23 - 6} = \frac{119}{17} = 7$$

Example 8:

$$\frac{2x-3}{3x-2} = \frac{5}{6}$$

$$x = \frac{-10+18}{12-15} = \frac{8}{-3}$$

EXERCISE 23.3

Solve the following:

1. $\dfrac{x+2}{x+1} = \dfrac{5}{3}$ 2. $\dfrac{x+3}{x+1} = \dfrac{6}{5}$ 3. $\dfrac{x-2}{x-5} = 4$

4. $\dfrac{x-1}{x+1} = \dfrac{1}{2}$ 5. $\dfrac{x+6}{x+2} = 2$

TYPE – IV:

$$\frac{m}{x+a} + \frac{n}{x+b} = 0$$

After all the LCM's, cross multiplications and the transpositions, we get:

$$x = \frac{-mb - na}{m + n}$$

Example 9:

$$\frac{1}{x+3} + \frac{7}{x+11} = 0$$

$$x = \frac{-11 - 21}{1 + 7} = \frac{-32}{8} = -4$$

Example 10:

$$\frac{2}{x+5} + \frac{3}{x+2} = 0$$

$$x = \frac{-4 - 15}{2 + 3} = \frac{-19}{5}$$

Formulae for finding solutions for four types of equations can be summarized as:

Types	Equation format	Value of x
Type I	$ax + b = cx + d$	$x = \dfrac{d - b}{a - c}$
Type II	$(x + a)(x + b) = (x + c)(x + d)$	$x = \dfrac{cd - ab}{a + b - c - d}$
Type III	$= \dfrac{ax + b}{cx + d} = \dfrac{p}{q}$	$x = \dfrac{pd - bq}{aq - cp}$
Type IV	$\dfrac{m}{x + a} + \dfrac{n}{x + b} = 0$	$x = \dfrac{-mb - na}{m + n}$

EXERCISE 23.4

Solve the following equations using an appropriate formula:

1. $5x + 3 = 3x + 11$

2. $2x + 7 = 5x - 11$

3. $(x + 4)(x + 15) = (x + 5)(x + 3)$

4. $(x - 7)(x - 9) = (x - 3)(x - 2)$

5. $\dfrac{2}{3} \quad \dfrac{1}{4} \quad \dfrac{4}{5}$

6. $\dfrac{x - 6}{2x + 3} = \dfrac{1}{4}$

7. $\dfrac{6}{x - 2} + \dfrac{3}{x + 5} = 0$

8. $\dfrac{7}{x + 5} + \dfrac{2}{x - 3} = 0$

9. $(x + 3)(x + 15) = (x + 9)(x + 5)$

10. $\dfrac{1}{x + 2} + \dfrac{1}{x + 3} = 0$

LINEAR EQUATIONS (Special Types)

There are several special types of linear equations which can be solved practically at one sight with the help of a special formula called *"samuccaya"*.

"Samuccaya" merely says: "when the samuccaya is the same, equate it to zero". *"Samuccaya"* is a technical term which has several meaning in different contexts and we will try to understand them one by one in each of the special types of equations.

TYPE I: Samuccaya as a common factor

Here samuccaya means a term which occurs as a common factor in all the terms concerned. So, if there is a common factor in all the terms on both sides, then that factor is equated to zero.

Example 1:

$$3x + 4x = 7x + 7x$$

Since x is a common factor in all terms on both sides,

So, $x = 0$

Example 2:

$$107(x + 7) = 97(x + 7)$$

Since, $(x + 7)$ is a common factor on both sides,

So, $x + 7 = 0$

∴ $x = -7$

Example 3:

$$3(x + 5) + 6(x + 5) = 7(x + 5)$$

Since $(x + 5)$ is a common factor on both sides,

So, $x + 5 = 0$

∴ $x = -5$

EXERCISE 24.1

Solve the following:

1. $7x + 3x = 4x + 5x$

2. $3(x - 1) = x - 1$

3. $4(x - 2) = 7(x - 2)$

4. $(x - 3)(x - 3) = 3(x - 3)$

5. $4x + 5x = 2x$

TYPE II: Samuccaya as a product of the independent terms

When the products of the independent terms are equal on both sides, equate it to zero.

Example 4:

$$(x + 7)(x + 9) = (x + 3)(x + 21)$$
$$7 \times 9 = 3 \times 21$$
$$63 = 63$$

So, $x = 0$

Example 5:

$$(x - 9)(x - 8) = (x - 18)(x - 4)$$
$$-9 \times -8 = -18 \times -4$$
$$72 = 72$$

So, $x = 0$

Example 6:

$$(x + 1)(x + 2)(x + 3) = (x + 1)^2(x + 6)$$
$$1 \times 2 \times 3 = 1^2 \times 6$$
$$6 = 6$$

So, $x = 0$

Also, by type I, since $(x + 1)$ is common factor on both the sides, so, $x + 1 = 0$

i.e. $x = -1$

EXERCISE 24.2

Solve the following:_

1. $(x+4)(x+6) = (x+3)(x+8)$

2. $(x+1)(x+9) = (x+3)^2$

3. $(x+6)(x-3) = (x+2)(x-9)$

4. $(x+3)(x-4) = (x-2)(x+6)$

5. $(x+7)(x+6) = (x+3)(x+14)$

TYPE III: Samuccaya as the sum of the denominators of two fractions having the same numerical numerators

When the two fractions have the same numerical numerators, samuccaya says to equate the sum of the denominators to zero.

Example 7:

$$\frac{1}{3x-1} + \frac{1}{2x-1} = 0$$

Since, the numerators are same, so the sum of denominators = 0

$$(3x-1) + (2x-1) = 0$$
$$5x - 2 = 0$$
$$x = \frac{2}{5}$$

Example 8:

$$\frac{3}{x-4} + \frac{3}{3x-8} = 0$$

Since, the numerators are same, so the sum of denominators = 0.

$$x - 4 + 3x - 8 = 0$$
$$x = \frac{12}{4}$$
$$x = 3$$

EXERCISE 24.3

Solve the following:

1. $\dfrac{2}{2x-1}+\dfrac{2}{x+1}=0$

2. $\dfrac{x}{x+3}+\dfrac{x}{x+4}=0$

3. $\dfrac{3x}{x-7}+\dfrac{3x}{x+4}=0$

4. $\dfrac{1}{2x+1}+\dfrac{1}{3x-4}=0$

5. $\dfrac{5}{7x-3}+\dfrac{5}{x+11}=0$

TYPE IV: Samuccaya as the sum of numerators and the sum of denominators

When the sum of the numerators $(N_1 + N_2)$ is equal to the sum of the denominators $(D_1 + D_2)$, then equate the sum to zero.

$$N_1 + N_2 = D_1 + D_2 = 0$$

Example 9:

$$\frac{2x+9}{2x+7}=\frac{2x+7}{2x+9}$$

Here $N_1 + N_2$ = sum of numerators = $4x + 16$

and $D_1 + D_2$ = sum of denominators = $4x +16$

Since, $N_1 + N_2 = D_1 + D_2 = 4x +16$

So, by the application of samuccaya, sum = 0

$$4x + 16 = 0$$

$$x = -4$$

So, we see that no laborious cross multiplications of N_1 by D_2 and N_2 by D_1 and transpositions, etc. are required in the vedic method.

Example 10:

$$\frac{2x-3}{2x-5}=\frac{4x-9}{4x-7}$$

Since the total of numerators and denominators are both $(6x -12)$,

$$\text{so, } 6x -12 = 0$$

$$x = 2$$

Note: If in the algebraic total, there be a numerical factor, that should be removed.

Example 11:

$$\frac{2x+13}{x+7} = \frac{6x+35}{3x+17}$$

Here we have $N_1 + N_2 = 8x + 48 = 8(x+6)$

and $D_1 + D_2 = 4x + 24 = 4(x+6)$

Removing the numerical factor, we get the sum $(x+6)$ for both.

So, $x + 6 = 0$

and $x = -6$

EXERCISE 24.4

Solve the following:

1. $\dfrac{2x+1}{3x+6} = \dfrac{2x+7}{x+2}$

2. $\dfrac{3x-3}{x+1} = \dfrac{2x+1}{4x-3}$

3. $\dfrac{3x+4}{6x+7} = \dfrac{5x+8}{2x+5}$

4. $\dfrac{5x+12}{5x+7} = \dfrac{3x+4}{3x+9}$

5. $\dfrac{7x+4}{4x+3} = \dfrac{2x+5}{5x+6}$

Samuccaya in case of quadratic equations:

In case of last three examples, it can be observed that the cross multiplication of the coefficients of x gives us the same coefficient for x^2, indicating the equation to be linear. But when the cross multiplication of LHS and RHS gives the different coefficient of x^2, this reveals that the equation is not linear, but quadratic.

That means there will be two roots of the equation.

The first root will be found as earlier:

$$N_1 + N_2 = D_1 + D_2 = 0$$

For the second root, we will take into account the difference between the numerator and the denominator on each side and if they are equal, equate that difference to zero.

$$N_1 - D_1 = N_2 - D_2 = 0$$

Example 11:

$$\frac{2x-3}{x+4} = \frac{x-9}{2x-16}$$

Since, mental cross multiplication reveals that the x^2 coefficient on LHS and RHS are 4 and 1 respectively. So it is a quadratic equation and we will have two roots for the equation.

First Root:

$N_1 + N_2 = D_1 + D_2 = 3x - 12$

So, $3x - 12 = 0$

and $x = 4$

Second Root:

We see that $N_1 - D_1 = N_2 - D_2 = x - 7$

So, $x - 7 = 0$

and $x = 7$

So, the two roots are $x = 4$ and $x = 7$.

We see that we have solved a quadratic equation at mere sight without going into long cross multiplications and transpositions.

TYPE V: Samuccaya as the sum or total of denominators on both sides

When the sum or total of denominators on LHS = the sum of the denominators on RHS, other elements being equal, then we equate the sum to zero.

$$D_1 + D_2 = D_3 + D_4 = 0$$

Example 12:

$$\frac{1}{x-7}+\frac{1}{x-9}=\frac{1}{x-6}+\frac{1}{x-10}$$

Here, on LHS, $D_1 + D_2 = x - 7 + x - 9 = 2x - 16$

on RHS, $D_3 + D_4 = x - 6 + x - 10 = 2x - 16$

Since, $D_1 + D_2 = D_3 + D_4 = 2x - 16$

so, according to vedic formula:

$2x - 16 = 0$

$x = 8$

Example 13:

$$\frac{1}{x-7}+\frac{1}{x-4}=\frac{1}{x-5}+\frac{1}{x-6}$$

$D_1 + D_2 = D_3 + D_4 = 2x - 11$

So, $2x - 11 = 0$

$$x = \frac{11}{2}$$

EXERCISE 24.5

Solve the following:

1. $\dfrac{1}{x+5}+\dfrac{1}{x+11}=\dfrac{1}{x+4}+\dfrac{1}{x+12}$

2. $\dfrac{1}{x-7}+\dfrac{1}{x+10}=\dfrac{1}{x+12}+\dfrac{1}{x-9}$

3. $\dfrac{1}{x-8}+\dfrac{1}{x-9}=\dfrac{1}{x-5}+\dfrac{1}{x-12}$

4. $\dfrac{1}{x+12}+\dfrac{1}{x-3}=\dfrac{1}{x-6}+\dfrac{1}{x+15}$

5. $\dfrac{1}{x+2}+\dfrac{1}{x-7}=\dfrac{1}{x-10}+\dfrac{1}{x+5}$

SUMMARY

Types	Samuccaya as	Value of x
I.	Common factor	Factor = 0
II	Product of independent term	Variable (x) = 0
III	Sum of denominators of 2 fractions having same numerator	Sum of denominators = 0
IV	Sum of numerators and sum of denominators	$N_1 + N_2 = D_1 + D_2 = 0$
	in quadratic equation for second root	$N_1 - D_1 = N_2 - D_2 = 0$
V	Sum of denominators on both sides	$D_1 + D_2 = D_3 + D_4 = 0$

APPLICATION IN WORD PROBLEMS

Q.1   36 pens and 24 pencils together cost ₹ 702. While 24 pens and 36 pencils together cost ₹ 558. Find the cost of a pen and that of a pencil.

Solution:

Let the cost of one pen be ₹ x
and the cost of one pencil be ₹ y

Then, $36x + 24y = 702$ .... (i)
          $24x + 36y = 558$ .... (ii)

On Adding (i) and (ii), we get:
          $60x + 60y = 1260$
          $x + y = 21$ .... (iii)

On Subtracting (ii) from (i), we get:
          $12x - 12y = 144$
          $x - y = 12$ .... (iv)

Adding (iii) and (iv), we get:
$$2x = 33$$
$$x = \frac{33}{2} = 16.5$$

Substituting value of x in (iii), we get:
$$y = 21 - 16.5 = 4.5$$

$\therefore$ cost of each **pen** = ₹ **16.50**

and cost of each **pencil** = ₹ **4.50**

Q.2 The monthly income of A and B are in the ratio 8:7 and their expenditures are in the ratio 19:16. If each saves ₹ 500 per month, find the monthly income of each.

Solution:

Let the monthly income of A and B be ₹ 8x and ₹ 7x respectively. And let their expenditure be ₹ 19x and ₹ 16y respectively.

Then, $8x - 19y = 5000$
and $7x - 16y = 5000$

$$x = \frac{-19 \times 5000 + 16 \times 5000}{-19 \times 7 + 16 \times 8}$$

$$= \frac{-15000}{-5} = 3000$$

Monthly income of **A** = 8 × 3000 = ₹ **24000**
Monthly income of **B** = 7 × 3000 = ₹ **21000**

EXERCISE 24.6 (MIXED TYPES)

Solve the following equations using an appropriate application of samuccaya:

1. $(x - 1) = 3(x - 1) + 2(x - 1)$

2. $(x + 3)(x - 4) = (x - 2)(x + 6)$

3. $\dfrac{1}{2x + 1} + \dfrac{1}{3x + 2} =$

4. $\dfrac{5}{2x + 3} + \dfrac{5}{9 - 5x} = 0$

5. $\dfrac{5x + 11}{5x + 14} = \dfrac{3x + 5}{3x + 2}$

6. $\dfrac{3x + 4}{6x + 7} = \dfrac{5x + 6}{2x + 3}$

7. $\dfrac{3x + 4}{6x + 7} = \dfrac{x + 1}{2x + 3}$

8. $\dfrac{2x + 1}{x + 2} = \dfrac{2x - 3}{3x - 4}$

9. $\dfrac{x + 2}{2x + 1} = \dfrac{x + 1}{2x + 5}$

10. $\dfrac{1}{2x + 9} + \dfrac{1}{2x + 3} = \dfrac{1}{2x + 5} + \dfrac{1}{2x + 7}$

SIMULTANEOUS LINEAR EQUATIONS

Simultaneous linear equations are a set of equations having two variables, say x and y. Both the equations are solved together to get the values of the variables x and y. Mostly students solve these kind of equations using substitution or elimination method.

In elimination method they multiply each equation by a suitable number so that the coefficients of either x or y become the same in both the equations, which can then be eliminated by addition or subtraction, leaving a single equation in the other variable. Solving this resulting equation we get the value of one variable, which on substitution gives the value of other variable.

Conventional Method:

__Example 1:__

Solve for x and y:

$$2x + 3y = 17$$
$$3x - 2y = 6$$

The given equations are:

$$2x + 3y = 17 \qquad \qquad \dots (i)$$
$$3x - 2y = 6 \qquad \qquad \dots (ii)$$

Multiplying eq.(i) by 3 and eq.(ii) by 2, we get:

$$6x + 9y = 51 \qquad \qquad \dots (iii)$$
$$6x - 4y = 12 \qquad \qquad \dots (iv)$$

Subtracting (iv) from (iii), we get:

$$13y = 39$$
$$y = 3$$

Substituting the value of $y = 3$, in (i), we get:

$$2x + 3 \times 3 = 17$$

$$2x = 17 - 9 = 8$$

$$x = 4$$

So, $x = 4$ and $y = 3$

This method is very lengthy. Also, when the coefficients of x and y are big, then it becomes very difficult to equate them by multiplying them with suitable numbers.

The current method of cross multiplication taught in schools is a good and short method of solving simultaneous linear equations, but the major drawback of this method is that many-a-times students sometimes get confused over (+) and (−) sign.

The vedic sutra *"Transpose and apply"* enables student to give the correct answer easily by a small mental calculation.

Vedic Method:

Example 2:

$$2x + 3y = 17$$

$$3x - 2y = 6$$

The values of x and y in the form of $\dfrac{\text{numerator}}{\text{denominator}}$ can be directly found through the following steps:

Step 1:

For calculating the value of x, we start with the y coefficient and cross multiply with the independent terms:

$$2x + 3y = 17$$
$$3x - 2y = 6$$

Numerator is obtained by cross multiplying (3×6) and subtracting from it the cross product of (-2×17) as shown by the arrows in the diagram above.

$$\textbf{Numerator} = (3 \times 6) - (-2 \times 17)$$

$$= 18 + 34 = 52$$

Step 2:

Denominator is obtained by cross multiplying (3×3) and subtracting from it the cross product of (-2×2) as shown below:

$$2x + 3y = 17$$

$$3x - 2y = 6$$

Denominator $= (3 \times 3) - (-2 \times 2)$

$$= 9 + 4 = 13$$

So value of $x = \dfrac{\text{Numerator}}{\text{Denominator}} = \dfrac{52}{13} = \mathbf{4}$

Step 3:

For calculating value of y, substitute value of x in equation $2x+3y=17$

$$2 \times 4 + 3y = 17$$

$$3y = 17 - 8 = 9$$

$$y = \mathbf{3}$$

So, $x = \mathbf{4}$, $y = \mathbf{3}$.

Note: While calculating both numerator and denominator, we started with the y-coefficient of the first equation.

<u>***Example 3:***</u>

$$3x + 5y = 19$$

$$2x + 3y = 12$$

Value of $x = \dfrac{\text{Numerator}}{\text{Denominator}}$

Numerator	Denominator
$3x + 5y = 19$	$3x + 5y = 19$
$2x + 3y = 12$	$2x + 3y = 12$
$(5 \times 12) - (3 \times 19)$	$(5 \times 2) - (3 \times 3)$
$60 - 57 = 3$	$10 - 9 = 1$

So, $x = \dfrac{3}{1} = 3$

Now, substituting the value of x, we get:

$3x + 5y = 19$

$3(3) + 5y = 19$

$5y = 10$

$y = 2$

So, $x = 3, y = 2$

Example 4:

$$10x + 3y = 75$$

$$6x - 5y = 11$$

$$x = \frac{(3 \times 11) - (-5 \times 75)}{(3 \times 6) - (-5 \times 10)}$$

$$= \frac{33 + 375}{18 + 50} = \frac{408}{68}$$

$$= 6$$

Substituting the value of x, we get:

$6x - 5y = 11$

$6(6) - 5y = 11$

$$y = \frac{11 - 36}{-5} = \frac{-25}{-5} = 5$$

So, $x = 6, y = 5$

We can also calculate the value of y first and substitute its value to get the value of x.

Example 5:

$$2x + 3y = 13$$

$$5x + 2y = 16$$

Step 1:

For finding the value of y, we start with cross multiplication of coefficient of x and independent terms. For numerator, cross multiply (13×5) and subtract from it the cross product of (16×2), i.e.

$$2x + 3y = 13$$

$$5x + 2y = 16$$

Numerator $= (13 \times 5) - (16 \times 2)$

$$= 65 - 32 = 33$$

Step 2:

Denominator is obtained by the same cross multiplication and subtraction, as done in case of finding value for x, i.e.

$$2x + 3y = 13$$

$$5x + 2y = 16$$

Denominator $= (3 \times 5) - (2 \times 2) = 15 - 4 = 11$

So, $y = \dfrac{\text{Numerator}}{\text{Denominator}} = \dfrac{33}{11} = 3$

Step 3:

Substituting the value of y in $2x + 3y = 13$, we get:

$$2x + 3(3) = 13$$

$$2x = 13 - 9 = 4$$

$$x = 2$$

So, $x = 2$ and $y = 3$.

Steps can be memorized with the help of an arrow diagram shown below:

Value of x:

Numerator	Denominator
$2x + 3y = 17$ $(-)$ $3x - 2y = 6$	$2x + 3y = 17$ $(-)$ $3x - 2y = 6$
$(3 \times 6) - (17 \times -2)$ $= 18 + 34$ $= 52$	$(3 \times 3) - (2 \times -2)$ $= 9 + 4$ $= 13$

$$\therefore x = \frac{\text{Numerator}}{\text{Denominator}} = \frac{52}{13} = 4$$

<u>Note:</u>

1. The flow of direction of arrows indicates the sequence of the operations to be done.

2. The arrow diagram of denominator is just the opposite or mirror image of arrow diagram of numerator, both arrows starting from the y coefficient of the first equation.

3. The coefficients will be multiplied with signs intact.

Value of y:

Numerator	Denominator
$2x + 3y = 17$ (−) $3x - 2y = 6$ $(17 \times 3) - (2 \times 6)$ $= 51 - 12$ $= 39$	$2x + 3y = 17$ (−) $3x - 2y = 6$ $(3 \times 3) - (2 \times -2)$ $= 9 + 4$ $= 13$

$$\therefore y = \frac{\text{Numerator}}{\text{Denominator}} = \frac{39}{13} = 3$$

<u>Note:</u>

1. While calculating both numerator and denominator the direction of the arrows is same.

2. But in numerator cross products of independent terms and coefficients of x are subtracted.

3. In denominator, cross products of x–coefficients and y–coefficients are subtracted.

Some more solved examples:

<u>*Example 6:*</u>

$$5x + 4y = 3$$
$$2x - 3y = -8$$

$$x = \frac{(4 \times -8) - (3 \times -3)}{(4 \times 2) - (5 \times -3)}$$

$$= \frac{-32 + 9}{8 + 15} = \frac{-23}{23}$$

$$x = -1$$

$$y = \frac{(3 \times 2) - (5 \times -8)}{(4 \times 2) - (5 \times -3)}$$

$$= \frac{6 + 40}{8 + 15} = \frac{46}{23}$$

$$y = 2$$

So, $x = -1$ and $y = 2$

Example 7:

$$4x - 3y = 20$$
$$5x - 2y = 32$$

$x = \dfrac{(-3 \times 32) - (20 \times -2)}{(-3 \times 5) - (4 \times -2)}$	$y = \dfrac{(20 \times 5) - (4 \times 32)}{(-3 \times 5) - (4 \times -2)}$
$= \dfrac{-96 + 40}{-15 + 8} = \dfrac{-56}{-7}$	$= \dfrac{100 - 128}{-15 + 8} = \dfrac{-28}{-7}$
$x = 8$	$y = 4$

So, $x = 8$ and $y = 4$

<u>Note:</u> 1. Instead of finding both the values by the above method, you can find one value first and the other can be found by substituting the value of first in any of the given equations.

2. Though you can compute either of the value of x or y first and substitute its value for the other variable, but if the coefficients of x are big numbers, then calculate x first and then substitute its value to find y, because then you have to deal with y coefficients twice, thus avoiding the big x–coefficients and vice versa.

Example 8:

$$21x + y = 5$$
$$36x + y = 35$$

$$x = \frac{35 - 5}{36 - 21} = \frac{30}{15} = 2$$

Substituting the value of x, we get:

$$y = -37$$

If we find the value of y, then

$$y = \frac{(5 \times 36) - (21 \times 35)}{36 - 21}$$

$$= \frac{180 - 735}{15} = \frac{-555}{15} = -37$$

In finding y first, calculation of bigger numbers is involved. So in some cases, it is better to give preference of finding value of one variable first over the other.

EXERCISE 25.1

Solve the following equations for x and y:

1. $x + y = 8$
      $2x - 3y = 1$

2. $3x - 5y = 19$
      $-7x + 3y = -1$

3. $2x + 3y = 0$
      $3x + 4y = 5$

4. $2x - 3y = 13$
      $7x - 2y = 20$

5. $11x + 15y = -23$
      $7x - 2y = 20$

SOME SPECIAL CASES

There are some special cases in simultaneous linear equations which can be solved on mere observation.

Special Case I:

Some simultaneous linear equations which may involve big numbers also, but owing to a certain ratio between the coefficients, can be solved easily.

This comes under the vedic sutra or formula:

If one is in ratio, the other one is zero

The application can be understood by the following example:

Example 9:

$$3x + 2y = 6$$
$$9x + 5y = 18$$

Here we note that the coefficients of x, on the LHS, are in the same ratio as the independent terms on the RHS, i.e. $3:9 = 6:18$

According to the vedic sutra, if x is in ratio, the other one,

i.e. y is zero or $y = 0$

if $y = 0$, then x can be easily found by substituting y in $3x + 2y = 6$, which gives $x = 2$.

So, $x = 2$ and $y = 0$

Example 10:

$$426x + 128y = 512$$
$$792x + 256y = 1024$$

Since ratio of y–coefficients = ratio of independent terms, i.e.

$$\frac{128}{256} = \frac{512}{1024} = \frac{1}{2}$$

So, the other one, i.e. $x = 0$

Now, substituting $x = 0$ in $426x + 128y = 512$, we get:

$$y = \frac{512}{128} = 4$$

$$y = 4$$

So, $x = 0$ and $y = 4$

> *Doesn't it look like a magic to give solutions of such big equations on mere sight!*

Special Case II:

Simultaneous linear equations, where the x–coefficients and the y–coefficients are found interchanged, can be solved easily by the use of vedic formula: *"by addition and by subtraction"*

Example 11:

$$71x + 37y = 253$$
$$37x + 71y = 287$$

Add them once and subtract them once. This reduces the large coefficients into workable coefficients.

On addition, we get $108x + 108y = 540$

$$108(x + y) = 540$$
$$x + y = 5 \qquad \text{... (i)}$$

On subtraction, we get $34x - 34y = -34$

$$34(x - y) = -34$$
$$(x - y) = -1 \qquad \text{... (ii)}$$

Adding (i) and (ii), we get:

$$x + y = 5$$
$$+ \quad x - y = -1$$
$$\overline{ 2x = 4}$$
$$x = 2$$

Substituting $x = 2$ in $x + y = 5$, we get $y = 3$

So, $x = 2$ and $y = 3$

No matter how big and complex the coefficients may be, we can give the solution by mere simple addition and subtraction, without doing those long multiplications.

Example 12:

$$217x + 131y = 913$$
$$131x + 217y = 827$$

On adding both equations, we get:

$$348x + 348y = 1740$$

$$348(x + y) = 1740$$
$$x + y = 5 \qquad \qquad \text{... (i)}$$

On subtraction, we get:
$$86x - 86y = 86$$
$$86(x - y) = 86$$
$$(x - y) = 1 \qquad \qquad \text{... (ii)}$$

Adding (i) and (ii), we get:
$$x + y = 5$$
$$\underline{x - y = 1}$$
$$2x = 6,$$
$$x = 3$$

So, $x = 3, y = 2$

EXERCISE 25.2

Identify the special cases and solve for x and y:

1. $37x + 43y = 123$
        $43x + 37y = 117$

2. $12x + 8y = 7$
        $16x + 16y = 14$

3. $9x + 2y = 2$
        $3x + 5y = 5$

4. $41x - 17y = 99$
        $17x - 41y = 75$

5. $12x + 78y = 12$
        $16x + 16y = 16$

Application of Vedic Maths in Competitive Exams

1. In which of the following groups, fractions are written in descending order?

   (a) $\dfrac{1}{2}, \dfrac{5}{6}, \dfrac{7}{8}$ (b) $\dfrac{1}{2}, \dfrac{7}{8}, \dfrac{5}{6}$

   (c) $\dfrac{7}{8}, \dfrac{5}{6}, \dfrac{1}{2}$ (d) $\dfrac{5}{6}, \dfrac{7}{8}, \dfrac{1}{2}$

   Solution:

   In option (c) only, first fraction $\dfrac{7}{8} > \dfrac{5}{6}$.

   So, **(c)** is the correct option.

   (*refer chapter 12*)

2. Among $\dfrac{2}{15}, \dfrac{3}{10}, \dfrac{5}{21}$ and $\dfrac{7}{21}$, which is the least?

   Solution:

   Comparing the four fractions, $\dfrac{2}{15}$ is the least.

   (*refer chapter 12*)

3. Find the area of the square field with each side 45 feet.

   Solution:

   Area = Side² = 45² = **2025** sq. ft.

   (*refer chapter 10 for squares ending in 5*)

4. In a field, trees are planted in equal number of rows and columns. If each row has 123 trees, how many trees are planted altogether?

    Solution:

    Total number of trees = 123^2 = **15129**

    (*refer chapter 11*)

5. Which is the greatest 9 digit number, which is a perfect cube?

    Solution:

    A 9 digit number will have a cube root of 3 digits and largest 3 digit number is 999. So, its cube will be the greatest 9 digit number, which will be the perfect cube.

    i.e. 999^3 = 997 / 003 / $\overline{001}$

    $\qquad$ = **997002999**

    (*refer chapter 17 for cubing*)

6. What is the least number that must be given to * to make 451*603 divisible by 9?

    (a) 2 $\qquad$ (b) 6 $\qquad\qquad$ (c) 7 $\qquad\qquad$ (d) 8

    Solution:

    For a number to be divisible by 9, its Digital Root (D.R.) should be 9.
    D.R. of 451*603 = 1 + *
    So, value of * should be 8.
    So, option **(d)** is the correct answer.
    (*refer chapter 6*)

7. Find the total surface area of the cube whose volume is 17576cm³?

    Solution:

    Volume = 17576cm³
    Each side (a) = cube root of 17576 = 26
    (*refer chapter 16*)
    Surface area = $6a^2$ = 6 × 26^2 (*refer chapter 11 for squaring*)
    $\qquad\qquad$ = 6 × 676 = **4056** cm²

8. A total land of 46089 sq. ft. is to be distributed equally among 81 people. How much area would each person get?

    Solution:

    Each person will get area = 46089 ÷ 81 = **569 sq. ft.**

    (*refer chapter 14 for division*)

9. If the marked price of an article is Rs. 320 and a discount of 8% is given on it, what is the selling price?

    Solution:

    Selling price = 92% of Rs. 320 = $\dfrac{92}{100}$ × 320

    $\qquad\qquad$ = 9.2 × 32 (*vertical & crosswise multiplication*)
    $\qquad\qquad$ = **Rs. 294.40**

10. Find the largest number of 4 digits which is exactly divisible by 103.

    Solution:

    Largest 4 digits number = 9999
    So, 9999 ÷ 103 gives remainder as 8
    (*refer chapter 13 for division*)

    So, required largest 4 digits number which is exactly divisible by 103 = 9999 – 8 = **9991**

11. Given that 15ᵗʰ August 1947 was Friday, what will be the day on 15ᵗʰ August 2047?

    Solution:

    15ᵗʰ August, 2047
    $\quad$ 1 + 3 – 1 + 2 = 5
    5 stands for **Thursday**.
    (*refer chapter 20*).

12. Find if 42735 is divisible by 49?

    Solution:

    42735 is not divisible by 49

    (*refer chapter 19 for divisibility test*)

13. If in a stadium, 67081 students were made to stand in equal rows and columns, then how many students are standing in each row?

    Solution:

    Students standing in each row = $\sqrt{67081}$ = **259**

    (*refer chapter 15 for finding square root*)

14. 8756 × 99999 =

       (a) 875491244   (b) 875591244

       (c) 796491244   (d) None of these

    Solution:

    Correct answer is option **(b)**.

    (*refer chapter 3*)

15. 37245 × 24658 =

       (a) 918387210   (b) 819375210

       (c) 908173210   (d) 178342580

    Solution:

    Correct answer is option **(a)**.

    (*refer chapter 6 for checking answers using digital roots*)

16. Find $\dfrac{17}{19}$ upto 8 decimal places.

    Solution:

    $\dfrac{17}{19}$ = **0.89473684**

    (*refer chapter 18*)

17. $\dfrac{14}{79} =$

    (a) 0.1734   (b) 0.1772

    (c) 0.1372   (d) None of these

    Solution:

    Correct answer is option **(b)**.

    (*refer chapter 18*)

18. $\sqrt{93654} =$

    (a) 306.029   (b) 305.029

    (c) 315.026   (d) None of these

    Solution:

    Correct answer is option **(a)**.

    (*refer chapter 15*)

19. A group of 375 people are travelling in a train at the cost of Rs. 111 per ticket. What is the total cost of their tickets?

    Solution:

    Total cost = 375 × 111 = **41625**

    (*refer chapter 4*)

20. Find the amount of Rs. 8,000 for 3 yrs., compounded annually at 5% per annum.

    Solution:

    $$\text{Amount} = 8000 \left\{ 1 + \frac{5}{100} \right\}^3$$

    $$= 8000 \left\{ \frac{105}{100} \right\}^3$$

    $$= 8000 \left\{ \frac{21}{20} \right\}^3$$

    $$= 21^3 = 9261$$

Test Papers

Ideal time taken for each test paper is 10 mins.

Speed Enhancement Test – 1

Time Taken: _____
Marks Obtained: _____

(1)	$1000 - 243$	(2)	$1000 - 36.283$
(3)	436×11	(4)	72894×12
(5)	124×126	(6)	113×117
(7)	108×106	(8)	212×206
(9)	107×98	(10)	28^2
(11)	132^2	(12)	43^3
(13)	103^3	(14)	$4376 \div 31$
(15)	$\sqrt{20257}$	(16)	$\sqrt[3]{205379}$
(17)	$28934 \div 613$	(18)	2869×999999
(19)	$\sqrt{4397}$	(20)	$\dfrac{2}{3} + \dfrac{4}{7}$

Speed Enhancement Test – 2

Time Taken: _____
Marks Obtained: _____

(1)	$2000 - 43$	(2)	$10000 - 271.8567$
(3)	4872×9999	(4)	58196×999
(5)	102×111	(6)	9987×9986
(7)	2436×112	(8)	173×248
(9)	432×250	(10)	57×53
(11)	27^2	(12)	998^2
(13)	13^3	(14)	993^3
(15)	$\sqrt{8354}$	(16)	$\sqrt{93}$
(17)	$\sqrt[3]{474552}$	(18)	$2398 \div 42$
(19)	$0.32596 \div 78$	(20)	$\dfrac{5}{12} + \dfrac{7}{32}$

Speed Enhancement Test – 3

Time Taken: _____
Marks Obtained: _____

(1)	$10000 - 124.739$	(2)	$5000 - 92.4926$
(3)	9374×111	(4)	1111^2
(5)	999^2	(6)	126^2
(7)	197×193	(8)	47×39
(9)	706×521	(10)	999×6342
(11)	1013×987	(12)	41^3
(13)	991^3	(14)	28^3
(15)	$\sqrt{8314}$	(16)	$\sqrt{92061}$
(17)	$35426 \div 123$	(18)	$28942 \div 71$
(19)	50428×1234	(20)	$\sqrt[3]{912673}$

Speed Enhancement Test – 4

Time Taken: _____
Marks Obtained: _____

(1)	2896×11	(2)	43029×111
(3)	539×999	(4)	832×714
(5)	248×112	(6)	997×991
(7)	998×98	(8)	1421×124
(9)	106×118	(10)	1012×992
(11)	583×118	(12)	127×123
(13)	4283×99	(14)	83^2
(15)	98^2	(16)	993^2
(17)	1012^2	(18)	112^2
(19)	58^2	(20)	162^2

Speed Enhancement Test – 5

Time Taken: _____
Marks Obtained: _____

(1)	$60000 - 253$	(2)	$1000 - 43.76$
(3)	$400 - 27$	(4)	119×102
(5)	1018×1012	(6)	101×79
(7)	998×989	(8)	9889×10011
(9)	246×642	(10)	58362×14
(11)	325^2	(12)	421^2
(13)	78^2	(14)	32^3
(15)	92^3	(16)	$3542 \div 91$
(17)	$58392 \div 73$	(18)	$7246 \div 174$
(19)	$\sqrt{3136}$	(20)	$\sqrt[3]{250047}$

Speed Enhancement Test – 6

Time Taken: _____
Marks Obtained:

(1)	43×52	(2)	76×81
(3)	241×365	(4)	146×64
(5)	112^2	(6)	989^2
(7)	207^2	(8)	509^2
(9)	1122^2	(10)	33^2
(11)	99^3	(12)	108^3
(13)	$\sqrt{243.76}$	(14)	$\sqrt{3236}$
(15)	$\sqrt{0.053}$	(16)	$\sqrt[3]{195112}$
(17)	$56123 \div 152$	(18)	$7321 \div 8123$
(19)	$82915 \div 2024$	(20)	$17539 \div 621$

Vedic Mathematics Sutras

Vedic Mathematics Main Sutras

	SUTRA	TRANSLATION
1.	एकाधिकेन पूर्वेन Ekadhikina Purvena	By one more than the one before
2.	निखिलं नवतश्चरमं दशतः Nikhilam Navatashcaramam Dashatah	All from 9 and the last from 10
3.	ळ्ध्वर्तिर्यग्भ्यामं Urdhva-Tiryagbyham	Vertically and Crosswise
4.	परावर्त्य योजयेत् Paraavartya Yojayet	Transpose and Apply
5.	शून्यं साम्यसमुच्चये Shunyam Saamyasamuccaye	If the Samuccaya is the Same it is Zero
6.	ग्रानुरूप्ये शून्यं ग्रन्यत् (Anurupye) Shunyamanyat	If One is in Ratio the Other is Zero
7.	संकलन व्यवकलनाभ्यां Sankalana-vyavakalanabhyam	By Addition and by Subtraction
8.	पूरणापूरणाभ्यां Puranapuranabyham	By the Completion or Non-Completion
9.	चलनकलनाभ्याम् Chalana-Kalanabyham	Differential Calculus
10.	यावदूनं Yaavadunam	By the Deficiency

11.	व्यप्टिसमप्टि: Vyashtisamanstih	Part and Whole
12.	शेषाण्यडेन चरमेण Shesanyankena Charamena	The Remainders by the Last Digit
13.	सोपान्त्यद्वयमन्त्यं Sopaantyadvayamantyam	The Ultimate and Twice the Penultimate
14.	एकन्यूनेन पूर्वन Ekanyunena Purvena	By One Less than the One Before
15.	गुणितसमुच्चय: Gunitasamuchyah	The Product of the Sum
16.	गुणकसमुच्चय: Gunakasamuchyah	All the Multipliers

The Sub-Sutras

	Sub Sutra	Translation
1	ग्रानुरूप्येण Anurupyena	Proportionately
2	शिष्यते शेषसंज्ञ: Sisyate Sesasmjnah	The Remainder Remains Constant
3	ग्राधमाधेनान्त्यमन्त्येन Adyamadyenantyamantyena	The First by the First and the Last by the Last
4	केवलै: सप्तकं गुण्यात् Kevalaih Saptakam Gunyat	For 7 the Multiplicand is 143
5	वेष्टनम् Vestanam	By Osculation
6	यावदूनं तावदूनं Yavadunam Tavadunam	Lessen by the Deficiency

7	यावदूनं तावदूनीकृत्य वर्गं च योजयेत् Yavadunam Tavadunikrtya Varganca Yojayet	Whatever the Deficiency lessen by that amount and set up the Square of the Deficiency
8	ग्रन्त्ययोर्दशकेऽपि Antyayordasake'pi	Last Totalling 10
9	ग्रन्त्ययोरेव Antyayoreva	Only the Last Terms
10	समुच्चयगुणितः Samuccayagunitah	The Sum of the Products
11	लोपनस्थापनाभ्यां Lopanasthapanabhyam	By Alternative Elimination and Retention
12	विलोकनं Vilokanam	By Mere Observation
13	गुणितसमुच्चयः समुच्चयगुणितः Gunitasmuccayah Samuccayagunitah	The Product of the Sum is the Sum of the Products
14	ध्वजाङ्क Dhvajanika	On the Flag

NAMES AND APPLICATIONS OF SUTRAS OF VEDIC MATHEMATICS USED IN THE BOOK

Name	Translation	Applications
Nikhilam Navatascaramam Dasatah	All from nine and last from ten	Complements, Subtraction, Multiplication by 9 & base method, Division by 9 and numbers less than the base.
Antyayoreva	Only the last 2 digits	Multiplication by 11.
Sopantyadvayamantyam	The ultimate & twice the penultimate	Multiplication by 12.
Ekanyunena Purvena	By 1 less than the 1 before	Multiplication by 9.
Anurupyena	Proportionately	Multiplication by working base & cubes.
Urdhvatiryagbhyam	Vertical & crosswise	Multiplication, equations and squares.
Paravartya Yojayet	Transpose & apply	Division of numbers more than the base.
Ekadhikena Purvena	By 1 more than the 1 before	Square of numbers ending in 5.
Antyayordasakepi	Last totalling to 10	Multiplication of numbers whose units add to 10.

Avadunam Tavadunikrtya Varganca Yojayet	Whatever the extent of its deficiency lessen by that amount and set the square of the deficiency	Squares of numbers close to the base.
Dwandwa yoga	Duplex combination	Squares of all numbers.
Yavadunam	By the deficiency	Cubes of numbers close to the base.
Vilokanam	By mere observation	Square roots & cube roots of exact squares & cubes.
Dhvajanka	On top of the flag	Straight division.
Sankalana Vyavakalanabhyam	By addition & subtraction	Alternate remainders.

ANSWERS

Chapter 1: Two basic concepts of Vedic Maths

1.1

1. F	2. F	3. F	4. T
5. T	6. F	7. F	8. F
9. T	10. F		

1.2

1. 757	2. 269	3. 8702	4. 5237
5. 15944	6. 2940	7. 300	8. 19100
9. 0900	10. 19950		

1.3

1. 361.74	2. 275.150	3. 693.998	4. 70653.17
5. 41400	6. 71691	7. 18181	8. 8798.950
9. 17350	10. 3590.80		

Chapter 2: Multiplications with 99999.... in less than 5 seconds

2.1

1. 2376	2. 731268	3. 400599	4. 6633
5. 831168	6. 17648235	7. 99870012	8. 8567014329
9. 39236076	10. 789525210474		

2.2

1. 41958	2. 36963	3. 9009099	4. 759924
5. 8129187	6. 1699983	7. 9819018	8. 56699433
9. 639936	10. 38000961999		

2.3

1. 93654	2. 657	3. 19008	4. 162261
5. 42273	6. 8428563	7. 52074	8. 5562432
9. 388773	10. 90054855		

Chapter 3: Magic with 11

3.1

1. 352	2. 4961	3. 5379	4. 51931
5. 16456	6. 12452	7. 48576	8. 88506
9. 74591	10. 26334		

3.2

1. 43179	**2.** 4773	**3.** 60606	**4.** 357864
5. 236643	**6.** 779922	**7.** 904872	**8.** 2323101
9. 547723	**10.** 193029		

Chapter 4: Multiplying by 12 *without using 12*

4.1

1. 288	**2.** 864	**3.** 5436	**4.** 2592
5. 4104	**6.** 106944	**7.** 57168	**8.** 257184
9. 68808	**10.** 371496		

4.2

1. 7952	**2.** 9408	**3.** 59808	**4.** 189504
5. 473712	**6.** 1018592	**7.** 927408	**8.** 3037984
9. 788408	**10.** 6517432		

4.3

1. 7008	**2.** 6526	**3.** 141355	**4.** 180288
5. 5208	**6.** 4680	**7.** 171228	**8.** 7059
9. 35532	**10.** 576656		

4.4

1. 559	**2.** 1392	**3.** 4199	**4.** 16055
5. 70794	**6.** 42780	**7.** 14514	**8.** 8051442
9. 109044	**10.** 24408		

Chapter 5: Subtraction at one look

5.1

1. 54	**2.** 6	**3.** 41	**4.** 72
5. 754	**6.** 5715	**7.** 858	**8.** 604
9. 5092	**10.** 63		

5.2

1. 923	**2.** 9935	**3.** 99363	**4.** 9997
5. 991.95	**6.** 0.762	**7.** 9125.1	**8.** 7.0036
9. 27.58	**10.** 99827.754		

5.3

1. 512	**2.** 47669	**3.** 7962	**4.** 168
5. 1021	**6.** 3714.64	**7.** 667.957	**8.** 6565
9. 6976.4	**10.** 4762		

5.4

1. 1419	**2.** 1606	**3.** 6640	**4.** 4536
5. 983	**6.** 2037	**7.** 28931	**8.** 2506
9. 38262	**10.** 316508		

Chapter 6: Checking your answers (*removing silly mistakes*)

6.1

1. 5	**2.** 3	**3.** 9	**4.** 1
5. 9	**6.** 4	**7.** 3	**8.** 7
9. 9	**10.** 5		

6.2

1. Correct	**2.** Incorrect	**3.** Incorrect	**4.** Correct
5. Corrent	**6.** Incorrect	**7.** Incorrect	**8.** Correct
9. Correct	**10.** Incorrect		

6.3

1. By 3 and 9	**2.** By 3	**3.** Not Divisible	**4.** By 3
5. By 3 and 9			

Chapter 7: Multiplication of numbers near the bases

7.1

1. 8918	**2.** 8188	**3.** 987022	**4.** 900099
5. 98950306			

7.2

1. 11554	**2.** 10908	**3.** 1023132	**4.** 100200096
5. 12402			

7.3

1. 10094	**2.** 1003779	**3.** 9879	**4.** 1007952
5. 100989694			

7.4

1. 827.7	**2.** 990.021	**3.** 98389.5	**4.** 88.74
5. 100019.857			

7.5

1. 4556	**2.** 3599	**3.** 649627	**4.** 91416
5. 36630306	**6.** 89984	**7.** 639068	**8.** 157608
9. 49140075	**10.** 159192		

7.6

1. 88288	**2.** 92736	**3.** 9909088	**4.** 1199109
5. 1008576	**6.** 1040609	**7.** 9199632	**8.** 9990937
9. 10109099	**10.** 963072		

7.7

1. 778596	**2.** 995879484	**3.** 1018077060	**4.** 1037952
5. 1165136			

Chapter 8: Multiplication by 5, 25, 50, 250, 500....

8.1

1. 210	**2.** 180	**3.** 3650	**4.** 4200
5. 28000	**6.** 45500	**7.** 7000	**8.** 33000
9. 335	**10.** 2450		

Chapter 9: Vertical & Crosswise Multiplication

9.1

1. 713	**2.** 2226	**3.** 6106	**4.** 1504
5. 1215	**6.** 3999	**7.** 80784	**8.** 93555
9. 254826	**10.** 287716		

9.2

1. 10388	**2.** 13206	**3.** 28575	**4.** 14484
5. 4034536	**6.** 22935550	**7.** 7420068	**8.** 531854
9. 5113570	**10.** 744804632		

Chapter 10: Interesting squares

10.1

1. 2025	**2.** 3025	**3.** 4225	**4.** 9025
5. 18225			

10.2

1. 7216	**2.** 15621	**3.** 4224	**4.** 11009
5. 1100196			

10.3

1. 8464	**2.** 1012036	**3.** 10404	**4.** 11881
5. 990025	**6.** 13225	**7.** 99700225	**8.** 998001
9. 7744	**10.** 1050625		

Chapter 11: Finding squares in one line

11.1

1. 16	**2.** 28	**3.** 96	**4.** 18
5. 41	**6.** 66	**7.** 52	**8.** 6
9. 72	**10.** 77		

11.2

1. 2704	**2.** 5041	**3.** 1296	**4.** 841
5. 7921	**6.** 1024	**7.** 8464	**8.** 196
9. 4489	**10.** 529		

11.3

1. 63001	**2.** 15129	**3.** 188356	**4.** 389376
5. 674041	**6.** 107584	**7.** 18671041	**8.** 7873636
9. 535552164	**10.** 108264025		

Chapter 12: Fractions

12.1

1. 17/12	**2.** 37/40	**3.** 16/15	**4.** −31/105
5. 41/84	**6.** −11/48	**7.** 25/36	**8.** 1/3
9. $3\frac{8}{15}$	**10.** $4\frac{5}{84}$		

12.2

1. 1/7,   2/9,   6/11   **2.** 2/5,   3/7,   5/9

3. 2/7,   1/3,   8/9   **4.** 9/11,   11/13,   8/9

5. 3/11,   4/13,   6/17

Chapter 13: Division

13.1

1. Q = 26	**2.** Q = 335	**3.** Q = 680	**4.** Q = 779
R = 7	R = 7	R = 4	R = 1
5. Q = 1258			
R = 4			

13.2

1. Q = 24	**2.** Q = 570	**3.** Q = 494	**4.** Q = 23
R = 39	R = 54	R = 20	R = 8243

5. Q = 41
   R = 5
6. Q = 11
   R = 2475
7. Q = 103
   R = 76038
8. Q = 42
   R = 597

9. Q = 83
   R = 9637
10. Q = 75
    R = 634

13.3

1. Q = 103
   R = 2
2. Q = 108
   R = 252
3. Q = 923
   R = 24
4. Q = 278
   R = 413

5. Q = 408
   R = 71
6. Q = 2
   R = 814
7. Q = 54
   R = 4394
8. Q = 117
   R = 1025

9. Q = 222
   R = 39
10. Q = 63
    R = 43

Chapter 14: Long division in one line *(the crowning glory)*

14.1

1. 56
2. 66.304
3. 12.808
4. 9.161

5. 80.25
6. 0.905
7. 5209.602
8. 61.812

9. 171.125
10. 151

14.2

1. 22.333
2. 116.972
3. 0.445
4. 121.844

5. 739.031

14.3

1. 3.334
2. 182.547
3. 622.343
4. 10.451

5. 13.877

14.4

1. 6.442
2. 0.00016
3. 16.722
4. 5.490

5. 0.0093

14.5

1. 0.089
2. 0.062
3. 0.00091
4. 0.543

5. 0.00028

Chapter 15: Square roots in one line

15.1

1. 83
2. 91
3. 74
4. 68

5. 24
6. 31
7. 37
8. 57

9. 46
10. 52

15.2

1. 721	**2.** 5.291	**3.** 37.242	**4.** 70.121
5. 512	**6.** 914	**7.** 266.501	**8.** 86.612
9. 17.219	**10.** 71.007		

Chapter 16: Cube roots at a glance

16.1

1. 56	**2.** 13	**3.** 39	**4.** 88
5. 95	**6.** 78	**7.** 46	**8.** 63
9. 17	**10.** 14		

Chapter 17: Cubes

17.1

1. 17576	**2.** 29791	**3.** 91125	**4.** 357911
5. 50653	**6.** 551368	**7.** 804357	**8.** 6859
9. 157464	**10.** 314432		

17.2

1. 753571	**2.** 614125	**3.** 1092727	**4.** 1018108216
5. 994011992	**6.** 970299	**7.** 1061208	**8.** 1001200480064
9. 1003303631331	**10.** 997601919488		

Chapter 18: Magic Division

18.1

1. 0.52525252	**2.** 0.29411764	**3.** 0.66666666	**4.** 0.31578947
5. 0.82758620			

18.2

1. 0.34210526	**2.** 0.71590909	**3.** 0.17857142	**4.** 0.91025641
5. 0.24576271			

18.3

1. 0.12903225	**2.** 0.156862745	**3.** 0.37254901	**4.** 0.51612903
5. 0.11801242			

18.4

1. 0.22727	**2.** 0.09375	**3.** 0.04464	**4.** 0.10975
5. 0.01612			

18.5

1. 0.25925925	**2.** 0.30769230	**3.** 0.78723404	**4.** 0.4230769
5. 0.5625			

Chapter 19: Check divisibility by prime number

19.1

1. 5	**2.** 9	**3.** 13	**4.** 13
5. 26	**6.** 28	**7.** 7	**8.** 14
9. 7	**10.** 10		

19.2

1. Divisible	**2.** Not Divisible	**3.** Divisible	**4.** Divisible
5. Not Divisible			

19.3

1. 4	**2.** 2	**3.** 5	**4.** 7
5. 14	**6.** 11	**7.** 8	**8.** 11
9. 12	**10.** 9		

19.4

1. Divisible	**2.** Divisible	**3.** Divisble	**4.** Not Divisible
5. Divisible			

Chapter 20: Dates and 500 years Calendar

20.1

1. Thursday	**2.** Saturday	**3.** Saturday	**4.** Tuesday
5. Monday			

20.2

1. b	**2.** d

Chapter 21: Algebraic Multiplication

21.1

1. $x^2 + 3x + 2$
2. $10x^2 - 7x - 12$
3. $3x^2 + 35x + 88$
4. $2x^2 - 5xy + 3y^2$
5. $4a^2 + ab - 3b^2$
6. $14x^2 + 55xy + 21y^2$
7. $10x^2 + xy - 24y^2$
8. $6x^2 - 13xy - 28y^2$
9. $4x^2 + 16xy + 15y^2$
10. $18x^2 - 41xy + 21y^2$

21.2

1. $12x^2 - 23xy + 10y^2$
2. $8x^2 + 6xy - 9y^2$
3. $28x^2 - 68xy + 24y^2$
4. $34x^2 - 113xy - 21y^2$
5. $33a^2 - 105ab + 18b^2$
6. $21p^2 - 38pq + 16q^2$
7. $35m^2 - 29mn - 28n^2$
8. $18x^2 - 24xy - 10y^2$
9. $x^2 + 7x + 12$
10. $3a^2 + 7ab + 2b^2$

21.3

1. $6x^4 + 7x^3 + 19x^2 + 10x + 12$
2. $4x^4 + x^3 + 5x^2 + 17x - 10$
3. $10x^4 + 28x^3 + 27x^2 + 17x + 3$
4. $2x^4 + 15x^3 + 16x^2 + 15x - 12$
5. $2x^4 + 12x^3y + 15x^2y + 17xy^3 + 3y^4$

Chapter 22: Factorizing Quadratic Expressions

22.1

1. $(x + 5)(x + 11)$ 2. $(x + 2)(x + 3)$ 3. $(x + 4)(x + 3)$
4. $(x - 6)(x - 2)$ 5. $(2x + 3)(2x + 3)$ 6. $(2x - 5)(x - 3)$
7. $(x + 5y)(5x - y)$ 8. $(x - 4y)(3x - 2y)$ 9. $(x - 2y)(2x - 3y)$
10. $(x - 3y)(x + 2y)$

22.2

1. $(x + y + z)(x + 2y + z)$ 2. $(x + y + z)(x - y - z)$
3. $(x + 2y + 3z)(2x + y + z)$ 4. $(x - y - z)(3x - y + 2z)$
5. $(x + 2y + 3z)(2x + 3y + z)$

Chapter 23: Linear Equations in One Variable

23.1

1. $x = 5$ 2. $x = 8$ 3. $x = 2$ 4. $y = 5$ 5. $x = 1$

23.2

1. $x = \dfrac{7}{2}$ 2. $x = \dfrac{4}{5}$ 3. $x = 100$ 4. $x = \dfrac{13}{-7}$ 5. $x = 0$

23.3

1. $x\dfrac{1}{2}$ 2. $x = 9$ 3. $x = 6$ 4. $x = 3$ 5. $x = 2$

23.4

1. $x = 4$ 2. $x = 6$ 3. $x = \dfrac{-45}{11}$ 4. $x = \dfrac{57}{11}$ 5. $x = \dfrac{-11}{2}$
6. $x = \dfrac{27}{2}$ 7. $x = \dfrac{-8}{3}$ 8. $x = \dfrac{11}{9}$ 9. $x = 0$ 10. $x = \dfrac{-5}{2}$

Chapter 24: Linear Equations *(special types)*

24.1

1. $x = 0$ 2. $x = 1$ 3. $x = 2$ 4. $x = 3$ 5. $x = 0$

24.2

1. $x = 0$ 2. $x = 0$ 3. $x = 0$ 4. $x = 0$ 5. $x = 0$

24.3

1. $x = 0$ 2. $x = \dfrac{-7}{2}$ 3. $x = \dfrac{3}{2}$ 4. $x = \dfrac{3}{5}$ 5. $x = -1$

24.4

1. $x = -2$ 2. $x = \dfrac{2}{5}$ 3. $x \dfrac{-3}{2}$ 4. $x = -2$ 5. $x = -1$

24.5

1. $x = -8$ 2. $x = \dfrac{-3}{2}$ 3. $x = \dfrac{17}{2}$ 4. $x = \dfrac{-9}{2}$ 5. $x = \dfrac{5}{2}$

24.6

1. $x - 1 = 0, x = 1$ 2. $x = 0$

3. $5x + 3 = 0, \; x = \dfrac{-3}{5}$ 4. $-3x + 12 = 0, x = 4$

5. $8x + 16 = 0, x = -2$ 6. $8x + 10 = 0, x = \dfrac{-5}{4}$

7. $4x + 5 = 0, \; x = \dfrac{-5}{4}$ 8. $4x - 20, x = \dfrac{1}{2}$ and $x - 1 = 0, \; x = 1$

9. $2x + 3 = 0, \; x = \dfrac{-3}{2}$ 10. $4x + 12 = 0, x = -3$

Chapter 25: Simultaneous Equations

25.1

1. $x = \dfrac{1 + 24}{2 + 3} = \dfrac{25}{5} = 5 , y = 3$ 2. $x = \dfrac{5 - 57}{35 - 9} = \dfrac{-52}{26} = -2 , y = -5$

3. $x = \dfrac{15 - 0}{9 - 8} = 15 , \; y = -10$ 4. $x = \dfrac{-60 + 26}{-21 + 4} = \dfrac{-34}{-17} = 2 , \; y = -3$

5. $x = \dfrac{300 - 46}{105 + 22} = \dfrac{254}{127} = 2 , y = -3$

25.2

1. $x = 1, y = 2$ 2. $x = 0, y = \dfrac{7}{8}$ 3. $x = 0, y = 1$ 4. $x = 2, y = -1$

5. $x = 1, y = 0$

Speed Enhancement Test – 1

1. 757	2. 963.717	3. 4796	4. 874728
5. 15624	6. 13221	7. 11448	8. 43672
9. 10486	10. 784	11. 17424	12. 79507
13. 1092727	14. 141.161	15. 142.327	16. 59
17. 47.2006	18. 2868997131	19. 66.309	20. 26/21

Speed Enhancement Test – 2

1. 1957	2. 9728.1433	3. 48715128	4. 58137804
5. 11322	6. 99730182	7. 272832	8. 42904
9. 108000	10. 3021	11. 729	12. 996004
13. 2197	14. 979146657	15. 91.4002	16. 9.643
17. 78	18. 57.095	19. 0.0041	20. 61/96

Speed Enhancement Test – 3

1. 9875.261	2. 4907.5074	3. 1040514	4. 1234321
1. 998001	6. 15876	7. 38021	8. 1833
9. 367826	10. 6335658	11. 999831	12. 68921
13. 973242271	14. 21952	15. 91.181	16. 303.415
16. 288.016	18. 407.633	19. 62228152	20. 97

Speed Enhancement Test – 4

1. 31856	2. 4776219	3. 538461	4. 594048
5. 27776	6. 988027	7. 97804	8. 176204
9. 12508	10. 1003904	11. 68794	12. 15621
13. 424017	14. 6889	15. 9604	16. 986049
17. 1024144	18. 12544	19. 3364	20. 26244

Speed Enhancement Test – 5

1. 59747	2. 956.24	3. 373	4. 12138
5. 1030216	6. 7979	7. 987022	8. 98998779
9. 157932	10. 817068	11. 105625	12. 177241

1.3 6084   14. 32768   15. 778688   16. 38.923
17. 799.890   18. 41.643   20. 56   21. 63

Speed Enhancement Test – 6

1. 2236   2. 6156   3. 87965   4. 9344
5. 12544   6. 978121   7. 42849   8. 259081
9. 1258884   10. 1089   11. 970299   12. 1259712
13. 15.612   14. 56.885   15. 0.2302   16. 58
17. 369.2302   18. 0.901   19. 40.965   20. 28.243

TESTIMONIALS

"The techniques are very useful for students as well as teachers. It helps them in creating interest for maths and improving concentration power."

-Sunita Jain, PGT (Maths)

"We can really improve our mathematical calculation by doing this workshop. Long calculations can be made easy and very less tedious than before."

-Tanushree Sharma, 8th class,
D.P.S. , R. K. Puram

"Best stuff about maths I have ever thought."

-Shubham, 7th class,
G.D. Goenka

"Excellent way to solve maths problems very easily and fast."

-Yash Choudhury , 9th class,
Rukmani Devi School

"I found the methods quite interesting and useful. I would like to suggest it to many."

-Dr. Priyanka Shukla (M.B.B.S.)

"This is a very good mind sharpening workshop. This will be very helpful in my studies."

-Ridhi Sharma, 7th class,
Queen's Mary School

"I think Vedic Maths is a brilliant idea because this method makes our mind sharper."

-Aishwarya Sachdeva, 8th class,
Manavsthali School

"An excellent way of calculating mathematics sums fast and increasing one's mental ability. It has helped me a lot."

-Ajita Shukla, 8th class,
Presentation Convent School.

"Vedic Maths has changed my attitude towards Maths. Now I have made maths my new friend."

-Nidhi Meena, 10th class,
Prabhu Dayal Public School

"Vedic Maths tricks are fabulous."

-Akash Jain, 11th class,
Prabhu Dayal Public School

"Why are these techniques not being taught to us in school. It is a torture for us to use those long and boring conventional methods for calculations in schools when we can arrive at the answers directly without all the fuss. "

-Abhishek Gupta, 11th class,
Bal Bharti Public School

"The techniques were very useful and should be taught in every school. Efforts should be made to make Vedic Mathematics compulsory in schools."

-Yogesh Gupta, CA

"I am amazed at the comments I got in the PTM of the school of my son. Everybody was asking me how he can calculate so fast in school."

-Vandana Singhal, mother of Ansh Singhal, 6th class

"This is very nice and useful for all age groups."

-Anju Jindal, Housewife, B.Sc.

"I used to be afraid of numbers, they freaked me out, but thanks to your techniques I feel confident that with more practice, I'll become an expert!!"

-Safra Thawfeeq, ILMA International School,
Colombo, Srilanka